A TRAITOR'S WOOING

A TRAITOR'S WOOING

Headon Hill

General
Books

www.General-Books.net

Publication Data:

Title: A Traitor's Wooing
Author: Hill, Headon, 1857-1927
Publisher: London : Ward Lock
Publication date: 1909

1

A TRAITOR'S WOOING

CHAPTER I

TWO VILLAINS AND THE HEROINE

"'VT'OUR Highness will find your opportunity X now; Miss Maynard is for the moment alone," Mr. Travers Nugent whispered to his companion.

A guttural " Ah! " was the only answer as the individual addressed left the speaker's side and made his way through the crush towards a tall girl who had just dismissed her partner in the last dance. The ball-room at Brabazon House was almost inconveniently crowded on the occasion of this, the first great function of the London season, and progress was a little difiicult. A gleam of satisfaction crept into Mr. Nugent's steadily following eyes when at length the Maharajah stood bowing before the fair young Englishwoman.

The Indian Prince, a notable figure by reason of the jewelled turban that crowned his otherwise orthodox European evening dress, gave his arm to the girl, who greeted him with a pleasant smile of recognition, and together the pair strolled out through one of the French windows into the vast tropical winter-garden for which Brabazon House is celebrated. The dusky face of the Maharajah as it disappeared from view wore an expression of ecstatic rapture that caused Mr. Nugent's thin lips to curl in the ghost of a sneer.

"His Highness won't look like that when he comes back," the watcher muttered under his breath, as he leaned against a pillar and composed himself to wait. Mr. Travers Nugent spent much of his life in waitingâ with the consolation of knowing that there was generally a big stake to wait for. He was a well-built man of middle age and height, wearing a long, fair moustache that at first sight gave him rather a distinguished airâ an impression that was, however, negatived for any student of character by a hint of shiftiness in the close-set blue eyes.

A bachelor of good family, and of no visible occupation, Travers Nugent moved easily in the orbit of West End society. He occupied a luxurious fiat in Jermyn Street, and rented besides a pretty cottage in Devonshire, to which he retired after the fatigues of the season. He had a host of acquaintances, but very few intimates, and even to these latter the source of his income was a mystery. He was vaguely supposed to have inherited a small patrimony from an adventurous uncle who had died in America, and to whom he sometimes jocularly referred as his " avuncular oof-bird." As a matter of fact, there was a substratum of truth in this, to the extent of about a hundred a year, but as Mr. Nugent usually spent; 2, ooo in that period some other explanation was needed.

He could have furnished one readily, had he been so minded. He lived, and lived well, upon

TWO VILLAINS AND THE HEROINE ii the best asset with which kindly Nature can endow a man not otherwise provided forâ a clever, subtle brain, prompt to seize every chance that may come to it, and, failing such fortuitous aid, equally prompt to manufacture the chances for itself. To put it plainly, Travers Nugent lived upon his wits. A soldier of fortune, he belonged to the commissioned ranks of the great predatory army which sacrifices nothing to scruple, to compassion, or to honour. As cruel and as secret as the grave, he made a very good thing of it, and on its profits fed several unholy vices which no one knew that he possessed.

For the last three months he had been acting as self-appointed bear-leader to the arrogant Indian prince who had gone out into the winter garden with the loveliest of all the budding debutantes of the year upon his arm. There are many ways in which a not too scrupulous man of the world can be of use to an Oriental potentate whose civilization is only skin deep, and Travers Nugent had already estabhshed many claims upon the exalted visitor's gratitude.

His prophecy was quickly verified. Black thunder lowering on his swarthy brows, the Maharajah of Sindkhote came back through the window into the ball-room, and he came alone. Another dance was in progress now, but the Eastern barbarian, under the veneer of Western polish, had broken loose. Like one demented, yet with some remnants of savage dignity clinging to him, he strode straight across the floor to where Nugent still leaned against the pillar. The amused dancers who had to steer clear of his imperious path forgave much for the priceless jewels in his turban.

"Come away before I kill some one, Nugent," he said in a furious undertone. " Come round to my rooms at once. I must consult you on a matter of the utmost importance, in which I need your help."

Travers Nugent's help was always at the disposal of those who were willing, or could be forced, to pay for it. With the adroit tact for which he was noted he contrived to get the excited prince out of Brabazon House without a scene, forbearing to question him till a motor car had borne them swiftly to the great hotel where the Maharajah was staying. But as soon as they were alone in the dining-room of the suite which his patron for the time being rented there escaped him the two wordsâ

"She refused?"

Bhagwan Singh, Maharajah of Sindkhote, walked unsteadily to the sideboard and poured out half a tumbler of neat brandy. He drank it at a gulp, and then turned to his European mentor, restored to the outward semblance of his customary Oriental calm. A good-looking man with a pale olive complexion, jet black moustache and features of the full-faced Eastern type, he was by no means ill-favoured, though in his lazy eyes there were infinite possibilities of malevolent cruelty.

"Sit down, my dear Nugent, and talk," he said, tossing a gold cigarette-case across the table. " Yes, she not only refused my offer of marriage, but laughed at meâ treated me, the descendant of a hundred kings, as a joke. By God! I could have killed her twenty minutes ago, as she stood smiling disdainfully at me among the palms. But that brandy has steadied me for a better way. She shall be mine yet, though not as Maharanee now. I will have my way with her, and then she shall sweep out the harem."

"That is rather a tall order. Prince," rejoined Nugent, watching the other narrowly. " You will never accomplish that unless you kidnap her, and to convey an unwilling maiden from England to India presents, to my prosaic mind, a good many initial difficulties."

"Difficulties? Yes, but I will give you twenty thousand pounds to help me to surmount them. And I do not even ask you to devise the scheme for humbling this proud Englishwoman to the dust. When you told me that Violet Maynard would laugh me to scorn I did not believe you, but all the same I, Bhagwan Singh, prepared a plan for meeting the contingency. It depends, however, on one point. Has the girl a lover already?"

"No; I can reassure you as to that. She has admirers, of courseâ with her attractions that goes without saying. But she is perfectly heart-wholeâ so far," was Nugent's reply.

"Then success is certain, for I will provide her with a lover," the Maharajah rejoined, evidently expecting an outburst of surprise at the apparent paradox.

But his cunning eyes searched Travers Nugent's face in vain for signs of any such emotions. It was not that astute gentleman's way to show his inmost feelings, which at the moment were an intense curiosity to learn what was expected of him in return for the enormous bribe. It was characteristic of him that it was in his most indifferent manner that he said:â

"You are altogether too subtle for me, Maharajah, and I cannot think that you are quite serious. If you have finished poking fun at a jaded man about town, I think I'll go home to bed."

He half rose, as if to suit the action to the word, and that was the precise moment when the Hindoo once for all assumed the lead in the infamous partnership that was to bind them. And Bhagwan Singh gained and kept that mastery by the simple but efficacious expedient of throwing off all semblance of the equality on which they had muck-raked London together. In a blaze of haughty contempt he let his jackal see that he was understood and appreciated at his proper value.

"You are never jaded when there is plunder in view, and you have no intention of going from here till you have heard the proposal to which you will sit still and listen," said Bhagwan Singh, waving him with a commanding gesture back to his chair. " It comes natural to those of Royal blood, Mr. Nugent, to estimate truly those who serve them, and I know that you are a useful but expensive tool, as willing to be bought as I am to buy you. You have taught me some of your slang. I will act on the square with you if you will act on the square with me. If I pay you Â 20,000, and show you how to do it, will you, without any personal risk to yourself, aid me in achieving the desire of my heart?"

In a matter of business, and when there were no witnesses, there was not much pride about Travers Nugent. He tacitly waived his position as friend of the prince, and became his subordinate by replying:

"I should like to hear your plan before I commit myself, your Highness."

Now the project which the Maharajah of Sind-khote, after further recourse to the brandy decanter, proceeded to unfold, if put forward by any ordinary man, would have seemed on the face of it too wildly preposterous to be entertained for a moment. But Travers Nugent was aware that his patron's wealth was almost boundless, and that the lavish expenditure he was prepared to incur would discount most of the obstacles to the amazing abduction contemplated.

Bhagwan Singh, it transpired, had in his service as commander of his native body-guard a young Englishman who had been compelled by his extravagant follies to leave the British regiment in which he had formerly held a commission. He had incurred such debts in India that he would have been unable to leave that country even if he had possessed the price of a passage home, and, being thus stranded and penniless, he had accepted a mere pittance to drill the semi-barbarous matchlockmen of Sindkhote.

"He is mine body and soul, and the wretch is nearly desperate with home-sickness and misery," the Maharajah went on, warming as he saw that he had gripped Nugent's attention. " There are no Europeans for him to associate with in Sindkhote, and before his fall he was the most popular young officer at Simla and Calcuttaâ a good dancer, a crack shot and a grand polo player. He is as strong and as handsome as one of the ancient gods, and all the ladies adored him. I propose to return to India by the next mail boat, and I shall send him home to England, so that Violet Maynard may fall in love with him."

"What good is that going to do you? " asked Nugent, though his agile mind was already grasping the germ of the idea.

"It will be the task of this Leslie Chermside to induce Miss Maynard to elope with him on a fast steamer, ostensibly his own yacht, which I will furnish you with the funds to charter," the Maharajah continued. " It will be for you to select the crew and make all the arrangements, as well as secretly supervising Chermside's courtship and diplomatically working old Maynard so as to drive his daughter to consent to elope. Once on board, the rest will be easy, provided the embarkation is skilfully managed. She will make all speed round the Cape for Sindkhote, which is a maritime state, and the thing is done."

"And my twenty thousand will be paidâ when?"

"It will be placed to your credit the day Violet Maynard sets foot in my dominions. In any case, you will at once be supplied with the necessary money for preliminary expenses."

Nugent rapidly reflected. Win or lose the main stake, there should be some pretty pickings out of those preliminary expenses, and it ought not to be difficult in the event of failure so to cover up his own connection with the dastardly project as to escape unpleasant consequences for himself. It was a tempting prospect, but there was a flaw in the scheme from the point of view of one who would have sold his best friend for a song.

"You are sure of this fellow Chermside? " he said. " He won't play fast and loose with you, and chuck the whole job as soon as he gets quit of India and his embarrassments there?"

Bhagwan Singh's sensual lips creased in a cruel smile. " My dear Nugent," he said, "Mr, Leshe Chermside will not really be quit of his Indian debts till he has served my purpose. I shall buy them up, and hold them over him as a bond of good faith. If he shows signs of kicking over the traces it will be for you to put on the screwâ in your own way. Not that I anticipate anything of the sort from one who has sunk as low as he has, and I shau further secure his loyalty by the promise of a small pension contingent on his success."

Travers Nugent hesitated no longer. " Here is my hand on it," he exclaimed with an admiration that was not wholly feigned. " It would be flying in the face of Providence to stand out of a campaign planned on such masterly lines. Your Highness has supplied the strategy; I will devise the tactics."

"a screw loose somewhere"

A SMILING expanse of summer sea; hedges ablaze with wild flowers; the distant moorland one vast carpet of purple heather; and near at hand, dotted up and down on either side of a gently sloping coombe, some scores of pretty houses set in gardens of almost tropical luxuriance. Towards the lower end of the hill the private residences yielded pride of place to a little main street of more commercial aspect, which terminated in an unpretentious esplanade backed by a row of lodging-houses fronting the beach.

Westward from this spot the red cliffs shelved steadily upward till they culminated a mile and a half away in the Flagstaff Hill, a bold headland so called from the coastguard signal station thereon. Eastward of the esplanade, but hidden from it by a slight eminence, lay the marsh, formerly a broad estuary through which the river, then navigable for several miles inland, had emptied into the sea. In these later days the once broad river's mouth has become a mere stream by the action of a great storm which many years ago hurled a mighty dam of pebbles across all but a few 3ards of the outlet,

But the banks of the older watercourse remain, their steep red sides all verdure-clad and scored with cavities, hardly to be dignified as caves, concealed in the trailing undergrowth.

Such was the general configuration of the little town of Ottermouth in South Devon, for no fault of its own not quite a first-class seaside resort as yet, but slowly and surely worming its way into the affections of those who had discovered it. There was no pier, and therefore there were but few " trippers." But in the curious blend of brand-new brick villas and old-world houses of "cob" there dwelt men of varying fortunes, who in their time had helped to make history, and who had chosen this peaceful spot on the Devon coast as the one in which to end their strenuous days.

In one house you would have found a grey-headed veteran who rode into the valley of death at Balaclava; from another there strolled out on to the cliff front every morning to turn his dimmed eyes seaward one of the fast dwindling band who defended the Residency at Lucknow. And there were others of a younger generation, though also with finished careers, who had had their share in the Empire-building of the last half-century. There was, too, a sprinkling of rich business men, who only came to Ottermouth in the summer time to refresh themselves after toil in great cities.

In such an earthly paradise, where no one but the clergyman and the doctor ever pretended to do any work, there was naturally a clubâ as cosy and well-managed a rendezvous of the kind as could be found in many more populous resorts. The permanent members were all proud of it, and in their jealousy for its good repute were apt to regard stray visitors admitted to temporary membership with cold criticism till they had proved their title to more cordial consideration.

The club was the last building on the seaward side of the main streetâ a commanding position whence its windows on one side raked the esplanade, while those at the rear looked out to sea. About noon on a morning towards the middle of August three gentlemen were lounging in the general room, smoking and chatting in desultory fashion over the latest atrocities in Punch.

To them suddenly entered the club steward, who approached a tall, sun-burnt young man sitting a little apart from the others with the announcement: " There is some one who would like to see you, sir, at the door. I asked him into the hall, but he preferred to wait outside."

"Didn't he give his name?"

"No, sir; but I think he's a gentleman who has been staying at the Plume Hotel for the last week. I've seen him going in and out."

The tall young man reared his flannel-clad limbs from the depths of his comfortable chair, and went out, a half-stifled expression of annoyance escaping him. He had no sooner disappeared than one of the two remaining members, who had been leaning against the mantelpiece, with his back to the fireless grate, strolled over to one of the French windows overlooking the esplanade. He was an elderly man, very well groomed as to his person and clothes, and with a pair of alert, all-devouring eyes set in an ascetic face. Mr. Vernon Mallory had put in forty years at the Foreign Office and was now, in honourable retirement, reaping the reward of much useful work. He was known as a shrewd observer and a keen judge of character. It was now his pleasure, as it had once been his business, to know all things about all men.

"Chermside did not appear to be best pleased at the interruption," Mr. Mallory remarked. " Ah, there he goes, with the disturber of his peace, towards the marsh. I can understand his annoyance, for the man who called him out is a most unsavoury-looking person."

The other member, a fresh, clean-shaven youngster of not more than three-and-twenty, got up and joined his senior at the window.

"Who and what is this Mr. Leslie Chermside, anyhow? " he asked, after a prolonged stare at the two receding figures. " I rather like the chap, somehow, and yet there is a sort of shy constraint about him that is not altogether satisfactory."

"He arrived a month ago, bringing an introduction to our worthy honorary secretary from Nugent, on the strength of which he became a temporary member," Mr. Mallory replied, with a slight shrug of his shoulders.

Lieutenant Reginald Beauchamp, at present commanding a " destroyer " stationed at Plymouth, but spending his leave with his mother, was prone to merriment at all times and seasons. There was a dryness in the elder gentleman's tone which caused him to chuckle.

"You were never keen on Travers Nugent, I know," he said. " But you have not answered my question about Chermside with your customary enhghtenment, Mr. Mallor I asked who and what he is. My mother tells me that he has been making strong running with a pretty girlâ Miss Maynard, I think, the name wasâ whose people have taken the Manor House for the summer. You see, I only turned up last night for a short respite from my little tin ship, so I'm all agog for the local gossip."

At that moment the subject of their discussion and the man who had called for him disappeared from view, having rounded the corner of the slight eminence. The pair had struck into the footpath which would lead them along the marsh under the nearer bank of the vanished estuary. Mr. Mallory turned away from the window with an enigmatic smile for his young naval friend.

"I cannot tell you what Mr. Chermside is," he said when he had produced his cigar-case and selected a weed. " But the oibcial Army listsâ not the ones that are quite up to date, mind youâ record what he was. There seems to be an unexplained gulf between the termination of his military career and his presence in our midst. A hiatus, so to speak, of nearly two years since he was an officer in the 24th Lancers undoubtedly exists. His own account of himself is that he has recently come into money, and that he is playing about here while awaiting the arrival of a steam yacht on which he means to take an extended cruise. Beyond that, both my opinion and my scanty information coincide with yours. He strikes one as unobjectionable but reserved, and he has certainly been dangling after the daughter of old Maynard, who has rented the Manor House furnished for the season."

"What is Maynard? " demanded Reggie Beau-champ with persistent interest.

"A milhonaire maker of screws in Birmingham."

"Then it would be queer if there was a loose screw somewhere about his daughter's admirer," Reggie rejoined, and with a boyish laugh for his own jest he strolled off to the billiard-room in quest of a game.

In the meanwhile Leslie Chermside and his companion had reached the seclusion of the marshland path, at the same time plunging into a more private conversation than was advisable on the frequented sea-front. On their immediate left rose the tree-covered side, almost a miniature cliff, of the ancient river-bed; to the right of them there stretched to the opposite bank a quarter of a mile away the osiers and reeds that carpeted the mud-flats. There was no one to see or hear.

It did not need the presentation of a visiting card with his name on it to disclose Mr. Levi Levison's nationahty. The moment he opened his mouth to speak he stood revealed as a Hebrew of the Hebrews, and even before then, for apart from his lisping utterance he had all the bodily peculiarities of his race. The full red lips, the beaky nose, and the large conciliatory eyes that seemed to veil so much, could have belonged to no one but a Jew. His clothes were flashy, but none too clean. In age he was probably about thirty.

"I don't want to be harsh, but s'help me, Mr. Chermside, I ain't got any option in the matter," he was saying. " I've bought up your Indian debts in the ordinary courthe of business, and I can't afford to lose on the transaction. Here are the papers that you wanted to see. You'll find they're all ship-shape enough. And you must pardon my remarking that when you agreed toâ erâ act for the Maharajah in a certain delicate matter I sup-pothe you intended to keep faith with him."

Chermside took the proffered papers, glanced through and returned them. " Oh, yes; I intended to keep faith right enough," he replied rather wearily. " And I haven't said that I don't mean to do so, have I?"

"No, you'd hardly be such a juggins as that," Mr. Levison leered, exasperatingly. " But I've been here a week, Mr. Chermside, and kept my e3"es and ears open. I can find that things from his Highness's point of view are 'anging fire. What's a poor struggling feller to do? I bought up your little indiscretions in the Shining East, you see, on the understanding that his Highness, who sold them to me, would redeem them at a hundred per cent, advance on what I paid, directly you carried out his wishes; but that if not I was to put the screw on in the ordinary courthe of business. It wouldn't be nice for you to be therved with writs and thingsâ judgment summonses they'd soon blossom intoâ just when you're enjoying yourself in a pretty place like this."

Mr. Levison rolled his dark eyes over the picturesque landscape as if he had no thought but for the beauties of Nature.

Leslie Chermside made no reply, but paced on with downcast gaze.

"You see, I'm a little bit in the know," Levison went on, after a furtive glance at his tall companion's bronzed face. " Mr. Travers Nugent came down by the late train last night, and I've had a chat with him this morning up at that sweet little place of hisâ ' The Hut," he calls it. The steamer is lying at Portland, not thirty miles away, only waiting for you to throw your handkerchief to the girl, which, from what I've seen, she'll pick up fast enough. And, though expense is no object, it don't do to keep a crew of fifty toughs in harbour wondering why they don't start on a cruise that's to end in a pile of dollars for all of them."

A spasm crossed Chermside's face, and he dug the nails of his right hand into the palm as though he restrained some emotion with difficulty. " There was no time limit mentioned in my engagement with the Maharajah," he said hoarsely. " Nor did his Highness inform me that he had had my debts assigned to him. He gave me to understand that he had paid them."

Levison emitted a tantalizing laugh. " That's where the wily Hindoo had you on toast," he rejoined. " A wise precaution in case you should for any reason throw him over, as it begins to look as if you meant to. Your little affair with the lady seems to blow hot and cold, Mr. Chermside, which is why I'm pressing you a bit. Not that I'm 'ard-'earted by any means. Take till to-morrow night to think it over, and then, if you can give me a definite assurance that it will be all right in a week or so, I'll 'old my 'and."

Leslie Chermside breathed a sigh of relief. " Very well," he said, " by that time I may have news for you. Where shall we meet? It had better be somewhere where there is no risk of our being overheard."

The Jew glanced round the lonely landscape. Even at mid-day the marsh was deserted in favour of the superior attractions of the shore, the golf links, and the tennis field.

"We couldn't better this," he said. " There'll be a moon up, and there won't be a soul about at ten o'clock."

"That will suit excellently. I will meet you here at ten o'clock to-morrow night," replied Chermside. " And now as I am going on to lunch at the Manor House"

"You will be glad to get rid of yours truly," Mr. Levison interrupted. " Righto! Mr. Chermside. I'll go back the way we came, hoping that you will enjoy a sumptuous meal, and afterwards get a chance to put in some vicarious courtship. So long."

He turned on his heel, waving a be-ringed hand of insanitary aspect, and Leslie Chermside strode forward along the grassy footpath. His brows were knitted in a frown, and from time to time he shook his broad shoulders as though to free himself from an influence that oppressed the natural vigour of his strong frame.

He was well aware that he stood at the parting of the ways, with the disadvantage of not knowing where either of the two roads open to him would lead, except that they pointed to dishonour and misery. It was nearly three months now since he had been summoned to the Maharajah's presence in the tawdry palace at Sindkhote, and had been offered by his employer a way of escape from the bonds that held him in exile, in a position little better than that of a tinselled head flunkeyâ an appanage of Bhagwan Singh's barbaric splendour.

The task set him had been revolting enough; it had filled him with loathing for the gross libertine who was his tempter; but, homesick for England and wretched in the miserable Hfe he was leading, he had in reckless humour yielded, hating himself while doing so even more than the sardonic prince who was sending him home to England to commit such an outrage on an Englishwoman. After all, he had told himself, he didn't know the girl. Very likely she had brought her fate on herself by flirting with Bhagwan Singh in London, So he pledged himself to the foul errand, and sailed by the next mail-boat with a letter of introduction to Travers Nugent.

On his presenting it, Nugent had apprised him of the progress already made in the plot, and it was by no means inconsiderable. The Manor House at Ottermouth being to let furnished for the summer, it had not been difficult for the Maharajah's astute agent, who had a cottage in the little resort, to persuade Mr. Montague Maynard to take it. Indeed, the prospect of having the brilliant Travers Nugent as a neighbour during his holiday was in itself sufficient inducement to the wealthy screw manufacturer to fall into the trap. All that remained for the present was for Chermside to go down and commence operations by laying siege to Violet May-nard's heart, Nugent promising to follow later, when he had perfected the arrangements for manning and victualhng the swift turbine steamer he had chartered.

In sullen mood, and with rage in his heart against the cruel fate that had made a blackguard of him, Chermside had set out on his despicable mission. And from the very moment he had looked into Violet Maynard's pure eyes his purpose had begun to weaken, giving place to a greater horror of himself and the vile thing he had consented to do. If, in the depths of his misery out yonder, he had considered the matter at all, he had considered it in the shadowy abstract, as a means of escape from the hell-upon-earth exile he was enduring. But here in England, and in touch with the charming person-ahty of his intended victim, the scales were hfted from his moral vision, and he was left face to face with the enormity of his contemplated offence.

Yet his honour, if the word could be used in such a connexion, " rooted in dishonour stood," for he had pledged himself for what he beheved to be valuable consideration to go through with the iniquity. For the first few days of his stay in Otter-mouth he adhered rigidly to his contract. He presented the letters of introduction with which Travers Nugent had furnished him, and freely accepted Montague Maynard's lavish hospitahty. He posed as a gallant gentleman, and paid attentions to Violct which the gossips of the links and the tennis field described as " marked." And then as suddenly as he had apparently caught fire he apparently cooled. The spurious, perverted sense of duty which for a week or two kept him loyal to his tempter was shattered by a stronger force that would not be denied.

Violet's friendship, frankly given as to an equal properly accredited, her winsome ways, the careless abandon of a girl who trusted and evidently liked him, had conquered his heart.

Leslie Chermside was honestly in love with the woman whom he was pledged to entrap for delivery like a bale of goods to that sinister Oriental satyr, waiting in the palace at Sindkhote seven thousand miles away for the fulfilment of his mission. By the irony of fate, his love for the girl whom he had been hired to destroy was the first true passion of his life, and by the same strange kink in fortune's chain the first effect was to cause him to repress all semblance of love.

How could he do otherwise, when by no possibility could the suit of such a penniless wastrel as himself be crowned with success? And as to continuing his attentions on behalf of Bhagwan Singhâ well, he felt that he would cheerfully give many years of his life to wipe that vile episode from the page of his memory. So for the past week he had just drifted, avoiding any approach to more intimate relations, but loth to leave altogether the shrine at which it had been balm to his bruised heart to worship.

And now in some shape the end must come to the bitter-sweet interlude. The appearance of the Jew Levison on the scene left no room for doubt that if he refused to proceed with the Maharajah's dirty work, he would not be allowed to strut in false feathers much longer.

"I can have but one answer for that swine to- morrow night, and then he will take measures to wreak upon me Bhagvvan Singh's revenge," he told himself, as he quitted the marshland and struck into the road that presently brought him to the lodge gates of the Manor House.

OTTERMOUTH Manor was a place of importance in the county, and was only let furnished because its noble owner possessed so many other seats in different parts of the kingdom that for the moment he had no use for it. It is a practical age, and no one is so highly placed that he cannot without loss of dignity turn the nimble sixpence. The genial peer who had recently inherited the Manor, together with most of the ground-rents of the surrounding district, was no exception to the rule, and he had no objection to having his great rambling mansion and its appurtenances " kept up " at some one else's expense.

The consequence was that Mr. Montague Maynard found himself housed for the summer almost en-prince. Not that he was unaccustomed to luxury. Both in his splendid modern villa at Harborne, whence a thousand pound Mercedes car rushed him daily to his office in Birmingham, and at his London house in Park Lane, where he spent six weeks in the spring, he wanted for nothing that money can do for the assuagement of the sordid side of a commercial magnate's life. But at neither of those palatial abodes could he enjoy the sense of space, the glamour of feudal importance, and the pretence at majestic isolation which were included in the heavy rental he paid for the privilege of occupying Ottermouth Manor House.

It was approached on one side by a long carriage-drive under an avenue of ancient elms, and halfway up this Leslie Chermside saw three people advancing towards himâ a rather incongruous trio. No need for him to look twice at the tall girl in the simple white blouse swinging along with the graceful vigour of youth a little behind the other two. The sight of her set his pulses beating, for it was Violet Maynard herself, and Leslie felt sick with remorse at the glad smile of recognition she gave him. The remaining pair in this strangely-assorted party consisted of a diminutive old lady severely dressed in black, and of a foreign-looking man wearing ragged blue cotton trousers, who slouched along barefooted, carrying over his shoulder a stick from which depended several strings of onions.

The old lady appeared to be driving the foreigner before her at the point of her sunshade, while Violet entered an occasional half-laughing protest against her proceedings.

Chermside raised his hat as he drew near, and with a torrent of abuse and a final prod of her sunshade, the owner of the latter abandoned the pursuit, the two ladies turning to walk back to the house with the invited guest.

"No wonder you are astonished at Aunt Sarah's behaviour, Mr. Chermside," said Violet gaily. " She has been frightening that poor French onion-seller out of his wits and warning him off the premises for some reason that I have been unable to prevail on her to disclose."

"I am quite sure that Miss Dymmock would be actuated by no reason but a good one," Chermside replied politely. " I will wager that she had received strong provocation, and that the castigation I was privileged to witness was thoroughly deserved."

The little old lady, who was rapidly regaining her temper, cast a grateful glance at the speaker. At the commencement of their as yet short acquaintance she had taken a genuine liking for the handsome young soldier, and she had the firmest faith in her intuitions. Miss Sarah Dymmock was a personage to be reckoned with in the Maynard household. The aunt of Violet's mother, Montague Maynard's late wife, she had brought the girl up from childhood, and had incidentally governed the screw manufacturer's establishment with a rod of iron. Having a large fortune in her own right, and being suspected of a carefully-veiled kindness, her many eccentricities were forgiven her by those who knew her best.

"That's right, Mr. Chermside; I like a man who can stick up for an ugly old woman," she chuckled. " It's a pity a gallant gentleman of your sort didn't come my way when I was a lass, for I might have been a great-grandmother, instead of only great-aunt, to an impudent chit of a girl who has no respect for ageâ and venerableness. Well, I am venerable, ain't I? " she added, stopping and stamping her foot at Violet's merry laugh.

"Oh, yes, dearest Auntie; you are more than thatâ you are truly terrible at times," said the girl.

"I mean to be," Miss Dymmock continued austerely, resuming her progress. " As to my reason for chasing that monkey-faced Frenchy out of the grounds, I shall say nothingâ nothing at all till I have laid the facts before Mr. Travers Nugent, who is, I believe, to join us at lunch. I don't like Travers Nugent, mind you. But he is a man of the world, and I value his opinion as such. Personally, I wouldn't trust him with a shilling."

This was evidently the old lady's last word on the subject, but the rather awkward silence that ensued was due chiefly to the manner of her allusion to Nugent, Violet was rendered uncomfortable by her outspoken bluntness, because she knew that Leslie Chermside owed his presence amongst them to the introduction he had brought from the man so openly disparaged. And Leslie was ill at ease from the immediate prospect of having to meet one whom he had hitherto regarded as his partner in infamy, but from whom in his awakened repentance it would be his duty to dissociate himself at the earliest possible moment.

During the two or three days he had spent in London on his arrival from India he had neither been repelled nor attracted by the smooth-spoken gentleman who had taken him in tow. Beyond the brief discussion necessary to the elaboration of their arrangements Nugent had been far too wary to indulge in useless harping on the scheme in hand. It was not his cue to emphasize the heartless villainy of their compact. Indeed, he dismissed the moral aspect of the affair in a slurred and utterly mendacious justification, hinting that Violet May-nard had only herself to thank for having played fast and loose with the Maharajah. He even suggested that she had been really partial to the handsome Oriental, and would speedily become reconciled.

The black business being thus by mutual consent relegated to the background, Nugent had laid himself out to be a pleasant host without allowing it to be seen that he was making a minute study of the young man upon whom his own bribe would so largely depend. Leslie had not thought very much about him, except as one of the figures in what seemed more like a bad dream than reality.

But now all that was changed, and the personality of Bhagwan Singh's English wire-puller had for him a sinister significance. He had no doubt that the Cockney Jew Levison was acting in collusion with the more cultured scoundrel, and he wondered how the latter would take his revolt. Not kindly, that was fairly certain; but Leslie could not see how Nugent could injure him beyond inflicting the cunningly-provided punishment of financial ruin which he was powerless to resist. He could not expose the conspiracy without confessing his own part in it, and he felt that he would cheerfully prefer death to so abasing himself in Violet's eyes. At present his intention was to bask in the sunshine of fictitious happiness for one more day and then vanish to South America, New Zealandâ anywhere where a pair of strong arms could provide him with bread.

The opportunity for revolt was on him sooner than he expected. When they reached the Manor House

Mr. Maynard was at the hall door in the act of welcoming Nugent, who had arrived in his car, entering the park by the north lodge. The brilliant man-about-town turned to the ladies with effusion, receiving a courteous greeting from Violet and a sniff from Aunt Sarah, who, however, as she passed into the hall deigned to fling back at him: " You are as full of mischief as a ripe cheese is of maggots. I am going to take your opinion on a piece of mischief presently."

Mr. Maynard, a stout, florid man of sixty, gave a great guffaw. " The old girl always had her knife into you, Nugent," he roared, " but, hke all the rest of 'em, she can't do without you. Maggots in cheese! Lord love me, what' 11 she say next."

He turned away to direct the chauffeur to the stable-yard, and Chermside drew Nugent aside, saying, in a rapid whisperâ

"I am not going on with the damned thing!"

Travers Nugent, if he felt surprise, did not show it; nor was there any annoyance in his gently-murmured question: " You have counted the cost, I presume? You understand what defection will entail?"

"Oh, yes; that beast Levison has taken care of that," rephed Chermside. " I am to meet him tomorrow night on the marsh at ten o'clock to give him my final answer. But that was only to secure a day's respite, andâ and take leave of my friends. My mind is quite made up. I shall withdraw, and let him do his worst."

Again there was no trace of disappointment in Nugent's reception of this definite retirement. For an instant his right hand caressed his long, fair moustache, while his cold blue eyes rested meditatively on the slightly-flushed face of the recalcitrant, but the only note in his voice was one of unselfish concern as he said

"I am afraid you will find it very unpleasant, but I suppose that if you have scruples you are right to act on them."

There was no time for more, for Montague May-nard, having seen to the bestowal of the car and the chauffeur, came bustling back and conducted his two guests to the dining-room, where the ladies joined them at the luncheon table. Chermside managed to secure a seat next Violet, but in such a small party there was no chance for intimate conversation. On the whole, he was glad of it, for after to-dayâ to-morrow at latestâ it was improbable that he would ever see again the girl upon whom he would have inflicted such deadly wrong. Even now, in the midst of lightest chatter, she stabbed him over and over again with the frank confidence in her trusting eyes. He felt with a shudder that if he had pursued his fell mission to the end it would have been crowned with a horrible success.

Already his punishment had begun; he loved the woman whom he would have destroyed, and in a few hours he must say good-bye to her for ever. Yes, he was thankful that Aunt Sarah's quips and cranks, and Travers Nugent's scintillating small-talk rattled like musketry fire to the exclusion of all else.

Once or twice he stole a look at the man to whom Bhagwan Singh had accredited himâ natt ' in his grey summer tweeds, perfectly self-possessed and brimming over with tit-bits of harmless society gossip. Nugent's eyes were not prone to laughter, but his lips were, and they were laughing almost unceasingly now. Leslie Chermside wondered if this was altogether natural, or was it a pose designed to cover deeper emotions? The man had undoubtedly received a set-back in the last half-hour in the displacement of a programme that must have cost him much intricate scheming. The chartering of that steamer lying at Portland ready for her prey, and the engagement of a crew sufficiently unscrupulous, could have been no light work. How was it, then, that Nugent could accept with complacency the overthrow of the plan? Had he still hopes of success by some devious method at present carefully concealed?

Leslie comforted himself that that could not be. The steamer might rot at her moorings and the crew mutiny before any signal for her movement should come from him, and he would take good care before he vanished into the unknown that the same game should not be played with some pawn less susceptible than himself. He would anonymously warn Mr. Maynard of the Maharajah's design to kidnap his daughter, doing it in such a way that he should not be identified with the first abortive attempt. He clung desperately to the hope that he might remain a congenial memory to the unsuspecting girl at his side.

As soon as the butler and his satellites had served coffee and retired. Miss Sarah Dymmock straightened herself in her chair, and, with a bird-like glance and a shake of her grey curls, prodded her finger at Nugent.

"Now, you high priest of intrigue, I will consult your judgment," was her startling commencement. " The question is, was I right or wrong to eject from the grounds of this mansion an unwashed foreigner whom I caught using violent and insulting language to the French maid whose services I share with my great-niece?"

"When I came upon the scene it was Auntie who was using violent and insulting language to the unwashed foreigner," Violet remarked demurely.

"Silence, minx," the old lady retorted. " I found the maid, Louise Aubin, in tears in the shrubbery walk, with the creature bullying and threatening her. She explained that the fellow, who is one of the onion-sellers from a French lugger recently arrived at Exmouth full of similar vermin, knew her at her home in Normandy, and was, in fact, her lover there. On discovering her here by accident while disposing of his wares, he wanted to renew the old relations, and has been hanging about for the last month with that intention. He has found out that during the last week Louise has been coquetting with some summer visitor staying in the town. She did not mention this second Lothario's name, but I gathered that he was putting up at the Plume Hotel."

"Ah! " said Nugent, who had been listening politely, " that does not tell us much, for I was informed this morning that the Plume is full to overflowing just now. Well, dear lady, I cannot presume to criticise your drastic measures. It seems to me to depend on Mademoiselle Aubin's inclinations. If she prefers the Frenchman, you have acted somewhat severely; if the gentleman at the Plume is the favoured swain, you have played the good mistress in protecting your servant from a nuisance."

Aunt Sarah, quaintly valuing the opinion of the man she disliked, nodded reflectively. " I'll find out which she likes best," she said. " It won't be the foreigner, I think, she being a girl of sense. She'd be as silly as Violet would have been if she'd accepted that blackamoor who had the impudence to propose to her at the beginning of the London season."

Montague Maynard let off one of his mighty bellows. " That was cheek if you like," he said, " though my little girl very soon sent him off with a flea in his ear. But you are forgetting. Aunt Sarah, that the boot was on the other leg in the case that made the Maharajah of Sindkhote the laughing-stock of London. The onion-seller is a compatriot of his inamorata. By the way, Nugent â you were pretty thick with his Highnessâ how did he take his knock-out?"

Travers Nugent looked across the table at Leslie Chermside through the wealth of hot-house flowers, pondering his reply with greater deliberation than it seemed to demand.

"As you know," he said at length, " the Maharajah left England within a few days of the ball at Brabazon House, where I understood that his discomfiture took place. I saw very little of him in the interval. Like all men worthy of the name who have set out to win a great prize and have met with failure, he was not one to admit defeat."

"Hear that, Vi? " said the screw manufacturer, rising. " His Highness means to come back and have another shy next season. There'll be a chance for you to be the pride of the harem yet, if you choose to think better of it."

Violet's laugh, as she also rose to join in the general movement, rang out merrily, proving how lightly she had treated Bhagwan's wooingâ how little she realized the smouldering danger that lurked for her in the steamer at Portland, lying ready to snatch her from peaceful Ottermouth to undreamed of horrors in the unspeakable East,

"I hope he won't trouble," she said lightly. " I let him down easy last time, but if it occurs again I shall have to be rude."

Leslie Chermside, following out of the dining-room, felt a prescience of coming peril for the beautiful speaker, and it was apart and separate from the plot in which he was to have taken such an ignoble part. From himself he knew that she would never have aught but loving fealty, and, so far as in him lay, protection. But in Nugent's words, uttered with such seeming carelessness, yet so well considered, there had, he could have sworn, sounded a note of menace, intended to be subtly conveyed to himself, that defeat was not admitted.

And the pity of it was that in a day or two at most he must fly from Ottermouth, unless he remained to be branded by that dirty little Jew as an impostor. In either case, his championship would be a sorry thing to stand between Violet Maynard and the fresh devices he feared were already hatching in Travers Nugent's cunning brain.

MR. NUGENT did not seekfurther private speech with Leshe Chermside while he remained at the Manor House. He acted in every respect as though he accepted the young man's renunciation as final, and after a saunter through the exquisite gardens with his host, asked that his car might be brought round. Having only reached Ottermouth the previous evening, he explained there were many things that claimed his attention at home,

"All right, dear boy," said Montague Maynard in his loud jolly voice. " Run out and see us whenever you can tear yourself away from golf and the delights of the Ottermouth Club. Old Sarah Dym-mock hates you like the devil, but she don't bite so long as people don't want to hurt my little Violet, and she's a good sportswoman. And you're too good a sportsman yourself to mind an old woman's whims."

"I thoroughly understand Miss Dymmock, and I have the most profound regard for her," responded Nugent cordially. " There is never likely to be any serious matter at issue between us, but if there were I should be very sorry to have to cross swords with her."

Yet his thin lips curled in a dreamy smile as he was whirled away in the serviceable little Darracq which had been presented to him by a titled idiot in gratitude for an introduction that had eventually ruined him.

"I hardly think that Miss Sarah Dymmock, useful as she has proved this morning, will loom on the horizon of present interests," he murmured softly to himself when he had directed his chauffeur to drive him home.

During the six minutes which it took to cover the distance from the Manor House into the town Nugent closed his eyes and leaned back, indifferent to the autumn glories of the fair Devon landscape. The fern-girt lanes, with occasional peeps of the blue sea and the red point at the mouth of the river, the golden harvest-fields, the lush orchards with their drooping loads of cider apples, the old cob-built farmsteadsâ all these flashed past him unheeded as he sat with folded arms wrapped in deepest reverie.

But when the car took the steep dip at the eastern end of the parade, and the road, first on one side only and then on both, became flanked with houses, he braced himself for social amenities. People were about in plenty, mostly known to him, and many of them eager for recognition by the cool-looking gentleman in the car who had the reputation of being a personage in London society. Nearly all the ladies of Ottermouth, at any rate, were proud of their Travcrs Nugent, and rejoiced greatly that for a month or two in the year he deigned to sojourn in their midst. And the dowdier the ladies and the less he had to do with them the prouder were they.

But the dowdy ladies at Ottermouth were an insignificant minority. Certainly not to be classed in that category was the winsome maiden, dressed in immaculate white flannel and carrying a tennis racquet, to whom Nugent raised his soft grey hat as the car struck into the main street. A vision of dainty, if very youthful, loveliness, Enid Mallory was smart from the crown of her well-poised little head to the soles of her natty shoes. She returned Nugent's bow with a trace of brusqueness, and immediately turned and made a grimace at the clean-shaven young fellow who was with her. Nugent, though not intending to do so, saw the grimace out of the tail of his eye, and frowned slightly when the car had passed.

"Old Mallory's daughter," he murmured. " She has done her hair up and lengthened her dress since last year, and she appears to have been infected Mdth the paternal antipathy. I must not forget that Mr. Vincent Mallory, formerly of the Foreign Office, is a resident in this Arcadian spot. He might, under certain circumstances, become a factor to be reckoned with."

Aloud he said to his chauffeur, who had come down with the car some days in advance: " Dixon, do you know who that young gentleman was who was walking with Miss Mallory?"

"It's Mr. Beauchamp, sir," was the reply. " Son of Mrs. Beauchamp, who lives in Lome Villas.

He's a lieutenant in the Navy, I've heard, commanding a torpedo-boat at Plymouth. He is at home on leave just at present, sir."

"Thank you, Dixon; you are always a mine of information," Nugent said with the suave urbanity he alwa3 s used towards inferiors.

But under his breath he added, "A curious combination, and one that may be worth watching."

The house in which Mr. Travers Nugent enjoyed his summer leisure lay on the hill beyond the western hmits of the town. Though he spoke of it as a cottage, it was really a luxurious bachelor abode, standing in a secluded garden and removed from the main road to Exmouth by a serpentine drive, not, of course, to be compared with the noble avenue at the Manor House, but long enough to separate the owner of The Hut from the madding crowd by quite a respectable distance.

Descending at his front door, Mr. Nugent passed through a porch smothered in purple clematis into a small, square hall, deliciously cool and shaded. Here he was met by a quiet-looking man of middle age, with a face like a sphinx, and wearing a black cutaway coat. Nugent was not one to make his confidential servant the receptacle of more secrets than he could help, but he knew that if he chose to do so this personification of reticence and discretion would never betray them.

"Well, Sinnett? " he said. They neither of them wasted words at any time in their communications.

"I heard the car, sir," was the reply. " I know you like to be prepared for visitors. Mr. Levison is waiting to see you in the smoke-room."

"Good! I will see him directly," said Nugent, glancing at the closed door of the room indicated. Then, dropping his voice, he added, "Come out into the porch a moment."

The effect of this manoeuvre was to place them beyond all chance of being overheard from the smoking-room, though the conversation was nevertheless continued with all precaution.

"I want you to go into Exmouth at once," said Nugent. " Dixon will take you in the car. At the quay you will find one of those French luggers which come over laden with onions to be peddled about the country by the crew. Inquire for a man named Pierre Legros, and tell him that I will buy as many strings of onions as he can carry if he will bring them over during the evening."

"Very good, sir," replied the manservant, who had absorbed the lucid but inexplicable instructions without the quiver of an eyelash. " Does Legros know you, sir?"

"He has never heard of me, nor I of him till this morning. I imagine, though, that the prospect of a good sale will bring him here. If, however, he demurs at all you might say that I have news to his advantage in connection with the Manor House. You understand, of course, Sinnett, that I am not really in need of onions?"

"You want the man, sir?"

"I must have the man."

With which the master of The Hut turned away in the certainty that he would get what he wanted, and, recrossing the hall, entered his cosy-smoking-room.

"Ah, Levison! Sorry to have kept you waiting," was his urbanely offhand greeting to the httle Jew who rose obsequiously from a big easy-chair. " I have been lunching at the Manor House, and as I met Mr. Chermside there I am able to forestall your report. He tells me that he intends to kick over the traces."

"Prethithely what he told me, Mr. Nugent, sir," replied the Hebrew. " And I reckon he means it. Though I'm only in the pawnbroking line, and an assistant at that, I flatter mythelf I played the blooming financier up to the nines, but he was as stubborn as Balaam's talking moke. He ain't given me his final answer, yet, though. I'm to meet him tomorrow night for that."

"So he said, and you must keep the appointment and do your level best to make him change his mind," Nugent went on. " You are a clever little chap, and I shouldn't be surprised if you succeeded. Mr. Leslie Chermside is suffering from a qualm of conscience which may be only transitory if you paint the alternative in sufficiently lurid colours."

"S'elp me, sir, but you can rely on me to rub it in thick."

"I am sure of that, though, by the way, I heard to-day that you have not been without your relaxations here while acting as my spy-glass," rejoined Nugent with an amused laugh. " How about the pretty lady's-maid at the Manor House, eh?"

Mr. Levison gazed at the speaker in blind consternation, but, finding nothing but playful tolerance in his employer's manner, he admitted the soft impeachmentâ boastfully, as is the way of such vulgar lady-killers.

"You're a fair caution, sir," he sniggered. " It licks me how you got hold of that; but there! you get hold of most things. The time was 'anging a bit 'eavy, you see. sir, and she's a dressy little bit of French goods. No 'arm done, I spothe, as it didn't interfere with business?"

"No harm whatever, Levison," said Nugent kindly. " I only mentioned it to show you what a paternal interest I take in your doings. Those who serve me well have no cause to be dissatisfied with the rewards they earn, and you will be no exception to the rule. Only don't relax your efforts with Chermside. Keep the appointment with him tomorrow night, and turn the screw till he squirms. Maybe he'll see reason yet."

And having fortified his visitor with whisky and a good cigar, Mr. Nugent put a graceful finish to his hospitality by conducting him to a side gate that led from the garden on to the moor.

"You came in this way? " he said carelessly as he opened the gate. " That is right. I want you to be particular about that whenever you have occasion to see me. It might complicate matters if your connection with me got to be talked of in this gossipy place."

"Dull little 'ole, I call it," commented Mr. Levison as he prepared to cross the purple heather. " Couldn't have stuck it for a week, I don't think, if it hadn't have been for Louise Aubin. A gent must amuse himself, and one misses the music-'alls. Well, so long, sir; I'll let Chermside 'ave it 'ot to-morrow night."

Nugent watched the mean-looking figure go stum- bling along the moorland track on a detour towards the town, and then, the acid smile on his lips in curious contrast with the thoughtful frown on his brows, he turned back into the house. He was the most abstemious of men, but on reaching his den he poured out a fairly strong brandy and soda and drank it at a draught.

"It's a big stake for reclaiming the rebel," he muttered. " But I think it will work out right if Sinnett's mission pans out properly."

But presently, when the laconic man-servant returned with his report that Pierre Legros would deliver several strings of onions during the evening, there was nothing in the manner of the master to denote whether he was satisfied or not.

"Thank you, Sinnett. Take care that he does not go away without my seeing him," was all that Mr. Travers Nugent vouchsafed in reply.

"OO that is Nugent, the London chap who lives
O at The Hut? " said Lieutenant Beauchamp, when the car had flashed past. " Why do you accentuate the information by making such disgustingly ugly faces, Pussy?"

Miss Enid Mallory tossed her dainty head in mock indignation. " You are perfectly horrid, Mr. Beauchamp," she snapped at him. " As if I could make an ugly face if I tried ever so. And I won't have you calling me Pussyâ now that Lm grown up."

"Grown up, is it, the little spitfire? " grinned the young sailor. " And I am to be Mr. Beauchamp, am I? Well, we used to be Reggie and Pussy when I was at home last, and, whatever you may do, the force of habit will be too strong for me. Even if I try to conquer it, which I shan't."

"That was three years ago, before you went to China," retorted Enid with dignity.

"What's the difference? We're neither of us very old yet, though Lm not sure I didn't like you better with a pigtail down your back than with all that crinkly bulge round your ears. However, to be serious, and stick to our muttonsâ what's the matter with Nugent?"

"Father doesn't Uke him," rephed Enid, still inclined to ride the high horse.

"I know that Mr. Mallory doesn't like him, but why not? " persisted Reggie. " I have the greatest regard for your father's judgment in all things. He is invariably right in his concl isions, but he is so jolly reticent as to how he arrives at them. I saw in the club this morning, when Nugent's name cropped up, that he didn't cotton to the johnny, but he refused to be drawn on the subject."

Enid was mollified at last, as she always was by any tribute to the acumen of the parent whom she adored.

"I don't know his reason," she said, as they turned to retrace their steps along the parade. ' But father, till he retired, was at the Foreign Office, as you are aware, and in the course of his duties he learned all sorts of secrets and came in contact with all sorts of shady men. I fancy his antipathy dates back to something that occurred during his official career, but you might as well try to open an oyster with your fingers as induce him to divulge what he knows."

Reggie Beauchamp nodded, really more interested in the sprightly hoyden he was talking to than in the subject of their conversation. " I see," he said. " li that's the way you figure it out, I shall be aware of Mr. Travers Nugent when I meet him at the club, H he's a dark horse he might rook me at billiards or bridge. I am obliged to you for this warning. Miss Mallory. You have probably saved an unsophisti- cated sailor from premature ruin and a suicide's grave."

Enid glanced up at him, her eyes dancing with mischief. " Bother Mr. Nugent! " she exclaimed. " Now that you have addressed me with proper respect, you may call me Pussy again if you wishâ till you misbehave again."

So for the next half-hour they reverted to earlier nomenclature, and forgot to play at quarrelling as they wandered up and down by the summer sea. And when at length they parted, Enid to go home to pour out tea for her blind mother, and Reggie to enter the club, they lightly made an appointment which was to have its grim bearing on the tale that has yet to be told.

"Look here. Miss Mallory," said the Lieutenant, with feigned solemnity. " I have to go into Exeter to-morrow to try on some new uniforms, and tonight I must stay at home and help the mater entertain a wretched curate whom she has invited to dinner. But I shall be at large to-morrow evening. What about a prowl along the shore or up the marsh? We might renew hostilities, and get some sort of a notion which of us is really right in the matter of our Christian names. I may change my mind, and come to the conclusion that you are, after all."

"Oh, may you, indeed, Reggie? " replied the girl, and with a roguish laugh she ran away without saying whether or no she would meet him. But he was familiar with his former playmate's impish ways, and it was in sublime confidence that the appointment would be kept that he loitered about on the sea-front on the evening of the following day.

Sure enough, a little after nine, when the sunset glow still lingered in the western sky, Miss Enid's white-clad figure was seen threading its way through the loungers on the parade. It was a beautiful evening, and the junior section of residents and visitors were about in plenty. Young men and maidens, hatless and in evening dress, strolled up and down the asphalte side-walk between the coastguard station and the club, for the most part chattering of the handicaps in the forthcoming tennis tournament, while some few exceptions, too busy making eyes at each other for such frivolity, worshipped at the love-god's shrine. Such public worship, however, has ever been considered bad form at Ottermouth, except among septuagenarians and the rosy-cheeked couples who on Sundays " walk out " together in the country lanes.

Perhaps it was because of this unwritten law of the place that Reggie Beauchamp and Enid Mal-lory, having duly greeted each other with flippant discourtesy, but having the germ of quite another sentiment in their irresponsible hearts, intuitively turned their steps to the further end of the parade, and came to a halt at the spot where the struggle between the feeble efforts of the urban council and the giant forces of nature ceased. In front lay the bank of shingle across the former river's mouth; to the left stretched the sedge-covered, dyke-sected bed of the old estuary.

"Shall we go back to the parade or take a turn up the marsh? " asked Reggie. And then, without waiting for a reply, he added, "By Jingo! Look out to sea. There is a cruiserâ the Terrible, I think, or one of her class."

Enid followed the direction of his pointing finger, and in the fast-fading twilight saw the great four-funnelled monster steaming slowly about two miles out at sea. Even as they looked, the big war-ship became little more than a huge blurred shape, barely discernible in the darkness that was swiftly blotting out land and sea.

"Well, she won't bite, I suppose," said the girl carelessly.

"No, but she might bark," laughed the Lieutenant. " I expect she's out for night practice with her heavy gunsâ with blank charges, of course."

The young people quickly lost interest in the ship, and, turning aside, struck into the path traversed by Leslie Chermside and Levison on the morning of the preceding day. It was raised above the level of the mud-flats which skirted it on the right; on the other side rose the umbrageous bank of the old water-course, increasing the shadows in which they walked.

Presently Enid's hand stole under her companion's arm, and they glided naturally into the frank comradeship which had prevailed between them long before the mutual banter which they had lately affected, and which was probably due to a desire to conceal the first stirrings of something stronger than a boy-and-girl attachment. They were both of the age when young folk are supremely susceptible, but have a self-conscious dread of being thought so. Out here on the marsh, in the kindly mantle of a moonless summer night, they could enjoy the pleasure of propinquity without fear of being laughed at.

"Let's sit down here for a bit while I smoke a cigarette," said Reggie, when they had gone half a mile along the marsh. " It is the old ambush, as we called it, where we used to picnic when I was a middy and you were a kid."

He ran down the side of the raised path into a little glade formed by some dwarf oaks at the base of the miniature cliff, and Enid followed, seating herself on the low-growing branch of one of the trees. It was quite dark nowâ so dark that though they were very close to the path they had quitted, they could not be seen from it. Even in daylight they would have been invisible behind their leafy screen.

"I suppose you executed that manoeuvre because you heard the footsteps behind us," said Enid in a whisper.

"Footsteps? I didn't hear any," replied Reggie.

"Hush! Don't speak. You can hear them now."

The sound of hurrying feet was distinctly audible now from the path, and a moment later a manâ the heavy tread left no doubt that it was a manâ went by. He was almost running, and they could hear his quick breathing, but it was impossible to tell whether he was tall or short, young or old, rich or poor, in the inky blackness that had swallowed up the marsh.

"A telegraph boy taking a short cut to the Manor House," suggested Enid when the steps had died away.

"Too late for thatâ the office closed two hours ago," replied Reggie Beauchamp carelessly. " More likely some poacher who has been setting snares for rabbits, and thought he heard a keeper behind him. The Ottermoiith fishermen used to be precious handy with a bit of copper wire and a bootlace."

The brief interruption passed from their minds, and they had been chattering for about ten minutes when once again the silence of the marsh was broken b ' the sound of advancing steps. This time the wayfarer came along in more leisurely fashion, and in this case also it was possible to guess from the heavy footfall that the passer by was a man. Perhaps a minute elapsed, and then, just as the young people were becoming absorbed in each other again, there came from further along the marshâ that is to say, from the direction to which both the successive pedestrians had been proceedingâ a sudden sharp cry, ending in a long-drawn wail.

"What on earth was that? " exclaimed Enid, jumping down from her bough.

"Goodness knows," laughed the careless sailor. " Either a bereaved cow or a curlew suffering from nightmare. Sit down again, Pussy; it was nothing to worry about."

"It struck me as being distinctly human," said Enid doubtfully, but she swung herself back into the tree, willing to be convinced that there was nothing wrong, rather than terminate a tete-d-tete that was rapidly gliding into a flirtation. Another pleasant quarter of an hour slipped by, and then at the beats of a distant clock in the town striking half-past ten she dropped from her perch.

"I must be getting back, or father will be wonder- ing what has become of me," she said as she made for the entrance of their lair.

Reggie's detaining hand fell on her arm.

"Half a second," he said. " There is some one coming along the pathâ one of those chaps who went by returning, perhaps. Better let him get ahead, whoever he is, before we break cover. We don't want company on our way back."

So they waited in the shadows, listening to the oncoming footsteps till the man who caused them was nearly opposite their hiding-place in the little glade. His identity was nothing to them; they had no thought but to enjoy their homeward stroll without having to tread too closely on the heels of any inconvenient outsider.

And then, suddenly, far out at sea a great shaft of light shot skyward, and, after steadying itself in a perpendicular gleam, swooped down upon the marsh, moving to and fro across the broad expanse, prying out its secret places and showing up each reed and sedge in an electric glare, that was twice as effective as lightning because it dwelt longer on its objectives. At first the radiant tongue played on the opposite side of the marsh, then it flickered on the central wastes, and finally darted on to the path close to Reggie and Enid just as the man they had heard advancing passed by.

Unseen themselves in the thicket, they had a clear view of him as he strode along the path, for, the latter being raised several feet above their level, his face was silhouetted against the dark sky beyond the electric beam. Their glimpse was only momentary, because as though dazzled, he raised his hand to his eyes, and altogether he was not ten seconds within the range of their vision, but it lasted long enough to enable Enid to whisper her companionâ

"That was Mr. Chermside, the young officer from India who has been staying down here for the last month. He's supposed to be awfully gone on Violet Maynard, the daughter of the rich Birmingham man who has taken the Manor House for the summer."

"Then I expect that is where he was coming from," suggested Reggie. " I met him in the club yesterday. Your father introduced him. He seemed a decent sort of chap, but down on his luck I thought."

"You have made two blunders in one statement," was Miss Enid's pert retort. " He can't have been coming from the Manor House because he wasn't in evening dress. And he can't be down on his luck because he's got heaps of money. Why, he's going to start on a cruise round the world soon in a steam yacht that is fitting out at Portland."

"Sorry I spoke," said Reggie. " Come, he's far enough ahead not to be a nuisance now; let me give you a hand up on to the path. I suppose that Mr. Mallory is prejudiced against Chermside, since he's a friend of Travers Nugent, eh?"

Disdaining the offer of assistance, Enid ran lightly up the slope on to the path before replying.

"On the contrary," she said as Reggie joined her, "I can't quite make father out on the subject of Mr. Leslie Chermside. For once in a way the dear old man is inconsistent, or so he seems to me. He won't commit himself to a definite opinion, but I

Their glimpse was only momentary, bfcause, as thoiigli dazzled, he raised his hand to his eves."

A Traito's Ji'ooinrg

Page iÂ can see that he is deeply interested in Mr. Nugent's friend, and in the relations existing between the pair. I think, from signs and portents knowti only to'myself, that father rather likes Mr. Chermside."

"Lucky for Chermside," Reggie absently mused aloud. " There! " he added with a quick return to nautical briskness. " Thank goodness that infernal searchlight has moved off us and found the town at last. I prefer being at the other end of the beastly thing to having it in one's eyes. There goes the first gun from the cruiser."

And under cover of the restored darkness arms were clasped again, and the young heads fell very close together for the rest of the way back to the town that was now being vigorously bombarded in mimic warfare.

Two miles out at sea the big guns flashed and boomed, and ahead of them on the marshland path the footsteps of the man they had seen in the rays of the searchlight were dying away, so quickly had he outpaced the lingerers. But Lieutenant Beauchamp and Miss Enid Mallory took no heed of either, little dreaming of the terrible significance that attached to what they had seen and heard that night.

" H, good morning, Chermside. So you have

V not, after all, left Ottermouth yet, as you led me to infer would be the case."

Leslie Chermside looked up from his newspaper to meet the steady gaze of Travers Nugent, who had just entered the reading room at the club. It was before the hour when the morning frequenters were wont to assemble, and for the moment they had the apartment to themselves.

"No," said Leshe shortly. " I have changed my mind, and shall stay on for a while."

Nugent carefully closed the door and came and stood with his back to the mantel-piece looking down at his late accomplice. " Does that mean that you have returned to your allegiance? " he asked softly.

"Certainly not," came Leslie's flash of indignation.

"Ah! then I presume that you found Levison amenable to reason, or, at least, that you persuaded him to grant you a reprieve when you kept your appointment with him last night? " said Nugent. Though he spoke with a great assumption of carelessness, applying a light to his cigarette the while,

THE CRY FROM THE TRAIN 6i his eyes never left the younger man's face for an instant, seeming to bum with a snake-hke ghtter.

Under this keen scrutiny Leshe reddened, and his reply came haltingly at first, as though he picked his words with deliberation. " I asked no favours of Levison. Heâ he can do his worst for all I calfe." And then, moved by a sudden impulse, the ex-Lancer added hotly: " See here, Mr. Nugent. My association with you, which I deeply regret, has not been an honourable one. It is not my province to blame you, seeing how culpable I have been myself, but the subject is distasteful to me, and at least I have the right to ask that you will not again refer to the disgraceful affair that brought us together. I shall hope shortly to obtain employment which will enable me to repay the money advanced by the Maharajah for my passage home, and, so far as I am concerned, that will be an end of the business. I do not consider that I am legally or morally bound to recognize the debts which his Highness gave me to understand he had paid voluntarily. As the bribe with which he tempted me was only a sham, I owe him no allegiance whatever."

Nugen-t listened with upraised brows to the angry outbreak, the flicker of a frosty smile playing about his lips. But if he had meditated a rejoinder he checked it. His quick ears had caught the chck of the hall door, and the hum of voices in the anteroom. He merely shrugged his shoulders, and was ready with a genial greeting for the members who trooped in. They were three in numberâ Mr. Montague Maynard, who had motored in from the Manor House; Mr. Vernon Mallory, whose pale, ascetic face reflected nothing of the interest inspired by finding Nugent and Chermside, obviously to his shrewd vision, concluding a heated discussion; and, lastly, but by no means least in his own estimation. General Kruse, formerly of the Indian Staff Corps.

The last-mentioned was somewhat unkindly behind his back called " the widow's Kruse," the nickname being founded on an erroneous rumour that he was pursuing with matrimonial intentions the wealthy relict of a London tradesman, who had settled in the neighbourhood. There was a still more unkind version of the origin of the nickname, and one i Vhich there was, unfortunately, just a spice of tfmli- that he was " always full." He was a big, burly man, with a rubicund complexion and a voice like a thunderstorm.

The three gentlemen had chanced to meet on the doorstep of the club, and the General had already commenced to impart to the other two an item of news which he had picked up on the way from his house. He now began it all over again for the benefit of the larger audience.

"Most extraordinary thing," he bellowed in his foghorn tones. " As I was just telling these feuows, Nugent, I looked in at the Plume Hotel as I came through the town, and they're in a rare pucker there. A chap staying at the hotel went out last night after dinner, saying he was going for a walk, and he hasn't come back."

"Bolted to save paying his bill, I suppose," suggested Nugent, stealing a glance at Leslie Chermside, who, however, was invisible behind his news- paper. " It is not an unprecedented occurrence at a seaside resort in the summer season, is it?"

But General Kruse with great gusto proceeded to demohsh any such commonplace theory. " It wasn't that," he roared. " The chapâ Levison his name wasâ had paid his charges pretty near up to the hilt. It is the custom to render bills weekly, and as he had been at the Plume a week yesterday, his account was presented to him. He paid it like a shot. There is only his last night's dinner owing for, and he has left luggage that would square that twenty times over."

"I expect he will turn up before the day is over," said Nugent, with the air of becoming bored with all this fuss about a stranger. And, as if to put an end to the General's prosing, he turned to Montague Maynard.

"When I was lunching with you the other day, Miss Violet consulted me about a picnic tea she was thinking of giving," he said. " Your daughter was good enough to want my advice as to a good camping-ground, and I told her I would take time to consider. Will you tell her from me that I should recommend that grassy patch on the marsh, half-way between the beach and the Manor House? It is sheltered from the sun at four o'clock in the afternoon, and that means everything at this time of year."

"Thanks very much; I'll tell Vi; she's sending out short invitations for to-morrow," replied Mr. Maynard, wondering why, in making a communication that concerned him alone of those present in the room, the speaker should have been looking at some one else. For, after claiming the screw manufacturer's attention, Nugent allowed his eyes to wander to Leslie Chermside, who was still hidden by the newspaper.

Mr. Vernon Mallory, of whom it had once been remarked that he noticed everything while appearing to notice nothing, happened to choose this moment for addressing a trivial but direct question to the diligent reader, calhng him by his name, and leaving him no alternative but for an equally direct answer. Leslie laid aside the paper and rephed courteously, but in doing so disclosed a twitching mouth, and a face from which every drop of red blood had fled, leaving it ashen grey.

Mr. Mallory did not pursue the subject of his interrogation further, but, turning to General Kruse, started a fresh and congenial topic by suggesting that that thirsty old warrior would be the better for a whisky and soda. The invitation being promptly accepted, Mr. Mallory, who eschewed spiritual indulgence in the morning, ordered a cigar for himself, and plunged into a discussion of the delinquencies of the urban district council, in which Travers Nugent and Mr. Maynard were presently included.

Under cover of these amenities Leslie Chermside rose and, followed by two pairs of observant eyes, left the club. Avoiding the crowded parade, he crossed the pebbly beach to an upturned and discarded boat, and flinging himself down in the shade of it, abandoned himself to his thoughts. Gradually the colour came back to his cheeks, and the agonized expression which Mr. Mallory had surprised yielded to one of dogged determination.

"The prospect of the picnic at that spot is simply horrible, but after all it is a mere detail, and I must go through with it," he murmured presently. " The fact remains that, within limits, I am now free to stay here and thwart the new scheme which I am convinced that Nugent is hatching. If I could have but one glimpse at the cards he holds."

For an hour Leslie lay in the shadow of the boat, vainly striving to penetrate the veil which he felt sure Nugent had thrown over his designs. It was futile to formulate plans for combating them till he had discovered what the designs were. That the Cobra, the big turbine yacht that had been chartered, would stiu be retained as the principal feature in the programme was probable, since Nugent would naturally be reluctant to waste the expense already incurred, and, except on a vessel controlled by the Maharajah's emissaries, the abduction of Violet Maynard to India would be practically impossible. But how, without the co-operation which he had withdrawn, Nugent could hope to convey an unwilling passenger on board the steamer Leslie could not surmise. He could only wait and watch, in the full knowledge that his former colleague and present antagonist was a man of infinite resource, and endowed with an inborn cunning which it would be folly to despise.

One thing was certain, he told himself, as he rose and strolled back to his lodgings on the main streetâ day and night he must keep vigil for the appearance of the Cobra off the coast, and he must also cultivate close relations with Violet, so as to learn of anything that might indicate the ruse by which it was intended to inveigle her on board.

To sustain the pretence that he had recently inherited a fortune, and had means which would justify the possession of a large steam yacht, he had established himself, by the advice and introduction of Travers Nugent, at the best and most expensive rooms in the place. Here he shut himself up for the remainder of that day, refraining from going to the club or to the tennis field, and brooding over the resolves and apprehensions which unfitted him, as he knew, for the society of his fellow-men.

By the last post he received an informal note from Violet, inviting him to a picnic tea on the following day. The party was to assemble at the Manor at four o'clock, afterwards making its way on foot to the spot selected, which was within easy reach of the house. Leslie shuddered as he read the concluding words, but having braced himself to sit down and pen an acceptance, he went out in the dusk and posted it.

The next day was favoured with ideal weather for an al fresco entertainment, and when the guests assembled at the appointed hour it was at once evident that Violet's picnic tea had been hailed as a popular function. Every one who had been asked put in an appearance, to the number of about a hundred. Hired conveyances deposited a mixed assortment of residents and season visitors from Ottermouth; a few old-fashioned barouches brought representatives of such of the neighbouring county families as had deigned to recognize the Birmingham magnate; while motor cars in plenty accounted for many of the arrivals.

Among the latter was Mr. Travers Nugent, well-groomed and debonair in his grey suit, and wearing an orchid in his button-hole from one of his own glasshouses at The Hut. On descending from his car he exchanged his motor-cap for a feather-weight Panama, and smilingly confronted the group at the main entrance. Mr. Mallory, who had arrived earlier, took particular notice of that smile, which lasted only just so long as it was wanted for the purpose of responding to the welcome of his host and hostesses. As soon as he had shaken hands with Violet and Miss Sarah Dymmock and Mr. Maynard, Nugent effaced himself unobtrusively among the guests, and Mr. Mallory's observant eyes following him perceived that the smile had given place to a look of preoccupation.

This in turn was chased away by a sudden start and a gleam of satisfaction when, among the last arrivals, Leslie Chermside was seen making his way on foot up the drive. Thence onward Mr. Travers Nugent's air of self-absorption left him; turning to those of his acquaintances nearest him he laid himself out to amuse and interest.

"Now, what does that portend? " the keen old diplomatist muttered under his breath. " It was almost as though Nugent had been afraid that Chermside was not coming, and that he was gratified when at length he appeared. I wonder what is the bond, if bond it is, between the young soldier with the mysterious blank in his life and the clever gentleman with so many irons in the fire that he ought to have burned his fingers long ago. There is something in the wind, but is the youngster from

India a dupe or confederate? I would give a good deal to know."

At the word from jovial Montague Maynard the now completed party set out for the picnic ground, a chorus of approval going up at the announcement of the spot selected. Even on a hot summer day the laziest could not object, for, once outside the Manor demesne, a quarter of an hour's saunter through the delightful scenery at the head of the marsh brought them to the little strip of pasture land reclaimed from the swamps, where the tea-tables had been set out in the shade of a group of elms. Cavillers might have complained that the railway embankment skirting the place on one side marred the aesthetic harmony of the whole, but if there were any such they remained discreetly silent.

The snowy damask of the tables laden with dainties and surrounded by a bevy of smart maidservants from the Manor made an inviting picture on the strip of verdure, and Montague Maynard's guests renewed their acclamations. Reggie Beau-champ, who had, of course, annexed Enid Mallory as his partner for the afternoon, expressed the opinion that it was " simply ripping."

"And, by Jove!" he added of malice aforethought, " look at that girl bossing the other maids. She seems to be in charge of the show. She is ripping too. Just the style of beauty I admire."

Enid cocked a sly eye at him, and catching the gleam of mischief refused to be drawn. " Yes," she said, following his gaze to the graceful brunette in black silk who was directing operations at the tables, conspicuous by the absence of apron and cap-streamers, "that is Louise Aubin, Violet Maynard's maid. She is certainly pretty, but she looks as if she had a temper. I shouldn't dare to find fault with her if she belonged to me."

"A bit of a spitfire, perhaps," assented the Lieutenant, finding that his harmless shaft had missed its mark. " Might give you beans with the brush, eh, if you slanged her for pulling out your hair by the roots?"

Miss Mallory sniffed contemptuously at the implied familiarity with the sacred rites of the dressing-table, and she might have expressed herself strongly on the subject had not their attention been distracted by the approach of a train along the embankment above them. It was beginning to shut off steam for the stop at Ottermouth Station, a mile further on, and the people in the carriages were plainly distinguishable by the picnic party.

Just as the train was sweeping past a cry from one of the third-class compartments drew all eyes that way. Looking up, the picnickers saw a man leaning from the window and frantically gesticulating â or, rather, vehemently pointing at some object on the marsh below. To those on the lower ground there was nothing visible to cause his agitation.

"What was that lunatic up to, and what was he howling about? " asked Reggie as the train disappeared round a curve.

"It sounded like ' the face of a fool," so far as I could make out," Enid laughed.

"I don't think it was that," said Violet Maynard, who, with Leslie and Mr. Mallory in attendance, had come up behind them. " It struck me that the excited passenger's cry was more hke' the face in the pool.""

"That was it, I expect," said Reggie lightly. " He must have seen the reflection of his own in one of those puddles of tidal water. That was the Otter-mouth section of the London corridor express, which has a luncheon car attached. The Johnny had probably been indulging too freely in the conveniences of modem travel."

Mr. Mallory said nothing. He was inwardly asking himself why Leslie Chermside, who, though obviously forcing himself to do so under intense nervous strain, had been pleasantly chatting all the way from the Manor House, should have suddenly turned pale, fiercely biting his underlip with strong white teeth.

DISCUSSION as to the exact words of theory from the train was cut short by a general adjournment to the tables, where for the next half-hour the guests did justice to their host's lavish hospitality. Mountains of sun-kissed peaches from the warm walls of the Manor gardens, gallons of fruit-salad and cakes in bewildering variety disappeared as by magic. The little green oasis at the brink of the marshes rang with laughter, presently blended with the strains of a small but select string band from London, hidden in a secluded nook behind the sheltering elms.

But if the episode of the excited passenger was generally forgotten it only remained in abeyance so far at least as the memory of one of Mr. Maynard's guests was concerned. It was not necessary for a man of Mr. Vernon Mallory's age to plead an excuse for an early desertion of the " aids to indigestion," as he called them, and he lighted a cigar and went off for a solitary stroll. Travers Nugent paused for a moment in his entertainment of a cluster of ladies to send a thoughtful glance after the tall, spare figure of the retired civil servant, and a curious gleam flitted over his inscrutable features. It could not have been wholly caused by dissatisfaction, for he resumed his amusing persiflage with enhanced sparkle.

Mr. Mallory's sauntering steps took him to the side of the reclaimed ground nearest to the railway line immediately under the embankment. To the casual observer his movements might have seemed somewhat erratic, and based only on a desire to get away from the chatter of the tea-tables and enjoy his cigar in peace. To any one really interested in his sudden detachment, however, it would have become apparent that there was system, carefully cloaked, perhaps, but none the less thorough, in every step he took.

The place where, by Travers Nugent's advice, the picnic camp had been pitched lay some two hundred yards beyond the little glade at the side of the raised marshland path where Reggie Beau-champ and Enid Mallory had rested on the occasion of their prowl in the dark two evenings ago. Here, for the purpose of raising the railway to the proper level, the bank of the old river bed had been destroyed for a short distance, and instead of the miniature red cliffs, with their leafy screen of brambles and dwarf oaks, the marsh was skirted by the ugly side of the embankment. This break in the beauties of nature caused by the exigencies of engineering was but a score or two of yards in length, and it was while the train had been in view on this short section that the third-class passenger had played such strange antics.

At the foot of the embankment the ground was swampy, nowhere yielding firm foothold, and here and there deepening into pools formed by the brackish water that had drained in from the tidal dykes at the other side of the path. For the most part the pools were surrounded and studded with sedges, which concealed them from passers-by.

It was among these offshoots of the marsh that, at the risk of getting bogged in the quagmires, Mr. Mallory pottered about by himself. Poking and prying everywhere, he, however, devoted most attention to the pools in the ground nearest the fence at the base of the embankment, which were furthest removed, and therefore less visible, from the path. Ten minutes must have been spent in this apparently unprofitable employment when he suddenly straightened himself, and, regaining the firmer ground, made his way slowly back to the gay gathering under the trees.

Many of the people had left the vicinity of the tables and were promenading the grassy strip while listening to the band. Montague Maynard, assiduous in his care for his guests, was a difficult man to catch, but Mr. Mallory managed to pin him at last as he was leaving one group to join another. Poles apart in temperament and in their life's experience, the genial manufacturer and the reserved old diplomatist had nevertheless conceived a sincere regard for each other during the former's sojourn in the neighbourhood.

"Just a word with you," said Mr Mallory in a low voice, leading his host aside.

"My dear fellow, certainly; but what is it? You look as though you had seen a ghost," replied the other.

"You will have to get all these folk away quietly," said Mr. Mallory, after assuring himself that they were out of earshot. " I have not seen a ghost, but the next thing to it. There is the dead body of a man in one of those pools close under the railway fence. Some of these youngsters will be sure to stumble on it if we remain here. Besides, we can't keep it to ourselves for a minute. The authorities must be notified at once."

Maynard emitted a low whistle, and his face clouded at a contretemps which, whatever else it might portend, bade fair to spoil Violet's party. But his brow cleared again as his eyes rested on the sombrely-clad diminutive form of Miss Sarah Dymmock, who, with a vivacity wonderful for her years, was holding court under one of the trees.

"Old Aunt Sally will manage it," he said. " You're quite right about clearing 'em off, and I'm deeply indebted to you, Mallory, for not raising a hullabaloo. It would never do to scare all these butterflies with a discovery like that. And, as you say, the pohce must be informed and a doctor sent for without a moment's delay."

He hurried off, and Mr. Mallory watched from afar the result of the whispered communication which he made to the aged spinster. It did not transpire till afterwards how Aunt Sarah contrived it, but after one or two comprehending nods the old lady turned to the group of which she had been the centre, and almost at once an electric spark seemed to have been communicated to the whole festive assembly. In twos and threes and larger clusters the picnic party began to move off the ground back towards the Manor House.

Having assured himself that the main object was gained, Mr. Mallory was free to study the details of the debacle he had caused. Travers Nugent, without a break in the lively conversation he was holding with a smart lady of local importance, had apparently accepted unquestionably the situation as propounded by Aunt Sarah, and was following the remainder of the flock with sheep-like docility. After Nugent, Mr. Mallory's eyes sought and found Leslie Chermside, and in his case there was more food for reflection. Mr. Mallory was at once aware that Chermside was observing him with equal interest; in fact, their eyes actually met in a quick thrust and parry of unspoken question on one side, and something that was curiously akin to defiance on the other.

The ex-Lancer was for the moment standing alone, and Mr. Mallory moved towards him as if to speak. But he was forestalled by Violet, who came up and evidently claimed Leslie as escort on the homeward walk, for they started in the wake of the others before Mr. Mallory, if such had been his intention, could make any attempt to detain them.

He was more fortunate in the case of Reggie Beauchamp, and he had his daughter to thank for the capture. Enid, not having outgrown her schoolgirl devotion to sweets, had lingered round the tables for a final ice, and the young sailor was still in faithful attendance. Mr. Mallory pounced on the pair just as they had realized that a general stampede was in progress, and were preparing to follow.

"Beauchamp, I wish you would remain with Mr. Maynard and myself for a little," he said. " There is a point on which I want to fortify myself with your opinion. We can walk back to the Manor afterwards."

Enid began to pout and toss her head, but she knew every phase of her idolized father's moods, and one glance at the network of creases round the keen eyes was sufficient to quell her incipient mutiny. The appearance of those filaments on the stem, ascetic face was a sure danger-signal that her father was not to be trifled withâ that the active brain was at work on some serious problem. She put her ice-plate down and, bidding the Lieutenant " make himself generally useful," ran away to overtake the fast-receding party.

She had hardly departed when Montague Maynard came bustling up, wiping his brow with a silk handkerchief. He stopped for an instant to order the wondering servants to pack up the crockery ready for the cart and to get home as quick as they could, and then he turned to Mr. Mallory, while Reggie, with instinctive modesty, fell back a pace or two.

"Aunt Sally is a masterpiece; I'll tell you how she did it later," he said, his eyebrows uplifted inquiringly in the direction of the young torpedo-boat commander.

"It is all right. He's wanted," interpolated Mr. Mallory shortly.

' Well, then this is what I have done," the screw magnate went on in a hoarse undertone. " I have sent a footman into the town direct for the police-sergeant, and another to hurry up one of the local medicos. All these maids will have skedaddled before either the sergeant or the doctor can turn up. Now shall we go and have a look at theâ the place? You have no idea who the poor fellow is, I suppose?"

"I am not sure; it is on that point that I want Beauchamp to corroborate me," was the reply. And, calling Reggie forward, Mr. Mallory told him, as the three went towards the swamps under the embankment, of the gruesome discovery he had made, and how he wished to learn if his view of the dead man's identity coincided with his own.

No more was said till they had picked their way over the firmest foothold they could find to the pool where the horrible sight awaited them. The body lay half in and half out of the water, the upturned face being afloat while the remains below the shoulders were embedded in the ooze at the brink and nearly concealed by the reeds.

"Miss Maynard was right, you see, as to what the passenger called out from the trainâ ' the face in the pool," " said Mr. Mallory. " The lower limbs were probably invisible up there. Now, Beauchamp; do you recognize the victim of this tragedy?"

Reggie looked blankly down at the features about which there lingered none of the majesty of death â mean, commonplace features, which nevertheless might have had their attraction for the unsophisticated by reason of a certain sensual fullness of lip and smoothness of the now marble-white skin. The wide-open eyes, staring skyward, conveyed the impression of sudden, awful fear.

"No, I can't put a name to him," said the lieu- tenant after a long scrutiny which he did not relax. " And yet there is a look about him that seems vaguely familiar. That, though, is not quite the word for it. I mean that I believe that I have seen him before."

"What about the French window in the reading room at the Club? " suggested Mr. Mallory. " Does that help your memory?"

"Of course! " came the quick rejoinder. " It is the chap who called for Chermside the other morning and walked away with him along the Parade. A cockney visitor, I should judge by his clothes. And, by Jove, I expect he's the man who is missing from the Plume Hotel. The club steward knew him by sight as staying there."

A frosty gleam shone in the old diplomatist's eyes. " You are probably correct in the latter surmise," he said. " But in any case we are in agreement as to his being Chermside's acquaintance. That was what I wanted to get from you."

"Not a very reputable acquaintance, I should imagine," said the great manufacturer, looking thoughtfully down at the bedraggled tawdriness of the dead man's attire. " If our young friend from India hadn't been vouched for by Travers Nugent, I should have put this poor creature down as a dun or a money-lender's tout. His features are distinctly Hebraic. I wonder how he got himself drowned in that shallow pool. A drop too much, eh, and a stumble in the dark?"

But Reggie Beauchamp, regardless of his immaculate flannels, had plunged knee-deep into the mire. His sailor's eye, used to note every detail, had perceived something that had escaped the two shore-going gentlemen with sight impaired by years of office work.

"He wasn't drowned! " he exclaimed, and then, moderating his voice so that it should not reach the maid-servants on the deserted picnic ground, he added: " His throat has been cut from ear to ear. By Jove"

But Reggie pulled himself up all short, and had no more to say. He had remembered the cry, weird and long-drawn, which Enid and he had heard from their cosy retreat at the marsh-side two nights ago. And he had remembered something else of even graver and more personal importâ a reminiscence of the prowl in the dusk which he discreetly forbore from disclosing till he should have had an opportunity for consulting his fair partner in that escapade.

MADEMOISELLE LOUISE AUBIN possessed all the attributes of her Gauic blood. She was vain of her voluptuous charms, susceptible to flattery, and prone to blurt out on the least provocation the scanty ideas in her empty httle head as soon as and whenever they entered it. She was further endowed with a fiery temper and an eager impetuosity, which often led her to act without thought of consequences.

In the last-named characteristics was to be found the reason why in the cool of the evening she set out to walk from the Manor House to Ottermouth in order to lay information with the police against the man she believed to be the slayer of Levi Levison. For once in a way she had said nothing of her purpose in the servants' hall, expecting to score a greater dramatic effect by announcing on her return that she had been the means of causing the murderer's arrest.

Long before the afternoon party had dispersed the reason for the hurried adjournment from the marsh back to the house had become knownâ first among the guests, from whom there was no longer any

INTERCEPTED i necessity to keep secret what was bound to be noised abroad in an hour or two, and then among the members of the domestic staff, to whom the news spread like wildfire.

The earliest intelligence had been quickly supplemented by further details of description and identification which left no doubt in the mind of Louise that the dead man was the hero of her three weeks' flirtation. Equally sure was she that he had come by his death at the hands of that older lover, the Breton peasant and sailor who had adored her in her native village long before she had dreamed of becoming femme de chamhre to the daughter of an English millionaire.

Yes, she told herself, assuredly Pierre Legros, the French huckster of onions, had killed her latest admirer out of insensate jealousy, and he should suffer for it if there was any power in a woman's tongue. Mr. Levison had held out glittering prospects, which it was galling to have destroyed by a persistent boor such as Pierre. Travers Nugent's human tool had described himself as " a financial agent "â a phrase which to the French girl's ears sounded the brazen tocsin of untold wealth, and which she could not know covered as many iniquities as that other comprehensive termâ " a resting actress." Pierre Legros must certainly pay the penalty for shattering her dreams of riches and luxury, and to secure that laudable vengeance she started for Otteimouth as soon as she had dressed her young mistress for dirmer.

The path skirting the marshes was her nearest way, but she dared not pass the spot where the crime had been committed, and where there would probably be a crowd of sightseers attracted to the scene. She chose the longer route along the high road, and by the time she had walked a mile between the leafy hedgerows she began to ask herself questions.

Coming of thrifty French parents, her first was: What was she to gain by making the disclosure and putting a noose round the neck of Pierre? Nothing at all, and, on the other hand, there was the chance that she might lose a situation in which she was extremely comfortable. Miss Sarah Dymmock, who was her virtual if not nominal mistress, would not be likely to tolerate lightly the scandal which she would bring upon Mr. Maynard's establishment. The old lady had shown her teeth the other day, when she had caught the onion-seller abusing her and had driven him out of the grounds at the point of her sunshade. Miss Dymmock's vituperations had not been all for the male delinquent. The rough side of Aunt Sarah's tongue was like a nutmeg-grater, and she had rasped out several rugged threats about not keeping a maid who was a bone of contention to violent " followers."

Again she was conscious, deep down in her fickle heart, of a soft spot for the faithful compatriot with vhom she had scrambled about the rocks of her native village when he had been a sunburnt fisher-lad and she a bare-legged hoyden of fifteen. For Levi Levison she had cared not one jot. If it had not been for the overthrow of the brilliant prospect which she fondly believed a marriage with him would have implied she would have borne Pierre Legros no ill-will for hacking his rival to death. It would indeed have been a delicate compliment.

So it was that as she walked the deserted country road she wavered, and as she wavered there came into view round a bend some way ahead a pedestrian sauntering so leisurely that he had more the appearance of keeping a tryst than of making for a destination. And, though the lady for whom he was waiting knew it not, Mr. Travers Nugent was, in a sense, keeping a tryst, and she was no less a personage than the damsel advancing to meet himâ Mademoiselle Louise Aubin herself.

As they met Louise was surprised to see the English gentleman stop and raise his hat to her. She had never before exchanged a word with him, or so much as given him a thought, though she knew him by sight as an occasional caller at the May-nards' house in London, and ha-d since learned that he had a summer retreat at Ottermouth.

"Pardon me for addressing you without formal introduction," said Nugent with the deference he would have used to a duchess, " but interest in this terrible murder must be my excuse. I recognize you, of course, as Miss Maynard's confidential companion. Can you inform me if any later intelligence has been received at the Manor House? There was nothing but vague rumour in the air when I left after the afternoon party."

He had to a nicety struck the correct note for " drawing" Mademoiselle Louise. The winning smile, the doffed hat would have gone far; but the promotion from lady's maid to " companion" made her conquest an easy matter. Yet, coquette as she was, she delayed the intended surrender which in her folly she regarded as a victory. She promised herself the pleasure of looking important in this affable gentleman's eyes, but it was a situation that must be prolonged for proper enjoyment.

"But no, M'sieu," she rephed. " It is not at the Manor House that you should inquire for news. They know nothing there, nor do they greatly care. How should they be distracted, my so kind friends, by a cr-rime which is to them but a bagatelle that has disturbed the pleasure of a summerre day? It is to the police in the town that you should apply."

Nugent's shoulders shrugged with Parisian eloquence. " I have already pursued inquiries in that quarter, but the police appear to be completely in the dark, except that they have verified the fact that the deceased had been staying at the Plume Hotel," he said, never forgetting for an instant to quahfy the baldness of his statement with a respectfully admiring glance.

Mademoiselle's opportunity for dramatic effect had come. It would be far more interesting to startle this so polite " Milor " than to scarify the servants' hall at the Manor House, and she could do that later as well. To the winds with all caution! She must brave Aunt Sarah's wrath if the old lady took a harsh view of her conduct. The chance to pose was irresistible and she took the stage there and then.

"M'sieu has been premature," she said, heralding her bomb-shell with a flash of her fine eyes. " If he returns and puts his questions to the sergent-ie-ville later in the evening he will doubtless be differently informed. For I, Louise Aubin, am now on my way to indicate to the authorities the assassin of that poor gentleman."

Travers Nugent's astonishment seemed to overwhelm him. He took a step back, eyed the girl with something like awe, and touched his lips with his tongue. " You are not serious? " he gasped. " Do you really mean that you witnessed the crime?"

The fair Louise lifted her hands in genuine horror. " Mon Dieu! Not so bad as that," she replied. " But it is all the same as if I had been there. It is the motive that I go to point out, and the name of the murderer that I go to give. I who speak to you was the motive, and the name is Pierre Legros. The scelerat is a seller of onions from a little French ship that is in the harbour of Exmouth."

And Mademoiselle Aubin proceeded to rattle off the history of her early courtship by Legros in her native village, and of his inopportune arrival while she was accepting the attentions of the " financial agent " from London. She volubly repeated her former lover's heated language to herself, and described the bloodthirsty threats he had used about his successful rival. His guilt was as clear as noonday, she avowedâ as clear as if that dreadful thing M'sieu had suggested had been really true and she had seen the deed with her own eyes.

"Pierre killed Monsieur Levison for love of me," she concluded, with a gesture worthy of the great Bernhardt.

Nugent's manner and attitude had almost imperceptibly and very gradually altered during the recital, though the theatrical young Frenchwoman had been so absorbed in herself that it was only when she had sounded the final flourish that she noticed the change. The look of surpriseâ of almost alarmed surpriseâ which had come into his face at her first profession of knowledge was gone, and was now replaced by an expression of chivalrous sympathy blended with just a trace of dissent.

"I can well beheve in the potency of the motive suggested by Mademoiselle," he said with a grave bow. " Any man might almost have free pardon for homicide committed for the sake of her favours. But it was not so in this case. The man whom I have good cause to suspect of having slain Mr. Levi Levison had never to my knowledge spoken with mademoiselle either in France or in England. That was why I was so astonished when you stated that though you had not witnessed the crime, you were on your way to denounce the criminal."

"Who, then, is it that you suspect, m'sieu " Louise, all taken aback, demanded in a sibilant whisper. " After all, Pierre was the friend of my youth, and it would be sweeter to take vengeance on other than he."

Travers Nugent appeared to be about to speak, but to check himself as an afterthought. " I do not think that it would be quite in accordance with a spirit of justice if I mentioned the villain's name, even to you, just yet," he said, after a pause. " I am morally convinced of his guilt, but there are one or two points to be cleared up before it can be proved. If it leaked out that he was under suspicion before the police had been furnished with enough evi- dence to arrest him he might evade us altogether.

This much, however, I can promise you, that as soon as I have Hnked up the chain you shau be the first to be informed of it. Surely you are entitled to be, as the adored of ce fauvre Levison. In the meanwhile, will you favour me with a description of Pierre Legros? I have a reason for asking which will commend itself to you."

Louise launched into an eloquent word-picture of the onion-seller, contriving with many deprecatory shrugs to convey her contempt for his rough appearance and for his humble calling, while taking full credit for having recognized him at all in her present exalted station. His fierce eyebrows, his swarthy skin, his blue jean garments were all in turn catalogued and tossed aside as so much rubbish not worthy of notice if their owner was not to achieve fame as a murderer.

"A thousand thanks! You are an artist in our language, mademoiselle, and have absolutely confirmed the innocence of your worthy fellow-countryman, though I commiserate with you on the reappearance in your life of one so gauche," said Nugent decisively. " You are entitled to my fullest confidence, but discretion confines me to this at present: Pierre Legros, so easily recognizable from your vivid description, could not have committed this crime. It would have been a physical impossibility. At the hour when the medical men say that Levison must have met his death Legros was creating a disturbance at the back door of my house because the cook would not purchase any of his wares. While I happen to know that the man I suspect had an appointment to meet some one on the marsh about the same hour."

One glance at the French girl's face as he made the last assertion told him that he had scored one trick at least in the game he had set out to play. There was no incredulity in the stare with which she drank in his statement, nor was there affectation in the sigh which escaped her, due partly to relief at the established alibi of her former lover, and partly to disappointment that she was not to achieve fame as the heroine of a murder mystery.

"I shall hold you to your promise, M'sieu," she simpered at last. " And as you have rendered my journey into the town unnecessary I will now return to the Manor House. Accept my best thanks for preventing me from committing a belise which would have anguished my soul. It would have desolated me to have accused that poor Pierre under a mistake."

So, after a few courtesies from Nugent, she turned and went back the way she had come, reflecting that, after all, there was compensation for her disappointment. Had she not been treated as an equal by a gentleman of position and fascinating manners? Certainly he was not so young as Levi Levison, but his eyes had rested on her charms with an admiration that seemed sincere. Who knew but what he might, after a little coy manipulation, step into the place in her affections vacated by the defunct Levi? But then she could not see the contemptuously satisfied smile on Mr. Nugent's face as he made his way back to the town, the contempt being for the fickle jade so easily duped, and the satis- faction for the complete success of the self-denial that had led him to postpone his dinner-hour and loiter about the country road on which an unerring instinct had told him that the dupe would be found.

"The treacherous little cat! " he murmured, caressing his long fair moustache. " Bereft of one lover, and on her way to get number two hanged, she was not too busy to make eyes at a possible third. With all your faults, Travers Nugent, you have cause to be thankful that a weakness for women is not among them."

REGGIE BEAUCHAMP'S mother, the widow of the late Admiral Beauchamp, R. N., lived in a small detached house prettily situated on the main road that extended from the High Street westward. A stout, comfortable-looking lady of some fifty years, she had but one aim in lifeâ the happiness and advancement of her sailor son. Following on his two years' absence in the China seas, she was having a glorious time this eventful summer, with her boy stationed at Plymouth, and able to run over to the little Devonshire resort as frequently as he could obtain leave.

As mother and son sat together at breakfast on the morning after the picnic tea she noticed with maternal solicitude that he seemed somewhat preoccupied. The town was in a ferment over the discovery of Levison's body, and though it was not like Reggie to take anything seriously she could only suppose that he was brooding over the small part he had played in that episode.

"When does the inquiry into this horrible affair take placc, dcar? " she asked, as she handed him his second cup of coffee.

He started as though she had read his thoughts.

"At two o'clock this afternoon, I believe," he replied. And then, knowing from experience that he could not deceive those loving eyes, he added: " I was just wondering if I should have to give evidence. I hardly expect to be called, as it was Mr. Mallory who was the first to actually find the body."

"Even if you were called it would not be much of an ordeal, I supposeâ little more than a mere formality? " persisted Mrs. Beauchamp, not wholly reassured by the shade of anxiety in his answer.

"How could it be, mother, when I didn't know the chap from Adam, and was not present when he was kiued," was the reply which was hardly out of the lieutenant's mouth when he sprang to his feet and made for the door. " Excuse me," he said, stifling an exclamation of relief, " there is Enid Mallory coming up the garden path. I have finished breakfast, and I'll go and see what she wants."

Mrs. Beauchamp smiled indulgently, and straightway forgot the momentary qualm of uneasiness called up by the half-tone of irritation in her son's reply to her questions about the inquest. Like the fond match-making mother she was, she had immediately jumped to the conclusion that her first diagnosis had been wrong, and that the boy's woolgathering was really due to the sprightly maiden whose knock was even now resounding on the front door. For the Admiral's widow, with happy memories of her own gallant husband to egg her on, had woven all sorts of fairy visions round the two young people who were now meeting on her doorstep. She approved of the lively Enid, was the devoted friend of her blind mother, and had the most profound respect for Mr. Vernon Mallory himself.,

"It is as it should be; they are outgrowing the old playmate stage, and are honestly falling in love with each other," the good lady murmured as she caught a glimpse through the Venetians of the pair strolling side by side across the dewy little lawn.

For, with set purpose, Reggie had not invited Enid into the house, but had suggested that they should betake themselves to a garden seat under the branches of a great horse-chestnut that grew in the boundary hedge. Mrs. Beauchamp, however, would have heard no lover-like phrases could she have listened to their matter-of-fact conversation.

"Well, have you decided what it is best for us to do? " said the girl, as soon as they were seated.

"For goodness sake don't screech like that," Reggie reproved her, with an apprehensive glance at the thick privet hedge that separated his mother's premises from those next door. " That beast Lowch is probably on the prowl over there, listening for all he's worth."

"That's where you're wrong," retorted Enid promptly, but, nevertheless, lowering her voice. " As I came up the street Mr. Lowch was up to his old gameâ walking up and down in front of the police station so as to get spotted for the jury by the sergeant."

Mr. Lazarus Lowch, Mrs. Beauchamp's nearest neighbour, was one of those freaks of humanity intended by an all-wise Providence to be as a thorn in the flesh of his fellow-men. His one idea of enjoying life was to creep about endeavouring to catch people doing wrong. He was known to carry a stop-watch for timing the speed of motor cars; he spent hours in " shadowing " small boys whom he hoped to detect stealing apples; he followed the municipal labourers about to see that they did not scamp their work; he had a finger in every one's pie, always with the intention of spoiling it; he was never really happy, but his nearest approach to the beatific state was when he was doing his level best to make some one else miserable.

A lean, cadaverous, lantern-jawed creature, more resembling the galvanized corpse of a dyspeptic ourang-outang than a man, he stalked the earth full of petty guile and mischief. His origin and reason for settling in the place were veiled in obscurity, though naturally there were many legends on the subject. Equally of course, he was not a favourite locally, and he would have been sorry to have it so. A man whose hand is raised against everybody neither courts nor expects popularity.

One of the eccentricities of this peculiar being was a morbid love of anything pertaining to the realm of the King of Terrors. He doted on funerals, and was always present at the cemetery when these solemn functions were being performed. Though somewhat stiff in the joints, he would run a mile to see a drowned man taken out of the sea; he had been heard to lament the fact that murderers were not hanged in public nowadays, and that he was consequently deprived of a spectacle that would have been as meat and drink to a starving man,

But his great opportunity came whenever it was necessary to hold an inquest in the bright httle resort. On these occasions he would thrust himself under the notice of the police with a view to getting summoned on the jury, and, as it saved trouble, his tactics were always successful. Moreover, since he occupied a superior social position to the general ruck of jurymen he was invariably chosen foreman, with the result that he reaped a double joyâ that of viewing the corpse and of making himself disagreeable to every one concerned.

Reggie Beauchamp, therefore, on learning how their uncongenial neighbour was occupied emitted a chuckle of mingled disgust and amusement.

"Up to his old tricks, is he? " he said. " Well, the coast being clear, let's consider what course to pursue. If we look at it from the point of view of what we ought to do there is no question but that we ought to come forward and say that we were on the marsh that night, and that shortly after hearing a blood-curdling scream we saw Chermside in the rays of the searchlight hurrying towards the town."

Enid's face fell. There was no heinous fault in her evening walk with her old playmate, and she did not in the least mind that coming to light, but she shrank from the publicity of having to appear as a witness whose evidence would be almost in the nature of an implied accusation against a man whom she could not regard for an instant as having anything to do with the crime. She had played tennis with Leslie Chermside, and liked him; besides which she had conceived a romantic affection for beautiful Violet Majniard, and had watched the undeclared love idyll between the young Indian officer and the millionaire's daughter with lively interest.

Possibly the cloud on Enid's frank face prompted Reggie to come to a decision more than half formed already.

"But," he went on without giving her time to reply, " one doesn't in this wicked world always do what one ought. Pussy."

"I never do," rejoined the girl, omitting to pretend to resent the use of the once familiar nickname. " I don't see why we should now."

"Nor, on the whole, do I," Reggie reheved her with his assent. " You see, it might put Cherm-side into the deuce of a hole, since he was undoubtedly acquainted with this chap Levison. He will have to own to that, anyhow, as he called on Levison once or twice at the Plume, and the police are sure to have got hold of that. But, though there's something mysterious about him, Chermside is a gentleman. I cannot imagine him carving a little Jew all to pieces simply because of a difference of opinion. He couldn't have had any real motive for doing such a horrible thing, since they say at the club that he's simply rolling in coin. And I don't suppose Levison can have been a rival for the hand of the peerless Violet."

"That suggestion is nothing short of sacrilege, you rude, crude sailor-man! " protested Enid. " Well, we are to lie low, then, and keep a stiff upper lip?"

"That's about the ticket," Reggie agreed, rising and stretching himself. " I don't see that one is even called upon to mention that we were on the marsh and heard that scream. Come, let's clear out of this and go up to the links. A little golf will be a tonic after the gruesome parliament we have been having."

So they went together, dismissing the unpleasant subject with the facility of youth, and in happy ignorance that a pair of sunken, hungry orbs were glaring after them from a tiny flaw in the privet hedgeâ a spy-hole which Mr. Lazarus Lowch had specially constructed for the purpose of keeping an eye on the comings and goings of his neighbour. He had returned from achieving his purpose of being summoned on the jury in time to hear the last words spoken by Reggie. The contortion which did duty with him for a saturnine smile creased his facial muscles.

"So they heard a scream on the marsh and don't mean to say anything about it, eh? I'll see about that," he muttered, rubbing his scraggy hands in a transport of malevolent triumph.

The inquest on Levi Levison was held that afternoon in the long room at the Plume Hotel â an apartment in much request for public functions of all kinds, from Volunteer dinners to sombre occasions like the present. According to precedent Mr. Lowch was chosen foreman, and, licking his lips with anticipation, went away with his brother jurors to gloat over the corpse of the little Hebrew. On their return the coroner at once announced that an adjournment would be necessary, as it had been found impossible as yet to trace the relations, if any, of the deceased. He would, however, take such evidence as was forthcoming that day, and leave the police to complete their investigations before the next occasion.

The first witness was the landlord of the Plume, who identified the body as that of a guest who had been stopping at the hotel for a week. Mr. Levison, he avowed, had been very reticent about the reason of his coming to Ottermouth, and he seemed to know nobody except a gentlemanâ a visitor of the name of Chermsideâ who had called on him twice during the week. The deceased had spent a good deal of time out of the hotel, especially in the evenings.

Leslie Chermside was then called and sworn. In answer to the coroner, he stated that he knew very little of Levison, but that the latter had made certain business proposals to him, and had, he beheved, come down to Ottermouth with the express purpose of making them. Levison came from London, but he did not know his address there.

"Have you any objection to informing the jury of the nature o' the business he had with you? " asked the coroner suavely.

Leslie faced his interrogator squarely, a slight frown of intelligible annoyance contracting his brows. " I should prefer not to," he made answer. " The business was of a very private nature."

"You can, perhaps, at least state to the Court what his occupation was?"

"I believe he called himself a financial agent," was the reply.

"One more question I am bound to ask you, Mr. Chermside," pursued the coroner with a deprecatory wave of his hand: " Were you in the company of the deceased on Wednesday evening last?"

"Most certainly I was not," said Leshe firmly. " I have not spoken to or been with Levison since the morning of the previous day, when he called for me at the club, and we discussed our business during a short walk."

The word had gone round that the bronzed young soldier from India, who occupied the best-furnished apartments in the town, was very wealthy, with a steam yacht lying at Portland, and this had been communicated to the coroner by the police sergeant, Leslie was therefore politely informed that he might stand down, though it might be necessary to recall him at the adjournment.

The next witness was Mr. Mallory. In brief snappy sentences he briefly described how he had found the body in the pool on the marsh while strolling about after the picnic-tea given by the tenant of the Manor House. Mr. Mallory's manner was distinctly that of the old official, who was aware of the fact that he was a merely formal witness. If only the coroner could have penetrated the thoughts which that sphinxlike demeanour veiled he would have started his officer hot-foot to fetch certain witnesses who were not in the room, even as spectators. Travers Nugent was playing pool at the club, and Mademoiselle Louise Aubin was attending to her young mistress's wardrobe a couple of miles away at the Manor.

Then followed the doctor, who described the dead man's injuries, and in doing so cleared the ground of all doubt as to it being a case of murder. Not only had Levi

Levison been slain, but he had fallen by the hand of some one who had literally " savaged " him to death. For the gash in the throat was but an item in a whole series of wounds inflicted on the hapless Jew's body. He had been stabbed three times in the back and once in the chest, any one of the wounds being in itself sufficient to kill.

Sergeant Bruce, in charge of the local force, and a singularly intelligent specimen of the provincial police officer, added his testimony, most of it being concerned with the condition of the ground. A careful examination had led him to adopt the theory that the fatal blows had been struck while the victim was on the footpath, and that the murderer had then carried the body across the swamp to the foot of the railway embankment, and had there flung it into the pool.

"That," said the coroner, " is as far as I propose to take the case to-day."

But it was not, it appeared, as far as Mr. Lazarus Lowch proposed to take it. Bobbing up from his seat like a jack-in-the-box, the foreman wagged a minatory finger at Reggie Beauchamp, whom he had singled out among the audience.

"Before we adjourn, sir, I should like to ask Mr. Beauchamp there a question. I have reason to know that he is concealing a material piece of evidence," Lowch declaimed in his husky voice, lowering at his prey.

Mr. Mallory, wedged in, alert and watchful, near the door, gazed thoughtfully across at his young friend. The lieutenant was already shouldering his way towards the witness-stand, and the old diplomatist noted not only a burning anger in the usually good-humoured boyish face, but a trace of something like consternation. The former sentiment he could understand, for it was nothing new for the methods of Lazarus Lowch to provoke wrath, but what could account for the dashing sailor's palpable nervousness?

At a nod from the coroner Reggie was sworn, and confronted the foreman with a defiant: " Well, sir, I presume that you were eavesdropping behind my mother's garden hedge this morning?"

Lowch ignored the innuendo. " Were you on the marsh late on Wednesday evening, Mr. Beau-champ? " he demanded, in the tone of a grand inquisitor.

"I was," admitted Reggie, shrugging his shoulders.

"In the company of a young lady?"

"Yes," with a scowl for the friendly titter that ran round the room.

"As a gentleman, I abstain from pressing for the lady's name, though doubtless it can be guessed by many in this assemblage," proceeded Lowch pompously. " Let me ask if you and your companion heard a scream on the marsh that night?"

"I am glad you labour the point of your being a gentleman," said Reggie sweetly. " Yes, we heard some kind of a cry. I thought it was a sea-bird, or possibly a snared rabbit."

"Then why did you not come forward when you knew that a murder had been committed and

THE INQUISITIVE FOREMAN loi inform the police of what you had heard? " came the supplementary query.

Mr. Mallory's wise old head was cocked a little on one side to catch the answer. From his attitude he seemed to set considerable store by it.

"Because," said Reggie slowly, "I didn't think that the cry necessarily had anything to do with the case. I know from experience that there are all sorts of queer noises on the marsh after darkâ hooting owls, barking foxes, and a hundred things."

Lazarus Lowch subsided suddenly into his seat with an air of great achievement, and Reggie, perceiving that he had exhausted his capacity for making himself disagreeable, turned with an engaging smile to the coroner. " I hope I have done nothing serious, sir," he said cheerily. " This person seems to accuse me of some terrible misdemeanour, but you will understand that unless one's evidence is really vital to the issue one doesn't want to be needlessly dragged into these Httle turn-ups."

The coroner, a good fellow with a taste for saltwater " breeziness," smiled in friendly fashion, and promptly adjourned the Court.

But Mr. Vernon Mallory was not so easily satisfied. " The boy is concealing something," he muttered as he allowed himself to be carried with the human stream out into the sunlight.

LESLIE CHERMSIDE walked away from the inquest like a man in a dream. It was only a few steps to the house where he lodged, and he at once sought the seclusion of his own sitting-roomâ a shady apartment with long windows opening on to a cool verandah, whence there was a distant view of the headland at the river's mouth and of the sea beyond.

"At any rate, I do not think that I am an object of suspicionâ yet," he murmured with a bitter laugh when he had stood staring from one of the windows with unseeing eyes for some minutes. " And, as I more than half expected, Travers Nugent did not disclose my appointment with that wretched little scally-wag."

Turning away, he lit his pipe and flung himself into a long chair to review the situation. At the best his position was a perilous one, and he was very conscious of the necessity of not lulling himself into a false security because of that day's immunity. But he had at least obtained a reprieve, and for the present he was free to concentrate all his energies on keeping watch and ward over Violet. That Travers Nugent had not abandoned his compact with the Maharajah because of his own defection he felt sure. For, looked at by the light of the event of that afternoon, the inactivity of Bhagwan Singh's agent seemed ominously sinisterâ the more so as it was entirely problematical.

If Nugent had played the obvious card of revealing what he knew about the meeting on the marsh arranged between Levison and Leslie, the latter would almost certainly have been arrested, and so had his wings clipped for further opposition to Nugent's plans. But this obvious and drastic course would have laid Nugent's flank open to the counter-attack of full confession by a desperate man, and he had been far too cunning to run that risk. No, he must be working by subtler and more tortuous methods towards the attainment of his purposeâ the embarkation of Violet Majoiard on board the turbine yacht Cobra.

Leslie gave his antagonist full credit for cold calculation of all the chances. He was under no illusion as to the apparent complaisance with which his rebellion had been accepted, and as to Nugent's quiescence in the matter of Levison's murder. He was assured that he was only sitting there at liberty because he was of more use to Mr. Travers Nugent in the freedom of that comfortable room than he would have been in a cell at the police-station charged with murder.

Rising from his chair with a sudden impulse, Leslie knocked the ashes out of his pipe. As always happens to the man in love, he had persuaded himself that the wisest course to pursue was the one which jumped with his inclinations.

"I will force his hand," he said half aloud. " I will spend all the time I can with Violet, and I will begin at once. My constant presence will be the best safeguard she can have."

Mounting his bicycle, he made short work of the two miles to the lodge gates of the Manor House, and as luck would have it whom should he see coming towards him along the drive but Violet herself. She was looking deliciously cool and dainty in a coat and skirt of white drill, which set off her tall, graceful figure to perfection. Leslie's pulses quickened at sight of the pleased surprise and heightened colour in her face as she saw him.

"I didn't expect you to-day," she said, when he had jumped off his machine. " I thought that you would be kept by that horrid affair in the town, but I suppose you couldn't shed any light on it."

"It was soon overâ adjourned for a week," replied Leslie. " As I was able to get away, I saw no reason why this should be a day entirely wasted."

Violet shot a glance at him from under the deep-fringed lids which had given the critics their cue for their ravings over her Academy picture. There was a warmth in the tone of the neatly-turned little speech that had been lacking in their intercourse of late. The millionaire's daughter had never disguised from herself the singular attraction which this sun-browned, well-knit young soldier from India had for her from the moment of their first meeting a month ago. And he had begun to woo her so bravely and openly, only to slacken his ardour after a week into an indifference which was almost insult after such warm beginnings.

No woman of spirit cares to be treated like goods sent out " on approval"â to be analytically inspected and then cast aside as not quite up to the mark. Especially if she happens to be the acknowledged beauty of the London season, and so lavishly dowered as to have had half the bachelor peerage at her feet. It speaks wonders, therefore, for the efficiency as a lover which Leslie Chermside had shown when he wasn't in love, that now, when he was, Violet should have behaved as she did.

"Let us go and be lazy on that seat by the sundial in the rose garden," she said, with a smile of invitation.

It was all that Leshe asked forâ to be near her, to worship her, to feel her gracious presence, and, above all, by his unceasing watchfulness, to avert the peril of the steamer with the giant horse-power lurking thirty miles away along the coast. That was all that was in his mind as he wheeled his bicycle at her side over the turf that lay between the drive and the rosery. But half an hour amid the late blooms of the old world pleasaunce was to alter all that modest scheme. Leslie Chermside had made the mistake of reckoning without heed to the power that had them in thrallâ the mighty power of love.

Neither of them ever knew how it came about. When they first sat down there was a shy constraint between them that seemed to hold them apart. They talked at random of trifles, with an obvious effort at searching for subjects. Violet even referred to the

inquest on Levison, though in such a manner as to show that she plainly took only a superficial interest in it. It made Leslie shudder to hear her
touch so lightly on a matter in which, though she was not aware of it, she was so nearly concerned.

Gradually and imperceptibly the awkward attempt at making conversation ceased, and the silence that supervened was threatening to become more awkward still, when Violet said suddenly:

"I believe that your heart is in India, Mr. Cherm-sideâ anywhere but in Ottermouth. You always â latterly at leastâ seem to me to be living in the past, or, perhaps, in the future. When your yacht is ready for sea, I suppose that you will lose no time in going back to the East?"

Leslie started, and came back to earth. " If you only knew the price I paid to get out of India you would not say that," he answered gravely. " And I am afraid that you are incorrect in your other surmises, Miss Maynard. I am neither living in a past which has nothing to recommend it, or in a future which is not alluring. As a matter of fact, I am just driftingâ and revelling in the present."

He did not look at her as he spoke. He was staring straight before him at a trellis arch groaning under a weight of crimson rambler roses, but at the suggestion of trouble in his voice the girl swayed nearer to him.

"I wish you would be as frank with me as I am with you," she said. " A woman's sympathy counts for much sometimes. Forgive me for saying that you puzzle me, and one isn't puzzled where one isn't interested. You don't convey the impression of a man with a discreditable career behind him, and from the accepted accounts of your position your prospects are assured from a worldly point of view, A month ago I thoughtâ I hopedâ that we were going to be friends. We had begun to exchange confidences in a mild sort of way. Will you not confide in me now more fully, and tell me if there is anything in which I can help?"

In that moment, listening to her sweet proffer of womanly aid, Leslie suffered the most exquisite torture. This was the girl whom he had lightly condemned to a fate worse than deathâ a fate which he had pledged himself to compass by deceitfully gaining her love. He turned and looked at her, and he knew that the priceless guerdon which he had played for as a mere counter in a disgraceful game had been won. And now that it was hisâ now that he valued it for its own sake more than all the treasures in the worldâ he could not take it. His reawakened sense of honour forbade him to think of such desecration. How could he, wastrel and pauper, have aspired to this queenly maiden, even if his soul had not been soiled by the memory of his infamous bargain?

"I am not worthy one passing thought from youâ still less to give you my confidence," he faltered. " Confidence! " he went on, with something hke a groan of anguish. " Why, I would rather lose the power of speech for ever than befoul your ears with the record of my shame."

Her eyes, like twin pools of shining radiance, were searching his face. " That is for me to judge," she said softly. " But I do not, on second thoughts, ask you for your confidence, Mr. Chermside. I have faith in my instinct. I do not believe that you have done anything really baseâ whatever, perhaps.

after sore temptation, you may have contemplated. You would have stopped short when you realized that you were on the brink of an evil deed. And â and if you hadn't stopped short Iâ well, I, perhaps, should have tried to make allowances. So, if you cannot give me your confidence, at least let me give you my help."

"Help? " came the man's sobbing cry, as the blood surged into his brain, and all barriers of conscience, expedience, and common-sense were swept away in a whirlpool of riotous passionâ " it is your love I want, my darling. The love of such as you means not only help but regeneration, life itself, to such as I."

By the great laws that govern us, these things happen so, and the love of Leslie Chermside and Violet Maynard had passed beyond the region of words and of petty sophistries. They were locked in each other's arms, eye to eye and lip to lip, at that moment of glad surrender in the solitude of the rose gardenâ a solitude that was not entirely solitary.

For from behind the high box-hedge that hemmed them in, the French maid, Louise Aubin, glided across the silent turf back to the house, her piquant features contracted in a venomous frown. She had come out to seek her young mistress on some trifling errand, but, having found her, decided to retreat without fulfilling it.

RUMOUR at Ottei-mouth had a trick of travelling as quickly as it does through the bazaars of the East. When the French maid turned away from the rose garden, after seeing Violet Maynard in Leslie Chermside's arms, she was already aware of the proceedings at the inquest held earlier in the afternoon. She knew, therefore, that the gentleman whose love affair seemed to be prospering so gaily had been called as a witness, and had owned to an acquaintance with her deceased admirer.

Now mademoiselle was an adept at swift deduction, and, putting two and two together, she had arrived at the conclusion that this Mr. Chermside, who had admitted having business relations with Levi Levison, must be the individual whom Mr. Travers Nugent suspected. Mr. Nugent had assured her that he had ascertained that Levison had appointed to meet some one on the marsh on the fatal evening. It followed as almost a certainty that the appointment must have been with the gentleman who had a mysterious connexion with Levison, the nature of which he refused to divulge.

And now this scelerat, this assassin who had ruined no A TRAITOR'S WOOING her prospects by untimely removing the amorous " financial agent," was making successful love to Miss Violet. It was preposterous, and not to be countenanced for a moment, that the murderer should carry off the great heiress, while his cruel crime had relegated her, Louise Aubin, to a probable future of celibate poverty. If only in her young mistress's interest, the atrocious thing must be nipped in the bud.

But mademoiselle was endowed with a fair share of French caution, the quality which kindly Nature supplies to balance French impulse, and she was not going to jeopardize a comfortable and lucrative situation by making a premature move. She must first put it beyond all doubt that the man whom Mr. Levi Levison had arranged to meet on the marsh was the man whom she had just seen in the rose garden, and to that end she must take counsel with that dear gentleman who had saved her from the error of denouncing Pierre Legros.

"Ce cher Monsieur Nugentâ 'e admire me just a leetle himself, I think," she murmured, as she tripped back to the house across the lawn. " I make 'im tell me all he knows."

Whereby Mademoiselle Louise Aubin showed herself to be of sanguine temperament, but a poor student of the art of reading men.

Nevertheless, when Mr. Travers Nugent was sitting in his cosy dining-room at The Hut that evening, peeling peaches and sipping his claret in the soft glow of shaded lamps, his sphinx-like manservant, Sinnett, entered, and, without a word, handed him a folded slip of paper. Nugent read it with a twitch at the corner of his mouth, and looked up sharply.

"Did any one beside yourself see this lady come?" he asked.

"Can't have, sir," was the reply. " She came to the front door, and I admitted her myself. It is pitch-dark outside, so none of the maids can have seen her walking up the drive."

"Then you can show her in," said Nugent. " It is business, Sinnett, but we don't want any village scandal. There are a score of gossiping old women in this place who would give their wigs to know that I had received a smart Frenchwoman in the seclusion of my dining-room, eh?"

A grim smile was the only answer, and presently the man of few words returned, ushering in Mademoiselle Louise. Faithful to his policy of treating her with all respect, Nugent rose with outstretched hand as she minced towards him. There was just enough pleased surprise in his manner to conceal the fact that by paying him this visit she was only fulfilling his calculated expectations.

"This is good of you, mademoiselle," he said in his soft accents. " You will be fatigued after your long walk from the Manor House. Sit down and let me give you a glass of wine from your own sunny France before you tell me how I can be of service to you."

The fair Louise simpered, and seated herself at the well-appointed dessert table. For that night, if for no longer, she had mounted several rungs in the social ladder, and in that thought was compensation for the loss of her " financial agent "â also encouragement for the future. This kindly-spoken gentleman of middle-age was evidently " taken " with her, and there could be no better way, she told herself, of winning and clinching his further regard than by professing a whole-hearted devotion to her last lover.

"I have some news for you, monsieur," she said, when she had sipped the claret poured out by her host. " And, in return, I come to demand, nay, to implore, some information from you."

"Then it must be my privilege to oblige you first, if it is in my power," smiled Nugent. " I trust, however, that you do not still suspect your fellow-countryman, Legros, of the foul deed that robbed you of your friend. Believe me, he is guiltless."

"It is not Pierre Legros that I suspect, monsieur, thanks to your guidance the other day," repued Louise coquettishly. " I was convinced then that the murderer of the poor Levison was the man who was to meet him on the marsh, and nowâ to-day, at the inquest, comes the straw that makes to show the blow of the wind. Monsieur Chermside was a witness, and admitted that he had affairs of business with Levison."

"Well? " Nugent purred gently at his pretty visitor.

"My little stupid wits figure from that, monsieur, that it was Chermside who was to meet the unfortunate one on the marsh. I have paid you this call, at so great risk to my reputation, to find out if for once my little stupid wits are right. You will not disappoint me. Say, I beseech you, if Chermside was the man with whom my poor one had arranged the rendezvous in that so desolate spot."

Nugent was moved with inward laughter at the impressive speech, at the ogling glances accompanying it. He was quite aware of the personal element the minx was endeavouring to import into their relations. Outwardly his face wore the semblance of a severe mental struggle.

"I cannot resist your appeal, Mademoiselle Aubin," he said at last, sighing a little as if in regret that his better judgment should be vanquished by the feminine charms across the table. " I had hoped to keep it to myself a little longer, while prosecuting inquiries which will bring the crime home to this black-hearted villain without allowing an outlet for escape. But I cannot deny you the solace of sharing the secret with me, knowing that, our aims being identical, you will preserve it till the time comes to strike. Yes, Leslie Chermside was the man who had promised to complete a certain transaction with Levi Levison at the spot where the latter was foully done to death."

It is easy to speak with your tongue in your cheek, and if the cheek is large enough no one need catch a glimpse of the tongue. At any rate, Louise Aubin did not. Confident in her potent fascinations, she swallowed the purposely grandiose words like so much milk and honey, and beamed ecstatically on the wily orator, more in delight at the sentiments she believed the communication to denote than at the communication itself. Levi Levison was beginning to take a very shadowy back seat in the affections of Mademoiselle Louise Aubin.

"Then, monsieur," she said, gracefully quaffing her glass at him, "I shall not be behindhand in civeelity. I shallâ what you call itâ place myself in your hands for the right time to punish Cherm-side, and in the meanwhile the secret is buried deep in my heart. Now for your repayment for your kind help, though it is only a tiny piece of news. The villain so despicable, upon whom we desire the avenge, is in love with myâ with Miss Majmard. I come from observing them this very afternoon, monsieur, in the rose garden, where they were embracing and using words of endearment."

And mademoiselle draped her eyes with their long, dark lashes, as though her maiden modesty quailed before the reminiscence.

As for Nugent, he did not disguise the fact that the information had for him the keenest interest. Rising from his chair, he lit a cigarette and began to pace the room.

"Really, I am greatly indebted to you for this information," he said. " The knowledge of Miss Maynard's infatuation for a man so utterly unworthy of her will alter my plans, or rather, hurry them to a crisis. I am, as perhaps you are aware, mademoiselle, a friend of Mr. Montague Maynard. I have, therefore, now a double incitement to bring Chermside to justiceâ that of saving my friend's daughter from a horrible mesalliance, and of securing for you the satisfaction which you so justly desire."

"Mr. Chermside is very rich, is he not? " asked Louise, her cunning but unequal brain beginning to weave an entirely new web, in which she was ultimately to entangle herself.

Travers Nugent shot a glance at her as she toyed with the stem of her wine-glass. For the moment her question caused him a trifling embarrassment. He would have liked to have answered it differently, but he reflected that it would be dangerous to do so, for this woman was by no means a fool. He was credited, rightly, with the introduction at Otter-mouth of Leslie Chermside as a man of wealth. His letter to the secretary of the club would be on file to prove it, and by that he must abideâ for the present.

"Mr. Chermside has the command of vast resources," was his guarded answer. " But I do not think that he will need to plead that argument with a girl of Miss Maynard's character. His worldly position will not weigh with her for an instant if she loves him. She is rich enough for two, you see."

But apparently mademoiselle did not see. Just then she had lost the thread of that newly-woven web on which her busy wits had set to work, and she was staring at one of the long windows. Travers Nugent was something of an artist by temperament, and on sitting down to dinner he had had the blinds left up so as to enjoy the dying after-glow in the western sky.

"The eyes! The peering eyes! " Louise exclaimed in a tense whisper.

Following the direction of her gaze, Nugent in four rapid strides reached the window, and, flinging it open, dragged into the well-lit room the lithe and sinewy form of a man dressed in blue jean. It was the French onion-seller whom Aunt Sarah Dymmock had driven from the precincts of the

Manor House at the point of her sunshade. Louise uttered a suppressed shriek as Nugent released his grip on the Frenchman's collar and carefully closed the window.

"Mon Dieu! it is Pierre Legros," she cried, looking from one to the other of the two men in sheer bewilderment, in which there was a trace of fear.

"Yes, it is Iâ Pierre," said the onion-seller in his native tongue, scowling at his fair compatriot. " Is it that you have acquired the habit of supping alone with gentlemen above your station, as well as of meeting them in the lonely places of the country? You have sadly changed, Louise, since we played barefoot together among the rocks of Dicamp."

In the dawn of her new ambition the reminder of her humble origin goaded the girl to a fury that dispelled her temporary fear. " Barefoot! " she shrilled. " Miserable one, you know quite well that I was never so, and that if you had the presumption to worship me it was from down belowâ as a pig may gaze at the stars. I came to this English gentleman to help me punish the murderer of my dear friend Monsieur Levison."

There was malice in every spitting syllable of the tirade, and more than malice in the baleful look she cast at the sullen Frenchman. Travers Nugent glanced at her a little anxiously, and hastened to intervene. It would not suit his book at all for Louise to revert, out of petty spite, to her original suspicionâ to the prejudice of the later one he had been at such pains to inspire.

"What mademoiselle asserts is absolutely true," he said in French, fixing Pierre's fierce eyes in a hypnotic stare. " She is greatly concerned to catch the murderer, and I hope to hand over to justice the Enghsh rascal who committed the crime on the marsh. And just a word of advice to you, Legros. You had better keep a civil tongue in your head, or you may find yourself in trouble. Mademoiselle Aubin and I, of course, know that you had nothing to do with the matter, but the police might think differently if they got wind of your jealous ravings."

Pondering on, and impressed by, the slight emphasis put on the word English, the onion-seller hung his head, muttering to himself. Nugent took the opportunity to touch the bell, and having done so turned to Louise.

"I think that we have concluded our affairs for this evening, mademoiselle," he said with a cool politeness, the purport of which the clever Frenchwoman was quick to appreciate. " You shall be kept informed of the latest developments, and now my servant shall escort you to the road, for I must have a private word with Legros. Sinnett," to the silent henchman who had appeared, " accompany this lady down the drive, please."

Sinnett understood by the ocular signal that his master flashed at him that Mademoiselle Aubin's departure from the premises was to be accomplished without witnesses, and he gravely followed the somewhat mystified visitor out. Neither by look or gesture did he express the slightest surprise at seeing an unkempt and none too clean foreigner in the room. Ten years in the service of Mr. Travcrs Nugent had killed the faculty of astonishment, or, at any rate, had taught him that the outward and visible signs thereof were inadvisable.

Directly the door was shut on them Nugent's manner underwent a rapid transformation. All the suave polish was gone. He became the brute and the bullyâ the man with the whip-hand. He was not in the least handicapped by having to express himself in French, because he spoke all European languages as fluently as his own. He showered every vile epithet he could think of on the onion-seller, calling him fool, dolt, and everything by turn, and then, when he had pulverized the still scowling but crest-fallen sailor into abject humiliation he demandedâ

"Why, in the name of all that is idiotic, did you disregard my instructions and come here to the house? I told you that nothing but the last extremity would warrant any intercourse between us."

Pierre Legros raised his bloodshot eyes in half-defiant remonstrance. " I came because I thought it was what you call the last extremity," he said. " There has been some one on the quay at Exmouth to-day asking questions of me. He also go on board our vessel and speak with my captain."

"You think he was a detective?"

"No, monsieur; he was not of the police. I believe him to be a gentleman. He lives here in Ottermouth. I see him often when I sell my onions up the streetâ an old man with no hair on his face, dressed in fine clothes, and having eyes that pierce like needles. Though of so great age, he walks very quick and upright."

Nugent took a turn up the room, frowning and biting his lips. " So! " he murmured to himself. " Mr, Vernon Mallory has to be reckoned with as still on the active Hst, eh? " And coming back to where Legros was standing, he added aloud, in more conciliatory tones: " You did right in bringing me this news, my friend. The gentleman is meddlesome, but there is no reason why he should become dangerous if you are discreet."

"I was discreet, monsieur," rejoined Legros. " The grey-head Anglais set springes as one sets them for birds, but I was wary, and walked all roimd. And Jules Epitaux, my captain, he make fool of the old man."

"I hope so," said Nugent drily. " But if it is a sample of your discretion that we have been having in this room to-night, my opinion of it is not high, Pierre Legros. You must learn to curb that insane jealousy of yours, or you will have Louise on to you like a wild cat. Your conduct was base ingratitude, seeing that I stopped her from setting the police at you."

"I am sorry, monsieur; I was taken by surprise, and I did not understand," replied the onion-seller submissively, as he passed out of the window which Nugent held significantly open.

But once outside in the darkness, setting out on the four-mile trudge back to his ship, he began to mutter to himself, and the refrain of the inaudible babble was always the same, recurring a hundred times as he stumbled along the moorland trackâ

"Louise goes to console herself, but not with Pierre. Poor Pierre! He will have to strikeâ always strikeâ if he is betrayed,"

THE COBR. rs SAILING ORDERS

NINE o'clock in the morning was a busy time in a mild way at the Ottermouth Railway Station. The budding resort was served by only a branch line with a single set of rails, and at this hour the first two trains of the day in each direction passed each other here.

Mr. Travers Nugent stood at the window of the booking office, waiting till the slide should be raised, and biting his long fair moustache in annoyance because out of the tail of his eye he had just discovered that the next intending passenger in the row behind him was Lieutenant Reginald Beauchamp. He had quite a poor opinion of the lieutenant's intelligence, but he was aware of his close acquaintance with the Mallorys, and there were reasons why he would have preferred to conceal his destination that day from the shrewd old civil servant.

However, the wooden slide was raised, and Nugent could not avoid asking for his ticketâ a first-class return to Weymouth. It was not till he had picked up his change and passed on that he affected to notice his successor at the window.

"Ah, Beauchamp! Going my way I hope? " he said genially. " I am compelled to go to Weymouth for the day, to look up a sick relative. Beastly nuisance having to play the good Samaritan in such hot weather."

Reggie, before replying, planked down his money and asked for a return ticket to Plymouth. " No," he replied as he joined Nugent. " As you heard, I am going in the opposite direction. My little torpedo craft requires my attention."

"Sorry I'm not to have the pleasure of your company," said the elder man courteously. " Surely your leave isn't up yet?"

"No," Reggie replied. " I have another ten days to run, but I have to see about one or two little matters of shipping stores and ammunition. I hope to be back to-night or to-morrow morning."

On the platform the two separated, Reggie getting into the train which would take him to the western naval seaport, and Nugent crossing the line by the footbridge to the east-bound train.

"I trust that that nautical noodle will have forgotten all about our meeting by to-morrow," Nugent communed with himself as he chose a comer seat in an unoccupied compartment. " It would not be advisable for Mallory, with his wonderful faculty for piecing trifles together, to know that I had paid a flying visit to the port where Chermside's alleged yacht is fitting out."

He leaned back in his cushioned corner and further reflected that even if Mr. Mallory was informed by young Beauchamp that he had been to Weymouth no irremediable harm could come of it. It was even possible that the incident might be converted into an advantage. He had good reason not to despise Mr. Mallory's capabihties, but that astute old gentleman could not thwart his scheme without a fuller knowledge of it, and that could only be gained from Leslie Chermside, who in his present circumstance as Violet Maynard's accepted lover would probably prefer death to confession.

"My immediate policy must be to preserve the renegade's life at all hazards, while threatening it by means of the fair Louise," Nugent smiled contemptuously. " Though what Bhagwan Singh will do to him when he is delivered at Sindkhote is another matter," the arch plotter added under his breath as he unfolded his newspaper and resigned himself to the tedium of the journey.

He reached Weymouth at noon, and at once made his way into the old town, where he turned to the left down the one-sided street of shipping offices and public houses that faces the harbour. The brick and mortar side of the street had no interest for him. His gaze was always for the long row of vessels moored to the quay wall. He walked on, past the wharf where the red-funnelled Great Western boats lay, and came to a halt opposite a large 2,000 ton steam yacht. A handsomely appointed craft she was, with something of the snake in her long, low, graceful lines, and evidently built for speed as well as comfort. The heavy gilt lettering on her stem proclaimed to all and sundry that she was called the Cobra.:,. rÂ

The gang plank was down, and Nugent stepped lightly across it on to the main deck, where his further progress was promptly barred by a bullet-headed ship's officer in a smart blue suit and a brass-banded cap.

"Here! you don't own the bally vessel," said this individual rudely. " Not quite so fast, if you please. What's your business?"

"I am a friend of Captain Brant's; if he is on board and if you will kindly have my card taken to him I have no doubt that he wiu see me," replied Nugent with his usual suave politeness.

The officer called a seaman, and, having dispatched him with the card, became roughly apologetic. " That's a horse of another colour," he growled. " Strict orders against strangers on this ship. Couldn't let you on if you were the skipper's own brother, and the skipper's the devil."

"My dear sir, I congratulate you on your discretion," rejoined Nugent affably. " I don't mind telling you that if you had let me on without orders you wouldn't have enjoyed your billet another hour. As it is, you will be like the nice little boy in the Sunday school who had a good mark put against his name."

The bullet-headed mate spat thoughtfully over the bulwarks, and then, as he realized the position, broke into an evil grin.

"I see," he chuckled. " You're the power behind the throne, eh? I guess if I'd known that I'd have given you a bit of stronger lip. What the blooming game is I don't want to know, but I can see it's going to be a funny sort of cruise."

The bluejacket, whose brutal features, Nugent observed with cynical satisfaction, were at curious variance with his trim, yacht-Uke attire, returned, and said that Captain Brant would receive the visitor at once. Nugent followed his conductor to a cabin under the bridge, the occupant of which, a little wisp of a man with an elongated, pear-shaped cranium, prominent teeth, and a yellow complexion, advanced with a strange, hopping gait to greet his guest.

"Ah! " he said with an uncanny hissing intake of breath, "I am charmed to see you, Mr. Nugent. The honour of your visit means that we are to get a move on us at last, I hope?"

"It points that way," replied Nugent guardedly as he took the seat offered him. " Your anxiety to be off means that you are having trouble with the crew, I am afraid, Brant?"

The repulsive captain twisted his features into a grimace that would have curdled milk, at the same time emitting a sound like the snarl of a wolf. " The maintenance of discipline among a lot of toughs like those I selected isn't child's play," he said. " It only wants a rule of three sum to find out how soon I shall have no crew at all if we are to lay idle here much longer. I've had to shoot one as dead as Queen Anne and crack the heads of four others for kicking over the traces."

The answer, delivered coolly and as a matter of course, seemed ludicrous coming from the undersized, deformed creature with the top-heavy head. But Nugent evidently knew his man, for he merely nodded comprehension and approval. " It is because you are such a holy terror. Brant, that I selected you for the job," he said. " There was bound to be trouble, at the start of a cruise for which the hands were induced to jom by the promise of a rich reward, if any hitch occurred."

"It is entirely the delay that caused the ructions," the captain assented. " You see, they don't know whether they're on a treasure hunt or what, and they're in a hurry to finger the pieces. To keep 'em from letting their jaw tackle run in the pubs I didn't allow much shore libertyâ none at all since I had to pump Black Jake, a fireman, full of lead for inciting to mutiny."

"But how about theâ erâ necessary formalities? " asked Nugent, genuinely interested in the drastic methods of his instrument.

Captain Brant uttered the unpleasant combination of croak and wheeze that did duty with him for a laugh. " You mean the inquest and funeral? We have no use for little extras like them on the Cobra. I'm the law on this ship. I took a kind of a trial trip out to sea for a couple of hours, and cremated Black Jake in his own furnace. That put the fear of the devil into the rest, and we're a happy family now. I wouldn't guarantee to hold 'em for more than a fortnight, though, tied up to this cursed quay. The officers are right enough. Bully Cheeseman, the chap who was at the gangway when you boarded us, is a fair scorcher. Twenty years ago he was suspected of being Jack the Ripper; and Wiley the second mate, as you know, has done time for manslaughter."

Travers Nugent gazed thoughtfully through the circular window of the deck-cabin at the teeming quay-side, and the array of public-houses across the road. He was not at all dissatisfied with the state of things prevailing on the Cobra. It had justified his choice of a skipper. If this frail little atomy with the body of an imp and the soul of a Thug, could isolate and hold in check a crew of cutthroats recruited from the slums of Limehouse, within sight of the drink-shops over the way, he was not likely to fail at the crucial moment.

And it was to expedite that crucial moment that Nugent had paid his surprise visit to the Cobra.

"I'm not finding fault, Brant," he said. " At least, not with you and your management of affairs. The blame rests on the mean-spirited cur who has kept the ship dallying here in port while he was going back on his bargain and playing a double game with me. However, you'll have him on board in a few days, I hope, and among your final instructions will be one to let him have a particularly warm time of it."

"I'll keel-haul the swine morning and evening if you like," growled Brant, " or give him a taste of the cat."

"Well, I don't want you to be tender with him," laughed Nugent, " so long as you leave enough of him for delivery to the consignee. But here is what I ran over to tell you. On receipt of a wire containing the one word ' Advance," you will leave port and steam to the westward at such a speed as will take you abreast of Ottermouth after sundown. Don't bring the ship nearer inshore than three miles, but lay to till you see a blue light, and then a green, shown about half a mile to the west of the town."

"Just a moment. Let's fix it up accurate,"

interrupted the captain. " We mustn't have any such words as ' about' in a job of this kind. Point out the exact place on this ordnance map, please."

"There, at the foot of that cleft in the cliff marked Coldbrook Chine," said Nugent, placing his finger on the map section which Captain Brant spread before him on the cabin table. " I have chosen the spot because it is hidden from the coastguard station by this jutting angle in the wall of cliff."

"The signal wouldn't be visible from the station? " croaked Brant.

"Quite impossible. When you see the blue and green lights, all you have to do is to send the electric launch, manned by three trustworthy and well-armed men, to the beach at the foot of the chine. The launch will pick up a passenger, and as soon as he has been put aboard the steamer, will return to the same spot and pick up another. On the second occasion I myself shall be there, and will hand your officer a sealed packet containing your final instructions. It is even possible that I may come aboard and hand them to you in person."

The weird Httle deformity laughed his horrible laugh. " Pleased to see you, I'm sure," he responded, when the convulsions in his throat had ceased. " You might be making the voyage with us, I reckon?"

"God forbid! " exclaimed Travers Nugent fervently.

CHAPTER XIII fool's paradise lost

LESLIE CHERMSIDE walked out of his lodgings in the Ottermouth main street and struck downwards towards the parade. He had promised to take Violet Maynard and Aunt Sarah Dymmock out for a sail in a boat he had hired, and, lover-like, he was nearly an hour ahead of the appointment he had made with the two ladies to meet him on the beach.

Three days had passed since the unpremeditated avowal of his love for the millionaire manufacturer's daughter. They slipped by like a happy dream, no care for the future, or the deadlock to which the future must inevitably bring him, disturbing the sweet dalliance of the present till the previous evening. He had dined at the Manor House alone with the family and, as they sat over their wine after the departure of Violet and Aunt Sarah, Montague Maynard had, quite kindly, put to him some pertinent questions, the drift of which there was no mistaking. Mr. Maynard would not have attained to his position in the commercial world had he not been a student of men and things, and, without definitely stating as much, he let it be clearly understood that he was not blind to what was going on. His manner imphed that he was not unfriendly, but, at the same time, in asking about the young ex-Lancer's resources, he spoke as if he had a right to the information.

He opened the battle in his usual blunt, jovial fashion, without any beating about the bushâ

"So, my young friend, you're a warm man, Travers Nugent tells me. Lucky chap, to possess inherited wealth, though I'm not sure that I wouldn't have preferred you to have made a pile by hard work, as I have."

Leslie suddenly finding himself on the edge of a precipice, clutched for the only available support â a deprecating and rather shamefaced laugh. " Mr. Nugent must be given to exaggeration, sir," he said. " I have never represented myself as a rich man. As a matter of fact I amâ not by any means what you would consider rich."

He thought grimly of the few 5 notes left to him out of the sum advanced by Nugent for current expenses during the bogus courtship of the girl now dearer to him than life. Something of the rueful irony in his mind must have been reflected in his face, for Mr. Maynard, after a sidelong glance at him and a sip of port, continuedâ

"Now, my lad, I've been and set your back up by hinting that you didn't earn your money. At any rate, you must be pretty well lined to be able to chuck the army at your age, and to possess such a steam yacht as Nugent has described to me."

"I am afraid, sir, that Nugent's imagination has run away with him," Leslie replied, flushing hotly. " The yacht at Weymouth, in which I had been going to travel, is not my own property."

"You have abandoned your intention?"

"Entirely."

A constrained silence fell upon the two men. The blue smoke of their cigars floated over the array of decanters, the luscious fruits and glittering plate. On one the demon of distrust had been unchained; on the other, a cloud of apprehension, threatening the short-lived bliss of the last few days, had swooped from an azure sky. It was Montague Maynard who broke the spell, going, as was his way, direct to the point.

"Look here, Chermside," he blurted out. " I like you, and so does old Sally Dymmockâ 'cute observers, both of us. But there's something not quite above-boardâ I don't say about you, but about your circumstances. I'm the last man to judge anybody hastily, and you may have the best of reasons for reticence; but I just want to warn you that if you come to me with a proposal which I need not define I shall expect perfect frankness."

Leslie's heart sank within him, for perfect frankness was what he would never be able to accord. How was he to explain the fact that he was a penniless man without prospects, in face of the impression which, if not actually inspired by him, he allowed to remain, that he was rolling in money? Still less could he explain the motive which had prompted him to acquiescence in Nugent's description of him. And the only alternative to explanation was once for all to abandon hopes of Violet, and to bear his loss as manfully as he could, accept- ing it as a punishment for his contemplated evil-doing.

"When I come to you with a definite proposal, sir, I shall naturally endeavour to satisfy you," was his long-delayed reply.

It was lame enough, but it served its immediate purpose of staving off the day of reckoning. For Montague Maynard rose abruptly from the table, flinging down his napkin with a gesture of impatience, and obviously restraining an impulse to press his guest for a declaration of his intentions.

"Come and join the ladies," he said curtly.

An uncomfortable half-hour had followed in the drawing-room, the air vibrant with an electric tension which all were conscious of, and, as is customary on such occasions, increased by their fatuous efforts to relieve it. Violet talked brilliantlyâ more brilliantly than usual, perhapsâ of things that did not matter, watching her father and lover with a pained surprise which her brave efforts could not wholly conceal. Aunt Sarah seized such opportunities as were offered to her of being openly rude to every one in turn, nodding her priceless lace cap to emphasize her points, stabbing her lean fingers at the successive victims of her caustic tongue, and galvanizing her mummy-like face into grimaces that would have terrified strangers.

But, so far as Leslie was concerned, it was reserved for the old lady to save the situation. When she got up to go she followed Mr. Maynard and Violet into the hall to speed the parting guest, winding up a stilted evening with the request that Mr. Cherm-side would take her and her great-niece on what she called " the water " the next day. She and Violet would motor out to the Ottermouth beach, and meet him there at 11,30 if " the elements were propitious."

Leslie had, of course, consented, though he had to conceal a certain amount of reluctance in doing so. After Mr. Maynard's plain speech he was not sure if it was not his duty to refrain from seeing Violet again. At any rate the time had come when he must quit the fool's paradise in which he had been living since the scene in the rose-garden, and seriously consider his position. But Miss Dymmock 's request was a command, and it had this meritâ that whatever course he decided on he would have one more hour in the company of his beloved.

Now, as he went to keep the appointment, he was no nearer a solution of his dilemma in spite of anxious deliberation through the long hours of a sleepless night. He was prepared to suffer the pain of giving Violet up, but from her own sweet confession he knew that in vanishing from her life he would inflict upon her a pain equal to his own. He shrank from dealing the cruel blow. And, again, the necessity of guarding her against the plot which he was all too sure was hatching in Nugent's brain was a strong inducement to remain on the spot as long as possible.

Racked with indecision, he loitered on the parade and absent-mindedly watched the bathers till one of the Maynard motor cars swept round the corner by the coastguard station, pulling up opposite the boat which the fisherman in his employ had in readiness. He thought that Violet looked pale and preoccupied as she stepped from the car, but Aunt Sarah was as alert and determined as ever, and, hardly deigning a word of greeting, started across the pebbly beach for the boat. Leslie and Violet followed, the sight of the little old lady's spindle shanks, as she trudged over the stones with skirts held high, for the moment taking them out of themselves.

A little later the boat was running eastward round the headland at the river's mouth before a gently favouring breeze. The wind being steady and the sea smooth, the boatman was left behind, Violet taking the helm and Leslie minding the sheet. Aunt Sarah, settled comfortably forward of the little stick of a mast, spent the first five minutes in a careful scrutiny of the sky, and then, finding that there were no outward evidences that she was to be drowned that morning, suddenly astounded her shipmates with the exclamationâ

"You two are in love with each other, and you can't deny it!"

There succeeded ten seconds of intense silence, and then Violet, who was famihar with her aged relative's little ways, laughed at the consternation on her lover's bronzed face.

"It is no use, Leshe," she said. " Aunt Sarah is a witch, and knows the secrets of our inmost hearts. We may as well confess."

"I don't suppose it is a crime," Chermside murmured weakly, in his confusion taking an unnecessary pull at the sheet and sending a spray over Aunt Sarah's mantle.

"No, 3'Oung man, it's not a crime," she snapped when she had recovered her balance and her equanimity. " I'm a bit of a character reader, and I don't think you're capable of crimeâ havn't got the backbone for it. But I know that you are weak, and that you're in some sort of a hobble that you ought to be pulled out of. Now just you be straight with me. If you had really been the man of the means you've been credited with in this gossipy little hole you'd have gone to my nephew Montague Maynard and asked him for his daughter three days ago, eh?"

"I admit that. There have been misunderstandings for which I am partly but not entirely responsible," said Leslie, marvelling at the almost uncanny insight with which the old lady had read between the lines, and wondering how much of his secret she had guessed.

She proceeded to cross-examine him after the fashion of a barrister handling a hostile witness. " Leaving aside for the moment the question of financial position," she continued, " is there any other cause or impediment why you should not be joined in holy matrimony to my great-niece? As a man of honour you will answer me truly and without reserve."

Leslie stole a glance at Violet and saw that she had become suddenly grave. Nurtured in the midst of luxury, she hardly knew the value of money, and had the most profound contempt for it; but she cherished the highest ideals of what a man's moral worth should be, and she was clearly awaiting his answer with eager interest.

"Yes," said Leslie, scarcely hesitating, " there is the strongest possible reason why Violet should not marry me. I have already urged it upon herâ that I am utterly unworthy."

"He is not so black as he would paint himself, Aunt Sarah," the girl pleaded. " Some quixotic idea"

"Mind your steering or we shall all be in the water," the old lady cut her short. " Now, Mr. Chermside, be explicit, please. Why are you unworthy to marry my niece?"

"Because," replied Leslie, who had expected the question. " I consented, under stress of peculiar circumstances, to aid and abet a base conspiracy for doing a great injury to an innocent person. It is true that I repented and left my tempters in the lurch, but I cannot hold myself white-washed on that account."

Miss Sarah Dymmock, not having a barrister's gown to hitch up, adjusted her mushroom hat before returning to the charge. " Has this piece of villainy you set out to do since been accomplished by the people who tried to mislead you? " she demanded.

"It has not," rejoined Leslie firmly. " And please God it never will. They have not, I believe, abandoned it; but I am devoting such feeble powers as I possess to thwarting them. I claim no leniency on that score. I tell you, Miss Dymmock, as I have told Violet, that the thing was a horrible thing, and that no decent woman ought to be joined to a man who, even in a mad lapse born of unspeakable misery, could have become a consenting party to it for a single minute."

Aunt Sarah nodded sagely once or twice, and let her keen old eyes rest for a while on the red cliffs past which the boat was gliding. " Reverting to the question of means," she resumed at length, " if you went to that greedy nephew of mineâ not a bad sort, but a money-grubberâ you would have to confess that you had no steam yacht to your name, or any of the other trimmings with which the Otter-mouth wiseacres have credited you?"

"I should have to confess that I haven't a blessed stiver," said Leslie grimly.

Aunt Sarah's stern features relaxed, and her smile could be very charming when she chose. " In that case, Mr. Chermside," she said, " you would be adding the sin of falsehood to your other real or imaginary iniquities. I yesterday arranged the preliminaries of a transfer to you of securities worth, roughly speaking, two hundred and fifty thousand pounds. I had an inkling that you were an attractive but quite harmless fraud, and as the present interview has confirmed that belief I shall wire my brokers to complete the transfer. I was aware that my dear girl's happiness was bound up in your ability to satisfy her father of your good faith, and I decided to place you in a position to do so. There is no need to thank me. It is only a little juggle with money for which an old woman has no use. In any case it would have been Violet's when I die."

"And you suggested a sail in order to tell us this? " Violet gasped.

"Yes; you see it is really a sort of plot in which we three must remain the only' conspirators," the old lady beamed at the fair young face flushed with joy. " A boat seemed the safest place for such business."

"You dear! " was all Violet could answer as she strove to keep back the happy tears.

As for Leslie, his first impulse was to reject the good fortune thrust upon him. The " coals of fire " heaped upon his head burned his brain and filled him with a greater shame; for he could not but think that if the real enormity of his offence were known this generosity would never have been shown him. His proper course, he felt, was to make still fuller confession, but that would be to stab his darling to the heart in the hour of triumphant love. All he could do then was to begin to stammer inconsequent but grateful protests which Aunt Sarah stopped at once with masterful insistence.

"Nonsense! " she snapped at him. " Just look to the sail and do what's necessary to put us ashore again as quick as may be. Lve got but a short patience with folk who don't know the butter side of a slice of bread."

So the boat was turned and went gaily dancing over the summer sea, under the red cliffs, and round the headland, to the beach. After the discussion on the outward run it was but natural that words should be few, and Leslie was glad of it for more reasons than one. They had the wind against them now, and the sailing of the boat claimed all his attention. A succession of short tacks was necessary before he landed his precious freight.

The motor car was waiting for the ladies, and when he had bestowed them in it, and given a promise to come out to the Manor House later in the day,

Leslie turned in the opposite direction to go to his rooms for lunch. As he neared the end of the parade, he saw Travers Nugent watching him from one of the windows of the club, and he averted his gaze so as not to catch the eye of his enemy. But the elementary tactics were of no avail. Nugent came out of the front door before he could pass.

"Come inside; there is need for a consultation," said the Maharajah's agent.

Leslie angrily shook off the detaining hand which had been laid upon his arm. " I don't wish to have anything to do with you. I'll be hanged if I come in," he said.

Nugent laughedâ the little musical laugh that women loved and men loathed. " My dear fellow, you have used an apt term in the reverse sense," he cooed. " You will certainly be hanged if you don't come in and listen to what I have to say."

For the second time that morning Leslie Chermside paled beneath his Eastern tan, and he meekly followed Nugent into the club.

THROUGHOUT the bewildering excitement in the boat consequent on Miss Dymmock's benevolence, Leslie had been conscious of a weak spot in his armour, which, if it had been detected by his antagonist, might prove his undoing. Nugent's ominous rejoinder suggested that the weak spot had been found, and that he was being led into the comfortable seclusion of the Ottermouth Club for the purpose of having it pierced.

"We had better go into the card-room," said Nugent. " There will be less chance of interruption there, though at present there is no one in the club. Every one has gone home to lunch."

The card-room was on the first floor, with a window overlooking the sea. Leslie remained standing just inside the door, but Nugent sat down at one of the card tables, his fingers drawing fantastic patterns on the green cloth as he seemed to consider how best to open the subject. Suddenly he raised his eyes, and Leslie saw with surprise that there was no hostility in themâ only a look of deep concern.

"You are in a tight place, my friend," he said. "Are you aware that you are under the gravest suspicion of having murdered Levi Levison?"

"I am not surprised to hear it, since you knew of my engagement to meet Levison on the marsh that night," repued Leslie. "I had more than half expected that you would give evidence to that effect at the inquest."

Nugent! brushed the insinuation aside with a contemptuous gesture. "My dear Chermside, if you are going to approach the matter in that spirit, we shall come to grief," he said. "Can't you see that our interests are absolutely identicalâ that if you fall I fall too. Not quite so far perhaps, but a good deal further than I care to contemplate. I don't pretend to any affection for you, after the way you have played the mischief with everything, but your arrest on this charge would mean my social ruinâ if nothing worse. The motive for your crime, and all that led up to it, would be sure to come to lightâ even if you did not plead guilty and put forward the motive as an extenuating circumstance."

This was selfish villainy, naked and unashamed, but it sounded like honest villainy. Leslie had realized from the first that if his appointment with Levison transpired, the case against him would be black indeed, but he had expected that Nugent would rejoice in that fact. It had not occurred to him that his former accomplice would be dragged down in his fall.

"It will be time enough to talk of motive when I admit that I killed Levison," he said, in a burst of indignation.

"You didn't kill him? There are no witnesses. Straight now, as from man to man, standing on the brink of the same precipice?"

"I'll swear I didn't."

The shrug and the raised eyebrows with which Nugent received the denial made Leslie itch to hit him, but his anger passed with the prompt semi-withdrawal of the implied accusation.

"If you didn't someone else did. Let me think a moment," said Nugent, and again he fell to tracing invisible patterns on the card table. Leslie leaned against the wall by the door, and stared vacantly through the window at faint specks on the horizon of the sunlit seaâ Brixham trawlers on the fishing-grounds twenty miles away. The dapper man in the immaculate grey suit, solving unseen problems on the green cloth, had disarmed him. Nugent's belief in his guilt, he told himself, had been genuine, but Nugent had been shaken in that belief. He was striving for some other explanation of the Jew's death. At last he raised his eyes.

"I have been trying to overhaul my knowledge of Levison's past in order to account for his murder by some other means than the obvious," he said. "And, with every desire to fit him with an appropriate murderer, I have entirely failed. There is no need to disguise the fact that he was my toolâ a dirty little shyster who has done odd jobs for meâ but he was not the sort of person to inspire a thirst for bloodshed. A mean-spirited little rascal, with no ideas beyond the price of a bill-stamp and overcharging what he called his ' exes." There was no one to kill him but you, my friend."

"Don't call me that," said Leslie hotly. "I repeat that I did not kill him."

Nugent shook his head with an incredulity the more exasperating because it seemed so thoroughly genuine. "At any rate, a judge and jury would find a difficulty in believing to the contrary. Let me state the case just to show you your danger. You have yourself admitted acquaintance and business relations with Levisonâ a stranger in the place, who is not known to have had dealings with any one else. Point one for the prosecution. It can further be proved that you had arranged to meet him at that lonely spot"

"Pardon me," interrupted Leslie hoarsely. " That cannot be proved unless you volunteer as a witness, and give away the whole vile story of the plot to abduct Miss Maynard."

The gentle tolerance of Nugent's smile was harder to bear than abuse would have been. " Really, Chermside, you are an impossible fellow to have as a partner in a losing game," he said. " At the risk of being wearisome, let me repeat that your trial would spell ruin for me. It is Louise Aubin, Miss Maynard's French maid, who is at the bottom of the trouble. Levison, like the vulgar wretch he was, amused himself with a flirtation with her. It seems that, most indiscreetly, he confided to her that he had some hold on you, and that it was either to be tightened or relaxed after an interview arranged for that night. Point two for the prosecution."

Leslie's heart sank as the remorseless indictment against him was unfolded. He had been naturally disposed to mistrust Nugent's profession of mutual interests, but with the introduction of this new and independent witness into the case this was explained. Louise Aubin, if she had been confided in by Levison, was certainly in a position to wreck the two of them. Yet once more his doubt surged up, and he put the quick questionâ

"Why has this woman imparted her suspicion to you? Why did she not take it to the police, and appear at the inquest?"

"Because, by the greatest good luck, I met her on her way to do so," answered Nugent promptly. " It was on the day of the picnicâ immediately after the discovery of the body. I was aware of her relations with the dead man, from what was said when we lunched at the Manor, and I guessed what she was up to. I managed to throw dust in her eyes for the time, and have contrived to hold her in check since, but she is growing restive, and threatens to appear at the adjourned inquest."

Leslie stared dully at the speaker. He could almost feel the hangman's noose at his neck. The bright vision of an hour ago had faded into Cimmerian gloom. Nugent's clever face suggested the only possible source of the advice of which he stood in such urgent need, and, almost against his will, the question escaped himâ

"What had I better do?"

"Cut and run for it. Avoid arrest at any price," was the ready reply.

"But I am not guilty. I did not murder the Httle Jew."

"You cannot prove that," Nugent rejoined, with a flicker of his hateful smile. " Besides," he added, " consider the execration you would incur in attempting to do so. What would your life be worth to you if you managed to save it by confessing your share in the Violet Maynard project?"

Leshe could frame no reply, and while he sought for one, a tiny sound, that under other circumstances would have been disregarded, reached his ears. Nugent, who was further from the door, evidently had not heard it. Somewhere about half-way up the staircase a loose board creaked, but the sound had been preceded by no footfall, nor, though he listened intently, could Leshe detect that it was followed by one. Some instinct, which he did not attempt to analyse then, but which he afterwards knew was a desire to dissociate himself from Nugent in any danger which that creaking stair might portend, prompted him not to call attention to it. But, to prevent any chance of the remainder of their conversation being overheard, he turned and closed the door smartly.

"If I make a bolt of it, where am I to bolt to? " he asked, lowering his voice and stepping to the table.

A gleam of triumph, instantly suppressed, flashed in Nugent's eyes. " I have considered that most carefully," he replied. " At the first hint of your departure, in the ordinary way, Louise Aubin would go to the police, and you would be traced and arrested. I propose, if you assent, to utilize the Cohra for your flight. She is the property of the Maharajah, and Bhagwan Singh is as much interested in covering up his attempt to gain an Enghsh bride by force as we are ourselves. Now that the vessel won't be wanted for her original purpose, she may as well earn her upkeep by helping to preserve the secret of our abortive scheme. Once smuggled aboard safely, she could put you ashore at some South American port, where you might carve out a new career, though you must forgive my saying that I doubt your success in any undertaking."

Leslie allowed the gibe to pass. He was prepared to make allowances for Nugent's disappointment, now that he was persuaded that he had definitely abandoned the plot against Violet, and was only concerned in hiding all traces of it. On the whole, the plan for evading arrest rather appealed to him. With a dull despair at his heart, he had already realized that the vengeful Frenchwoman had shattered his day-dream. Of what use to him would be good old Aunt Sarah's benefaction, when there was hanging over his head a murder charge which, even if he could refute it, would remove Violet beyond his pale for ever?

"I suppose you're right," he gave his tardy consent. " And if I have got to go, the sooner the better. When do you propose that I should start?"

Travers Nugent rose with a sigh of unaffected relief. " I expect it will be the day after to-morrow," he made answer. " But we will meet again to arrange final details. In the meanwhile, my dear fellow, let me congratulate you on the one gleam of common-sense you have shown throughout our disastrous association. All my energies must now be directed to chaining up that wild-cat of a French maid till you are safely on board."

Nodding curtly, he walked to the door, opened it, and, passing down the stairs, left the club. Les- lie, following more leisurely, was moved by a great curiosity to see if he could account for that ominous creak. He glanced into the reading-room, but there was no one there. It was too early in the afternoon for the assembly of members who came to chat and see the papers.

The click of balls, unusual at that hour, attracted him to the bilhard-room, and, entering, he was confronted with an enigma. The lean, ascetic form of Mr. Mallory was bending over the table, poising his cue for a difficult cannon, which he delayed for an instant because of the interruption, and then made with an unerring precision. His antagonist was the burly and rubicund General Kruse, who had his nose buried in a whisky and soda. On the lounge, watching the game with sardonic contempt, sat the cadaverous Mr. Lazarus Lowch, the foreman of the jury at the inquest on Levison, and but a rare visitor to the billiard-room.

Leslie walked to the scoring-board and noted the state of the game. It stood at 5-2, and could therefore have been only just begun. It followed that any one of these three gentlemen, so oddly occupied at an unaccustomed hour, when they ought to have been enjoying an after-luncheon siesta at home, might have caused the sound on the stairs a few minutes before.

Which of them could it have been? How much of that momentous interview, on which his liberty and his life might depend, had been overheard?

THE handsome pension which Mr. Vernon Mallory drew as a distinguished servant of the Foreign Office, added to considerable private means, enabled him to occupy one of the most important residences in the place. It had large, well-shaded tennis and croquet lawns, and here, later on that same afternoon, Mr. Mallory was sitting under a copper beech with his wife, a gentle, patient lady, who had the misfortune to be blind.

At the other side of the croquet lawn Lieutenant Reginald Beauchamp and Miss Enid Mallory were leaning on their mallets with every appearance of being engaged in a violent quarrel. The girl's face was flushed, and now and again she tapped the close-cropped turf impatiently with a neat brown shoe. The young sailor, viewed from the distance, had the air and attitude of saying rude things in a provoking manner.

"What are those two doing, dear? " Mrs. Mallory asked presently. " My ears tell me that they have stopped playing."

"They look," replied her husband, " as if they were hurling invectives at each other over a foul stroke. Knowing them as I do, my impression is that they are occupied in coming to an understanding. Their ideas of love-making are of the kittenish orderâ a pat and a scratch, and a pat again. But I think that they are both in earnest."

"Reggie has been suddenly recalled to his ship, has he not?"

"Yes, he has to rejoin at Plymouth to-morrow morning for some sort of manoeuvres or gun practice. That may account for the affair having come to a head to-day."

The blind lady sighed with contentment. " He is a brave, good lad, Vernon," she said. " You must be kind to him, and say ' Yes ' nicely when he asks you for our darling. They have been fond of each other since they were babies almost."

The ghost of a tender smile quivered at the comer of Mr. Mallory's stem mouth. " I shall not be rough with him, Margaret," he said gently, " but I am going to make a bargain with him for all that. He hasâ I believe both the young rascals have it â the key to something I want very badly."

Mrs. Mallory's sightless eyes turned towards her husband, and her voice spoke the affection they could not express. " The key to a secret, dear. To some mystery that is no concern of yours? When shall I be able to persuade you that you retired from the public service years ago? But they are coming this way, I think."

Her acute hearing, that blessed compensation granted to the blind, had told her truly. Reggie and Enid were crossing the la. wn. towards themâ a picturesque whirlwind of white flannel and flapping straw hats. Mr. Mallory composed his features into an acid contemplation of the approaching couple, though he had much ado to succeed. No sentimental nonsense here, but earnest, cocksure intent, after his own heart.

"We've come to ask your permission," Reggie began.

"Will you hold your tongue, sir? We have come to do nothing of the kind," Enid interrupted him. " We've come to give information, that's all. Father, dear, we have had an awful row about details, but we've patched it up, and are engaged to be married. You haven't any objection, I suppose? Of course Reggie is no great shakes, and I might have done better, but he suits me." And, after a pause, the minx added, with an impudent motie at her lover, " on the whole."

Mr. Mallory reared his tall, spare frame from the basket-chair in which he had been lounging, and, having pressed his wife's hand to reassure her that all would be well, turned with mock severity to the culprits.

"Come into the study," he said in his most judicial tone. " The remarks I have to make are not for the benefit of any chance passer-by, or of Mr. Lazarus Lowch if he is on the prowl."

The three passed into the house, and as soon as the door of Mr. Mallory's sanctum was shut upon them he laid an affectionate hand on the shoulder of each of his young companions. " Your little affair will be all right," he smiled at them, laying aside his judicial manner. " You were born to keep each other in order, and we ojd folks should have been disappointed had it been otherwise. But in return for my easy sanction, I want your fullest confidence about something very different. I was watching you the other day at the inquest, Reggie. What really happened that night when you two were sweethearting on the marsh?"

Two pairs of youthful eyes questioned each other, and each gave a mutely tentative answer in the affirmative.

"We saw something that night that might get some one into trouble," Reggie took upon himself to say. " Some one whoâ well, didn't strike us as the sort of chap to deserve it. So we decided to keep quiet about it."

"I am inclined to think that your discretion was praiseworthy," said Mr. Mallory gravely. " I hope, however, that for that some one's sake I may be honoured by your confidence. It was Leslie Chermside, was it not?"

"Well, yes; as you seem to be omniscient, sir, and friendly to him, we did see Chermside on the marsh that night," Reggie admitted.

"But we didn't see him murdering anybody," interposed Enid; adding inconsequently, "Dear Violet Maynard wouldn't be so keen on him if he was a murderer."

"You were not, I presume, an actual witness of the crime," Mr. Mallory said drily. He remained silent for a minute, walking up and down the room, and then continuedâ

"Now, look here, you two. There is some ugly mischief going on here, and it is my belief that Chermside, though mixed up in it, is more sinned against than sinning. You will best serve him by being perfectly frank with me, and if it will induce you to be so, let me say that the wire-puller in the business is Mr. Travers Nugent. You are both of you aware of my opinion of that gentleman, based on grounds of former official experience. I am certain that there is some deep-laid plot afoot in which Chermside is a mere pawnâ a plot which I somehow vaguely deem to be directed against the good people who have rented the Manor House. I have utterly failed so far to gain the slightest inkling of the nature or object of Nugent's machinations, but I have gathered this â that whether Chermside killed that little Jew or not Nugent is holding over him, as a means to effect his purpose, the probability of imminent arrest."

At that Reggie described fully how he and Enid had been " resting " in the bushes at the side of the marshland path, and how at short intervals two men, whom it was too dark to recognize, had passed by. He went on to repeat the evidence dragged from him at the inquest as the result of the eavesdropping of Mr. Lazarus Lowch, telling over again of the weird scream that had startled them a few minutes after the passing of the second unseen pedestrian. And he finished his narrative with the hurried return along the path of a man who, as he passed their lair, was shown by the searchlight on the battleship to be none other than Leslie Chermside.

Mr. Mallory pondered the statement, then asked suddenly, "Did you notice any pecuharity in the footfall of the invisible pedestrians?"

"Yes, we did," Enid answered quickly. " The first to come along was going rapidly, as though he was late for an appointmentâ almost running, in fact. We could quite plainly hear him puffing and blowing."

"Humph! Cannot yoa be a little more exact as to the time that elapsed between these four different incidentsâ the passing of the two unseen wayfarers, the scream, and the disclosure of Cherm-side by the searchlight? For instance, could the second of the two invisible passers-by have reached the spot where the body was found, when you heard the scream?"

"I couldn't say, sir," replied Reggie with a faint grin at his companion of the fatal night.

"Or whether, after the scream, there had been sufficient time for Chermside to traverse the distance from the same spot to where you were?"

"You see, father," Enid took up her parable as Reggie shook his head, " we didn't know then of any reason for paying attention to these matters. We were discussing things that seemed of far greater importance," she added demurely.

The old diplomatist was in too serious mood to give rein to his sense of humour just then. He allowed his daughter's naive confession to pass unheeded, and, walking to the window, tried, as men do when face to face with a knotty problem, to concentrate his thoughts by fixing his gaze on some immaterial object. The study window was at the side of the house, with a distant view of the red point at the mouth of the river, and his eyes unconsciously sought that soothing picture without causing any reflex action on the clever brain busy with affairs of more human interest. Close under the window ran the path leading from the tradesmen's entrance to the back door.

"Your vagueness as to time makes it uncet-tain," Mr. Mallory said presently, " whether Chermside was one of the two men who passed you in the first instance, going outwards from the town. By the way, was he in evening dress?"

"No," replied Reggie and Enid in unison. " He was wearing flannels."

"Then," mused Mr. Mallory aloud, " it is conclusive that he was not returning from dining at the Manorâ a point which could of course have been easily ascertained. He may have been one of those who passed you, but No, my good man, go away! We don't require any."

The sudden break-off, which drew Reggie and Enid's eyes to the window, was caused by a shabby, down-at-heels individual who was holding up a bunch of dangling bootlaces with the stereotyped smirk and inviting gesture of the street hawker.

Accepting his dismissal meekly, he went shambling off to the side entrance from the road.

"Reggie! " cried Enid.

"Madam to you."

"Did you twig who that was?"

"Can't say I did."

"He was the man who looked out of the train on the day of the picnic, and who called out about ' the face in the pool.'"

Mr. Mallory turned sharply round. He had been watching the exit of the tramp from the premises. " Are you sure of that? " he asked.

"Now that Enid has reminded me I am sure of it,"

Reggie replied. " He is dressed differently, but I remember the bloated, drinky face perfectly. And, by the way, I saw him coming out of the gates of The Hut this morning. Can it be that he was not in that train by chance, but was travelling at the instance of Nugent in order to ensure that the body of Levison should not remain there undiscovered?"

"Precisely what was in my mind," Mr. Mallory rejoined. " And he was probably hanging about this house as a spy in the interests of his employer, for I can see a connexion by which Nugent may have become aware of my active opposition. You went far to confirm my suspicions, my boy, when you told me of Nugent's journey to Weymouth the other day; what has just transpired is finally convincing that there is some villainy hatching with Chermside either as victim or catspaw."

"But you are entirely in the dark as to the purport of all this plot and counterplot? " said Reggie,

"Entirely; all I have been able to elucidate is that Nugent finds it necessary to threaten Chermside with implication in a murder which he may or may not have committed."

"Can't Reggie and I capture the bootlace man and stick red-hot needles into him till he confesses? " suggested Enid.

But her father smiled with grim tolerance. " You don't know Mr. Travers Nugent, my child," he said. " You may be very sure that' the bootlace man," as you call him, has not been admitted to the inner precincts of the mystery. Nugent, while pretending to trust his agents, never does so really. He is even capable of wiping them out of existence when they have served their purposeâ or failed in it."

"Then what is your game, sir? I should like to take a hand in it, whatever it is," said Reggie with the zest of the good sportsman he was. " To head off Nugent and give a shake up to old Lazarus Lowch too would afford me the greatest pleasure." Mr. Mallory took a turn up the room and came back. " The game," he said slowly, " is to find proof against the actual slayer of Levison before Nugent's blow, whatever it is, falls. As your leave is up to-morrow morning I am afraid there will be no time for you to help me in that."

"I hope that your researches won't lead you into danger, sir."

"Oh dear no," rejoined Mr. Mallory carelessly. " They are chiefly concerned with the movements on the night in question of a French onion vendor belonging to a lugger lying at Exmouth."

"Why not drop a hint to the sergeant of pohce? " But Mr. Mallory made a gesture of dissent. " Because I am far from sure that I am right," he said. " If the police were to push inquiries in that direction Nugent would get wind of it and make a counter-move. It isn't as if the catching of Levi-son's murderer was the chief desideratum. It is the cunningly veiled scheme in which that crime was only a detail that I have set myself to discover and foil. Given positive proof against the murderer, be he Chermside or any one else, and I would be at the pohce station with it inside five minutes. But it must be clear evidence, justifying an immediate arrest."

LOUISE AUBIN stood behind her young mistress's dressing chair, brushing the glorious tresses which her deft lingers would presently coil and coax into the latest fashionable mode. There was to be a small dinner party at the Manor House that evening. Mr. Vernon Mallory and his daughter were coming, also Leslie Chermside and Travers Nugent, as well as a few local people in whom we are not interested. It was the day following that on which Aunt Sarah had raised hopes for her protegees, which, so far as one of them was concerned, were so rudely dashed in the card-room at the club.

The maid glanced furtively at the beautiful face in the mirror opposite, and took note of the dreamy happiness in Violet Maynard's eyes. Violet had been consistently kind to her, and Louise, selfish though she was to the core, was not wholly ungrateful. She had deceived herself into the belief that she was about to do her mistress a genuine service, but it was characteristic of her that she rather enjoyed the prospect of inflicting'pain in the process.

"I should so like to consult you, mees, about an affair of my own," she began hesitatingly. There was no need for the hesitation, mademoiselle having been carefully coached for the part she was to play no later than that afternoon, when she had paid another surreptitious visit to The Hut. But a shy modesty was a weapon in her equipment for the fray.

Violet looked up quickly. The note of diffidence was unusual. " Of course, Louise, you can ask me anything," she said, wondering why the Abigail's gaze was so swiftly averted. " I should have thought, though, that you are much more capable of managing your affairs than I am."

The Frenchwoman contrived to show deprecation in the twirl she gave to the silver hair-brush. " In small things, mees, perhaps," she answered. " But this is not small, the thing in which I beg you to advise. It is an affair of the 'eart, and an affair of murderreâ the murderre of the gentleman who was killed on the marsh."

Violet with difficulty repressed a smile. The subject was a gruesome one, but, serene in her own love idyll, she had really paid very little attention to it. " You don't mean to tell me, Louise, that you killed that unfortunate man because he did not appreciate your charms?"

Mademoiselle was on her dignity at once; moreover, having marked down higher game, she could afford to be quite genuine in her repudiation of any partiality for Mr. Levi Levison.

"Mees will pardon her devoted maid for saying that it is hardly a subject for jest," came her prompt rebuke. " The shoe was what you call on the other foot. Mr. Levison, he admire me greatly, but I not think ver' moosh of 'im. All the same, he tells me things, and among others he tell me who it was he going to meet on the marsh. I blame myself for not having approach the police about it, and I desire to ask you, mees, if it is now too late."

Violet grew suddenly grave. A responsibility was being thrust upon her which she would have avoided if she could, but she felt it her duty to accept. Louise was a stranger in a strange land, the laws of which she could not be expected to understand, and who was there to advise her if not her mistress? Violet had not much doubt as to what her advice would be, for she knew that it was a serious matter to withhold information that would tend to the conviction of a criminal. The maid would have to be told to take the course she ought to have taken at firstâ to give the police the name of the man Levison was to meet.

But Violet intuitively shrank from uttering the word which might be the first step towards condemning a fellow-creature to ignominious death, however well merited, and perhaps it was to gain time that she askedâ

"How was it that you concealed this knowledge, Louise? Is the person whom you have been shielding a friend of yours?"

"On the contrary, mees, I 'ave neverre speak to 'im," came the glib reply. " I keep the secret because Mr. Travers Nugent, who I know to be honourable gentleman and well acquainted with m'sieu your father, because 'e guess I going to the police and persuade me to stop. 'E say it silly to stir up the mud for no good."

Now Violet Maynard had never yielded to the spell of Travers Nugent's social attractions. She had always been civil to him as one in whose well-informed society easy-going Montague Maynard found pleasure, but in her infrequent and superficial intercourse with the man-about-town she had been conscious of a vague mistrust. Quite naturally, therefore, she exclaimedâ

"Mr. Nugent should not have interfered. It was very wrong of him, and though I do not know much about such matters I imagine that he may have made trouble for himself as well as for you. Who was this person whom Mr. Nugent was at such pains to protect, Louise? He is fond of currying favour with the natives of this place, I know, but I should hardly have thought that his thirst for popularity would have led him to incur the risk of personal unpleasantness."

Mademoiselle Louise stole one glance at the mildly indignant face in the glass, then dropped her eyes demurely before firing the shot with which she had been primed.

"It was not about what you call native of Otter-mouth that he beg me to be silent, mees," she replied, using the hair-brush assiduously. " It was a visitor gentlemanâ very nice gentleman he seems and friendly with you, mees, and with m'sieu your father. But that I cannot 'elp. It was Mr, Chermside who arrange to meet Levison on the marsh at ten o'clock on the night when some one kill him."

Mademoiselle gave quite half a dozen strokes with the brush before she dared to look in the mirror again, and then she was impelled to do so by the quivering of the shapely shoulders. Was her mistress sobbing in silent anguish under the blow she had struck, or did the convulsion betoken restrained merriment? The glance into the glass settled it. The eyes of mistress and maid met, and Violet broke into a ripple of silvery laughter.

"Why, you foolish httle goose! " she cried, " there is no harm done after all. You had better go to the pohce with your story as soon as you like, or as soon as Mr. Nugent permits. Mr. Chermside would no more dream of murdering anybody than would Mr. Nugent himselfâ not half so much, indeed. It was nice of Mr. Nugent to want to save his friend annoyance, but he might have had more faith in him. Once more, you are a goose, Louise."

The Frenchwoman bore the rebuke in silence. She had fulfilled the instructions so carefully instilled into her artful but shallow brain, and all her efforts just now being devoted to pleasing her new cher ami, as she considered the master of The Hut, she was content to leave it at that. Nugent had not confided to her how he expected or wished Miss Maynard to behave on hearing what he had instructed Louise to tell her.

As soon as her toilet was complete Violet descended to the drawing-room, where Aunt Sarah was talking to the Mallorys, who were the only guests who had as yet arrived. In spite of having parted with Reggie Beauchamp that morning Enid was in high spirits, and looked delightfully fresh in her dinner dress of virginal white. She was merrily receiving somewhat pessimistic congratulations on her engagement from Aunt Sarah, who was laying it down that to marry a man liable to be drowned at any moment was simply flying in the face of Providence.

Nugent and Chermside arrived together, and when Montague Maynard came burst-ing in in the wake of the few remaining guests dinner was announced, and they adjourned to the dining-room. To Violet the meal was a tedious function that night. She was brimming over with mixed excitement over the implied aspersion cast by Louise on her lover, and she was longing to share the absurdity, as she considered it, with him. She had much ado to restrain herself from mentioning it at the dinner-table, but she realized that it was hardly a matter to be made fun of before the servants. Moreover, she noticed that Leslie was looking pale and preoccupied, and by no means in a mood to appreciate the humour of a jest so grimly personal. She was afraid he was going to be ill. On all accounts it would be wiser to postpone telling him till they were alone.

As it happened, it was not to Leslie that she was destined to first moot the subject of Louise's treacherous confidence. When the gentlemen joined the ladies in the drawing-room after dinner the human pack chanced to get so shuffled that Violet found herself for the moment paired off with Travers Nugent, and unable to obtain speech with her lover. It was not for her to know that Nugent had carefully arranged his entry into the drawing-room with a view to securing a tete-d-tetc with her. Eagerly awaiting Leslie's appearance, she had seated herself alone near the door, and Nugent, coming in ahead of the rest of the men, at once monopolized her.

"The Queen of the Manor is looking radiant," he said in his silky accents, assuming the air of deference which carried him far with most of his female acquaintances.

"I am not feehng very radiant, or even good-temperedâ with you," rephed Violet. Baulked of her wish to have it out with Leslie, she was seized with a desire to rend in pieces, figuratively, of course, this debonair gentleman who had busied himself to shield one who by no possible chain of circumstances could need any shielding.

"Is it permitted to inquire, fair lady, what has caused me to fall under the ban of your displeasure? " said Nugent smilingly. The smile was well managed, seeing that he was at the same time assuring himself that Leslie and Mr. Mallory, convoyed by their host, had passed on with the other men to where Aunt Sarah was holding a miniature court at the far end of the room. The smile deepened a little as he noticed that Mr. Mallory palpably overcame an impulse to join them.

"Yes," said Violet in answer to his question. " If you had not inquired I should have mentioned the matter myself. What is the meaning of this preposterous story brought to me by my maidâ that you prevented her from going to the police about Mr. Chermside's appointment with that poor man?"

The start which Nugent gave, if not natural, at any rate looked the genuine thing. He bit his lips as though annoyed and disconcerted, and an anxious expression crept into his eyes.

"So that stupid French girl has been frightening you," he said softly, "My dear Miss Maynard, I would not have had this happen for worlds."

"That is not an answer to my question," Violet persisted hotly. " Why did you pursue a course which may very likely get the girl into trouble? If you did it to save Mr. Chermside from unpleasantness your motive was all right, though I should have thought that a man of the world would have known that your action was very likely to have the opposite effect. If the police had been informed at once of this appointment on the marsh they would have laughed at the idea of a gentleman in Mr. Cherm-side's position having anything to do with the crime. But now, when they are informed of it, they will probably attach an exaggerated importance to the incident, and worry for explanations."

Travers Nugent sighed the sigh of the man who had been misunderstood. " I am glad that you give me credit for having acted from loyalty to my friend, even if you accuse me of folly," he replied.

"Why did you commit that folly? " demanded Violet, tapping her dainty shoe in imperious insistence.

The answer came as though dragged out by force and in the face of better judgment. " You leave me no option," said Nugent slowly, waving his soft white hand in a deprecatory gesture. " I took the course I didâ that of persuading Louise Aubin not to rush off to the policeâ becauseâ well, because"

He stopped abruptly, and then added with a strained little laugh, "I find this a difficult thing to say. Miss Maynard."

"I am waiting for you to say it," came Violet's inexorable rejoinder.

"Well, then, has it not occurred to you that if Chermside had wanted his appointment with Levison to be known to the police he would himself have informed them of it, whereas, though he was called as a witness at the inquest, he preserved silence about it?"

Violet Maynard was a beautiful woman, and she had never looked more beautiful than when she rose, majestic in her wrath, to champion the man she loved.

"Mr. Nugent," she suppressed her voice with an effort, " that implies doubtâ almost accusation. I am ashamed of you. How dare you think such an impossible thingâ to say nothing of putting it into words, to me of all people, who am his affianced wife!"

Nugent bowed as before an offended goddess, and a little flush came into his faceâ an unusual phenomenon in one whose emotions were so well controlled. " I somehow seem not to be able to express myself clearly to-night," he murmured plaintively. " You must forgive me if I point out that the suggestionâ the perfectly horrible suggestionâ came from you, and not from me. I was not charging Chermside with murder. The bare idea is ridiculous. I like the boy, and he brought me the best introductions from India, though personally he has not been communicative about his private affairs. I know this much, howeverâ that he had business with Levison, as he admitted at the inquest, which he does not want to be noised abroad and mouthed over by the wiseacres of Ottermouth. I surmise that he was to meet Levison on the marsh that night to discuss that business, and I therefore deemed it advisable in his interest to suppress all publicity about the intended meeting."

"You are inferring that the business, as you call it, was discreditable? " said Violet, mystified, and only half mollified.

"Not in the very least," rejoined Nugent glibly. " I do not know what the transaction was, but it is impossible to associate anything discreditable with Chermside. If I might make a suggestion it would be that you should yourself ask Chermside for enlightenment."

"Thank you, I shall certainly inform him of what has happened," said Violet coldly. " But it must rest with him whether he offers an explanation of his relations with Levison. I am content to trust the man who is to be my husband. In the meanwhile, Mr. Nugent, it is but fair that you should know that I have advised my maid to lose no further time in communicating with the police. It will be the shortest and most satisfactory way of getting this absurdity wiped out once for all."

Nugent bowed and stood looking after the graceful figure of the girl as she sailed away from him across the room. His long moustache hid the wicked curl at the corner of his mouth. " Ah, my lady," he murmured under his breath, " you will find that it is one thing to tender advice and quite another to get it acted on. The fair and flighty Louise is receiving her orders from your humble servant at present, and they will certainly not include an injunction to call at the police-station. But that bogey has been effectually set up, I think."

Leslie Chermside had been covertly watching from afar Violet's animated interview with Nugent, and seeing her coming towards him he hastened to meet her. That evening he grudged every moment not spent in her society, for on the morrow he would assuredly see her for the last time. Unless some miracle intervened there would be nothing for it, if he was to avoid arrest for murder and its consequent exposure, but to assent to Nugent's plan for flight on the Cobra. He had postponed giving his final decision, hoping against hope that something might turn up to save him, and also because at the back of his mind there still lurked the suspicion that Nugent's account of his danger might have been trumped up for some cunning purpose. But now he was to receive confirmation of the story of Louise Aubin's suspicions from a source there was no gainsaying.

"Take me into the orangery; I want to speak to you," said Violet, laying her hand on his sleeve.

The orangery at Ottermouth Manor was a huge glass structure in which oranges may have been gro Ti in Georgian days after the prevailing fashion, but which in modem times sheltered a wealth of tropical shrubs. In the great aisles of luxuriant foliage it was possible to lose oneself, as Violet and Leslie, after passing through one of the long windows, proceeded to do now. They halted at last under the spreading fronds of a giant palm, from a branch of which depended one of the electric lamps which the millionaire had installed in the old mansion.

"Leslie," said the girl, looking up into her lover's face, "I have done a strange thing to-night, as proof of my trust in you. That French maid of mine tells me that you had a rendezvous with the man who was murdered the other day, and that it was at or near to the spot where the body was found. I have been blaming her for withholding her knowledge from the authorities, and have advised her to rectify the omission without delay. You mustn't be angry with me if I have been unduly interfering, but I knew that you could have nothing to fear really in the matter of Levison's death, and that it would be better to scotch this ridiculous suspicion before it grows unmanageable."

Chermside laughed, keeping the bitterness out of the sound of it as best he could. To call it the irony of fate was beside the mark. It was really almost supernatural, the way he was being tossed hither and thither by the consequences of the crime he had abjured. Here was the woman who was all in all to him calmly telling him that she had taken a step which would snatch the last straw from his drowning hands. All hope was gone. He must run for it now, if the traces of his disgraceful lapse were to be covered.

"It is quite true," he said. " I had an appointment to meet Levison. But," and he laughed again as he made the addition, "I really didn't murder him, Violet."

The taper fingers, glittering with gems, closed on his arm. " Now don't be silly," came the quick answer from sweetly protesting lips. " Every one seems to be trying to be silly over this horrible affair â Louise, Mr Nugent, and now you yourself. I have just been calling Mr. Nugent over the coals for his preposterous counsel to that misguided French fool, and I told him what I now tell youâ that my trust in your incapacity for such a deed is invincible. I bum with indignation that even a fool like Louise should have thought the contrary. That is why I chanced the risk of offending you, dear, by forcing the issue."

"You have indeed forced the issue, but there is nothing in all the wide world that you could do to offend me," said Leslie, and his half-strangled sob carried conviction.

But Violet Maynard wanted more than conviction on a point on which she was already convinced. She hungered for the confidence which she was too proud to demand as her right. Yet her lover showed no sign of according it. He just stood there staring at her, and looking half dazed in the electric glow, but he had evidently no intention of explaining why he was to have met Levison in the marsh, and why he had concealed the fact.

"Is that all you have to say to me? " asked Violet quietly.

And then, when her question evoked no reply, she turned and threaded her way back amid the tangle of exotic luxuriance to the drawing-room, leaving Leslie to follow like a man in a dream.

ON the following morning Enid Mallory, clad in a serviceable jersey and a short skirt, and carrying her golf clubs, was walking up and down the lawn at her father's house, perusing a letter received from Reggie by the early delivery. She had already read it twice, once before and once after breakfast, but like all maidens in similar cases she wanted to make sure that she had missed none of its honey, implied or expressed.

She looked up as her father came out and joined her. " I have heard from my young man," she said, proffering the letter. " We don't indulge in sentiment or secrets. Read it and see how the poor boy is going to be worked to death in serving an ungrateful country."

But Mr. Mallory waved the letter aside with one of his fugitive smiles. " I wiu take your word for it, child," he said. " Those secrets used to be considered sacred in my courting days, but I am growing old-fashioned, I suppose. Reggie got back to his ship all right yesterday, then?"

"Yes, he is where he loves best to be I really believeâ on board his ' thirty-knot sardine-box," as he calls it," Enid replied. " He seems very pleased with himself and with the prospect of having plenty to do. He has got to take the destroyer out for torpedo practice every day for a week, leaving port at four in the morning."

"Ah well! " sighed Mr. Mallory, gently, " there is nothing like the strenuous life for the young. I often wish I was back in harness again instead of rusting here."

Enid stole an affectionately impudent glance at her father's keen face. " Why, for the past week you have been simply revelling in the atmosphere of intrigue, which is the breath of life to you, dad," she said with a little laugh. " I am due at the links to play golf with Mona Dartring, but I had to wait and ask you if there are any new developments. I mean about the French onion-seller in whom you were interested?"

Mr. Mallory shook his head. " I seem to have run up against a dead wall in that direction," he replied. " I am utterly unable to trace a connexion between him and Nugent, yet I am morally certain that they are both concerned in the murder of Levi-son in greater or lesser degree. Last night at the Manor House the air was charged with mystery which I could not pierce. At dinner Chermside was silent and preoccupied, while Miss Maynard was almost hysterically vivacious. Afterwards, in the drawing-room, she had a long confabulation with Nugent of the latter's seeking; then she withdrew into the orangery with Chermside for an interview from which they both returned as glum as if they had been mour- ners at their own funerals. There is some devihsh trickery going on, with Nugent pulung the strings, but I can do nothing but wait and watch."

"Watch Mr. Nugent? " suggested Enid with more than her usual gravity.

"Him and others. If one could spend a few hours inside The Hut in a state of invisibility much would be made clear. For instance, an unseen listener at a conference between either that coquettish maid of Miss Maynard's, or the onion-seller, or even Chermside himself, and Nugent would go far towards the solution I am striving for."

"What has Louise, the maid, got to do with it, father?"

"Possibly nothing. On the other hand, I think it extremely probable that she is the pivot of the whole situationâ so far as the murder of Levison goes. It is established that the onion-seller, whom the worthy Miss Dymmock chastised out of the park, was jealous of some one in respect of the maid; but unfortunately unless one has a chance of cross-examining the maid herself there is no way of proving whether Levison was the unknown admirer who had excited her compatriot's jealousy."

"I'll take that in hand," came Enid's eager answer. " I often see Louise when I am with Violet Maynard at the Manor. I'll pump the hussey as limp as a punctured tyre the next time I'm over there, and it's sure to be in a day or two."

Mr. Mallory patted his daughter's shoulder in mock encouragement. " Go ahead, Miss Cocksure," he smiled at her. " But, if I am not mistaken, you will find that Mademoiselle Louise carries too many guns for an honest English craft Uke my little Enid. There! that's a nautical simile suitable for a sailor's bride. Now nm away to your golf and leave an old fogey to worry the thing out as best he can. I am past the age for personal adventures in disguise, or I should be sorely tempted to explore The Hut in some other character than my own."

Enid pouted a little at the disparagement of her detective powers, and then, after a dutiful peck at the clean-shaven paternal cheek, shouldered her clubs and made for the garden gate. Half-way across the lawn she wheeled round and shouted backâ

"Don't wait lunch for me. Mona and I have arranged to have a snack on the links and go out for another round in the afternoon."

Mr. Mallory nodded and turned to re-enter the house. As a resident at a seaside resort where most people were engaged in amusing themselves, he had grown accustomed to the ordinary meals being movable feasts, sometimes omitted altogether so far as Enid was concerned. During the summer months she would frequently disappear after breakfast, and not be seen again till she arrived late but apologetic at the dinner table. Even that important function was occasionally allowed to go by the board when the popular little lady was intercepted on her way home and dragged into some neighbour's house to spend the evening.

To-day, keen sportswoman though she was, Enid's thoughts were chained quite as much by her father's self-imposed anxieties as by the game she loved. Passing by the entrance gates of The Hut, she looked in vain up the drive for any signs of the persons enumerated by her father as probably connected with the case, and it was only when she had reached the links on the breezy moor and had been duly chid by her waiting friend for unpunctuality that she shook off her absorption and gave herself up to the game. Conscious of her slackness, she forced herself to play rather better than usual, but at the close of the afternoon round she allowed her obsession to resume its sway.

Concocting some frivolous pretext, she avoided walking down the road to the town with other homeward-bound golfers, and contrived to shp away unseen along a moorland path which led to the town by another and longer route at the edge of the cliff. It had in Enid's eyes the merit of passing quite close to the rear of The Hut, whereas the road was separated from the house by the whole extent of a fairly long carriage drive. Somehow the secluded abode of Mr. Travers Nugent had for her that day the attraction of a magnet. She simply could not keep away from it.

There was no definite plan in her head, only an intense longing that something might happen which would enable her to fill the gap in her father's investigations. Before it struck out on to the cliff the path led her through a maze of gorse bushes very near the back gate out of which Nugent had shown Pierre Legros on the night of his first interview with him. When Enid came opposite this gate, which was of oak set in an impenetrable hedge of blackthorn, she was seized with an irresistible impulse to see if the gate was fastened. She fought against it for as long as it took her to walk resolutely ten paces by, and then there recurred to her her father's wordsâ

"I am past the age for adventures, or I should be sorely tempted to explore The Hut in some other character than m own."

The temptation was too strong for her. Retracing her steps, she picked her way across the few intervening yards of heather and tried the gate. To her surprise it was neither locked nor bolted, but opened inwards to the extent of the couple of inches for which she only dared apply pressure at first. Growing bolder, she pushed the gate further open and peered in. The house was partly visible fifty yards away through a screen of copper beeches, but an intense silence brooded over it, nor in the foreground of garden was there any sign of human life.

"Dad was pleased to be sarcastic about my ability to find out things," she murmured to herself. " All the same I think I'll do a little scout on my own account. It would be good fun to take the old dear a tit-bit of information that he hadn't been able to ferret out himself."

So at first tentatively, and then more surely, the gate was pushed wider still, and the trim figure in the short skirt stood with bated breath in the quiet garden. The coy retreat of Mr. Travers Nugent was beautifully kept. Tall trees and winding shrubberies afforded a grateful shade, and the well-shaven turf of the lawn was dotted with beds ablaze with brilliant summer flowers. In the bright yellow of the gravel walks never a weed showed. But it was past six, and the gardener who had wrought all this perfection was not there to make trouble for Enid on the threshold of her adventure.

Still without any definite plan except to " find out things," Miss Enid softly shut the gate and advanced a few steps towards the house, taking care to tread on the grass and not on the crunchy gravel. After all was said and done she could trump up an excuse if she was discovered. Mr. Nugent had always treated her with semi-paternal playfulness, and he was, ostensibly at any rate, on amicable terms with her father.

On the left the garden was bounded by a high brick wall covered with ripening peaches; on the right lay a thick belt of shrubbery, extending up to the house. Enid chose the latter as affording the best shelter from any one standing at the windows, and, darting into the friendly cover, she commenced her stealthy approach. With any luck, she told herself, Mr. Nugent might be in his library interviewing one or other of the people whom her father deemed his accomplices, and she might pick up some useful crumbs of information to take home.

She had traversed half the length of the shrubbery in safety when her heart was set thumping by a sound behind her. It was the chck of the latch of the gate through which she had so recentl entered the garden. Glancing over her shoulder she caught, through the foliage, a glimpse of a man who to her dismay was making straight for the shrubbery, taking a diagonal course across the lawn which would bring him to the very spot she had reached. Acting, as was her habit, on impulse, she did a thing the folly of which she only recognized when it was too late to remedy it. Just ahead of her, almost hidden in a tangle of thicket, was a small, one-storied structure built of stoneâ a sort of grotto or summer-house. Its walls were covered with green mould, never a ray of sun reaching them, and it looked damp, disused and forgotten. The doorway stood open, and Enid darted through, finding herself almost in darkness, for the place was only furnished with a small circular window, nearly obscured by ivy and high up in the wall.

It would serve well enough as a refuge if the man had not seen the fluttering of her white skirt amid the leafy screen. He would pass on his way to the house and all would be well. But if he had seen her, and was of an inquisitive turn of mind, her retreat would be cut off, for there were no signs of an exit at the rear. It was sure to be some one belonging to the house, or at any rate a privileged person, for the gate was a private one, intended only for the use of the master of The Hut. Would the man pass by, or would he come in and tax her with unwarrantable trespass? Her hasty glance had not told her whether he had a right to do so, as it had not enabled her to recognize him.

But a moment later she did, when the doorway darkened and on the threshold there stood the individual whom she had dubbed " The Bootlace Man "â the seeming pedlar who had sneaked in and out of the side entrance at her father's house two days before, and who in other garb had called out of the train to draw the attention of Montague May-nard's picnic party to " the face in the pool."

He blinked in his efforts to pierce the gloom of the dim interior, and then with a muttered oath produced a box of wax matches and struck a Hght. As the tiny flame flared up and showed him the pale but defiant face of the girl, he gave a little cackling laugh and puffed out his bloated cheeks in evil triumph.

"Golly, but this is a bit of all right! "his alcoholic exclamation smote Enid's ears and nose. " The governor will chalk this up to my score like the generous patron he is. Now you stay there, Missy, and meditate on the sin of curiosity tillâ well, till some one comes and lets you out."

With which he stepped back and slammed the door in the girl's face. A moment later the grating of the key in the lock told her that she was a prisoner.

ABOUT the time when the door of the stone grotto in the grounds of The Hut swung to on Enid Mallory, Mr, Travers Nugent's motor car was rushing up the avenue at the Manor House two miles away. At the main entrance of the mansion Nugent got down and rang the bell, and while waiting turned and spoke to his chauffeur,

"I shall want you to be busy this evening, Dixon," he said, "When we get home see that your tanks are full, and have the car ready for any emergency. I may want you at any moment."

The smart young fellow touched his cap, and the butler flinging open the door put an end to further possible instructions. Nugent, who was aware that the great manufacturer had gone to London that morning to attend a board meeting, blandly inquired if Mr. Maynard was in. On receiving the expected reply that the master would not be back till next day, he affected to consider deeply, caressing his long moustache,

"That is annoying," he said at last. " I wished to see him very particularly. Are the ladies at home?"

"Miss Dymmock is in the drawing-room, sir; but Miss Maynard is either in the park or in the gardensâ probably in the rosery, which is her favourite place," said the butler.

"Ah! " murmured Nugent, and again he seemed to be plunged into perplexity by Mr. Maynard's absence. " I had better see Miss Dymmock, perhaps. No, on second thoughts I won't trouble her, I will leave a message with Miss Maynard, if you will be good enough to show me where I shall be likely to find her."

So did this past-master in the art of chicane take elaborate pains to have it understood at the Manor that Violet was the last person whom he had originally set out to see. The butler called a footman to pilot the visitor to the embowered pleasaunce where four days earlier Leslie Chermside's declaration of love had been wrung from his headstrong tongue. With an unread book at her side, Violet was sitting on the same seat where her brief wooing had begun and ended. Nugent's eyes gleamed with momentary satisfaction as he noted the sadness in the beautiful face, the hstless droop in the attitude of the graceful figure. But by the time he reached her and bent over the proffered hand his manner was that of the courtly gentleman, tinged with a trace of grave concern which yielded to a semblance of uncontrolled agitation as soon as the footman had retired. His pose and facial expression was that of the bearer of ill tidings to the hfe. Violet, strung to a pitch of nervous tension by her lover's strange demeanour in the orangery the preceding night, read in Nugent's countenance the exact emotion he intended to show.

"This is not a duty call, Mr. Nugent? " she said, as she motioned him to a seat at her side. Nugent preferred to stand, looking down at her. He wanted to mark the effect of every word he had to say.

"No," he rephed, deftly throwing off his " society " manner, and, with the consummate skill of the genuine artist, speaking almost harshly. " I wish it was. Miss Maynard. I am here on very serious businessâ so serious that if I did not know you were a brave woman I should not dare to approach you about it. As it is I am sorely tempted to run away and leave matters as they are."

"I beg you will not do that." said Violet gravely. " It would be more cruel than if you had not come to me at all. I presume that it is about the suspicion that has been cast on Mr. Chermside?"

Nugent smiled inwardly as he noticed the change in her tone since last night. No longer did she heap contempt upon the inference as to Chermside's meeting with Levison. She was serious, and almost pathetically meek. Like Mr. Mallory he had watched the lovers on their return from the orangery to the drawing-room, and he had at the time gloated over the coolness that had evidently arisen between them. That ineffable idiot Chermside had, he congratulated himself, said or done something to shake her confidenceâ just as he, Nugent, had expected and intended.

But aloud he said, "Yes, it is about Chermside. Greatly against my will, I have consented to be his ambassadorâ to bring you a message from him, Miss Maynard. It will be kindest to break the worst to you without beating about the bush. Chermside is leaving England to-night. He is going to sail for South America in the yacht which has been kept in readiness for him at Weymouth."

' Sailing to-night? Without coming to say good-byeâ without a word of explanation? " And the sweet eyes brimmed with unshed tears at the conduct of the man who had so recently held her in his arms at that very spot.

"It is so hard to wound you," Nugent protested, and the faultlessly simulated note of self-pity with which he tinged his speech carried conviction. " He dared not come to you. Miss Maynard. Somehow the police have got wind of the appointment he had with the dead man, and he is in danger of arrest. He is in hiding, and it is touch and go whether he wiu get on board safely after dark. I am a selfish man, and I would give a good deal if Leslie Cherm-side's letters of introduction had been to any one but myself. All this has placed me in a most unpleasant position."

"But I do not understand," Violet protested. " Mr. Chermside has not committed this murder. Why does he not laugh at the charge, and stay and meet it? He must be able to prove his innocence."

Travers Nugent's shrug was eloquentâ so eloquent that Violet fired up instantly, rising and confronting him. " You cannot mean that you deem him guilty?" she demanded, with ominous restraint.

"My dear lady, noâ a thousand times no," came the quick repudiation. " But you must pardon my expressing the candid opinion that he is a fool, a chivalrous, misguided fool, perhaps, who is risking his future from some silly motive that would be brushed aside in a second if he would only enlighten his friends about it. I have pleaded with him to adopt that course but it was of no avail. Nothing would satisfy him but to fly the country, he avowed, till the murder of Levison had been cleared upâ I presume by the detection of the real criminal."

"And in the meanwhile he is going to wander about the world in exile, resting under a stigma which he does not deserve, till the end of his days?"

"I do not think he looks at it quite in that light," said Nugent, choosing his words carefully. "He is trusting that this cloud will blow over. Candidly, in my judgment, he is afraid that if he is brought to trial some episode in his life will come outâ as likely as not some harmless piece of youthful follyâ which he wishes to conceal."

Violet made a hopeless gesture, avoiding the falsely sympathetic eyes of this man, whom she intuitively disliked, but whose behaviour, she was bound to admit, was perfectly correct. Her unseeing gaze made a dumb appeal for comfort to the rich blooms of the rose-garden, to the blue sky overhead, to the aged yew hedge that girt the place where she had plighted her troth, but there seemed to be no comfort, no help anywhere. Nugent's statement talhed with the impression she had formed the previous night in the orangery exactly. Leslie had some reason, of which he was ashamed, for dreading the fierce light of a legal inquiry being thrown on his relations with the murdered Jew. It was to his credit, anyhow, and she hugged the remembrance because she loved him, that he had all along harped on some secret in his past career.

"Tell me," she said wearily, " what his message was. That can hardly have been all of itâ that he was running away?"

"No," replied Nugent, with the air of bracing himself for a distasteful task, " there was something more. And before I pass it on to you, let me assure you, Miss Maynard, that I tender no advice as to how you should treat Chermside's proposition. I merely impart it to you as his mouthpiece, and leave you to be guided by your own inclination and good sense. But this I beg of you to believeâ that if you decide to consent to his request, my willing services are at your disposal. He wants to bid you farewell, and he has commissioned me to arrange a meeting for to-night, before he sails."

In an ecstasy of eagerness Violet dropped some of her stately dignity and clasped her hands. " Meet him? " she cried. " Of course I will, but it will not be to say good-bye. If I have any influence over him, and I know that I have, it will be used to induce him to abandon tliis disgraceful flight and to face the accusation out. You have, indeed, been a good friend, Mr. Nugent, in coming to me. When and where can I see Mr. Chermside?"

"Not till quite late to-night," was the reply. " It will not be safe for the steamer to approach the coast and send a boat ashore till it is thoroughly dark. Should you have any difficulty in leaving the house here, say, at eleven o'clock?"

"Not in the least; I am my own mistress. I often go for a stroll in the park before going to bed when it is fine."

"Then if you will prolong your stroll to-night as far as the Ottermouth road, I will be waiting with my car about a hundred yards from the lodge," came Nugent's glib instructions. " I can easily run you to the place where the ship's boat is to come to pick up Chermside inside ten minutes. You may rely on me absolutely. I shall not fail you at the hour mentioned. And now, as there is much to arrange, I will leave you."

"I shall not keep you waiting," said Violet, shaking his extended hand warmly. " Punctually at eleven on the Ottermouth road."

But if she could have seen her kind helper's face as he turned his back on her to quit the rose-garden, she would have felt misgivings as to the honesty of his aid. Every line of it betokened an end gained by questionable means.

"Directly we're outside the lodge gates, drive to The Hut at top speed," he bade the chauffeur as soon as he reached the motor car. Glancing at his watch, he saw that it was nearly seven o'clock.

"In a little over four hours I shall have earned Bhagwan Singh's reward," he murmured to himself, as they slid down the avenue.

CAPTAIN BRANT, of the turbine steam yacht Cobra, walked the spotless deck of his vessel; and he walked slowly, for he was reading a letter which the postman had just brought on board. While he read his hideous features were twisted into the ape-like contortion that did duty with him for a grin. When he had mastered the contents of the missive, he thrust it into the pocket of his brass-buttoned reefer, and shouted for " Mr. Cheese-man."

An answering bawl was heard somewhere forward, and there came running aft the bullet-headed mate who a few days before had at first refused Travers Nugent admission to the ship.

"Know anything about ladies' underclothes? " asked the wicked-looking skipper, with a horrible leer.

"Can't say I do, sir; but if it's in the way of duty I can jolly soon find out," was the brisk reply.

"Yes, it's in the way of duty; and, by the same token, the need for the duds is a sign that we are soon to clear out of this beastly port," said the captain, scratcliing his cln'n. " I've heard from the bossâ the chap that was here the other dayâ and it seems that when we start we're to pick up a lady passenger, who will be in too great a hurry to bring her trunks aboard. So we're to buy some things for her, here in Weymouth.

I'll give you a ten-pound note, and you can go ashore straight away and buy what's necessary for a three weeks' voyage."

"Aye, aye, sir," replied the mate. " What about the size?"

' 'I forgot that," cackled Brant, and he referred to the letter. " My eyes! but she must be a strapping fine girlâ five feet ten high, and well proportioned as to other dimensions. That means that she ain't too broad in the beam, but just broad enough, I reckon. And there's another thing, Bully, my boy."

"Sir to you."

"It was thought that the lady's own maid would go the voyage with her, but it seems there's a doubt about it. Orders are to engage a woman to act as stewardess and general attendant to the passenger, it being owner's wish to show her every consideration in reason. While you're ashore after the nighties and things, you're to look out a female to suit the situation. Age and character immaterial. Any old geezer with a bad record will do, so long as she's got a good muscle on her."

"Right-o! " responded the truculent-looking mate. " Seems like a kidnapping job, but that's no business o' mine."

"And you wouldn't be chief officer on this ship for long if you were fool enough to make it so," Brant piped in his squeaky treble. " Now get ashore with you, and be back inside two hours with the drapery and the woman. I can see by the letter I've had that we may get saihng orders any minute."

Cheeseman made a pretence of touching his cap, and vanished shoreward over the gangway. The Cobra was still tied up to the quay at Weymouth, her highly-paid crew of scoundrels chafing against the delay which deferred their promised reward, but by this time thoroughly cowed by the vessel's weird commander. There was not a man on her who dared leave the ship without permission or definite orders. The grog-shops in full view of" the sleeping snake," as they had dubbed the steamer, had no longer temptation for men who knew that if they yielded to it, retribution would be swift and sure. It was wiser, they argued amongst themselves, to observe discipline and reap a harvest of shekels when the Cobra's mission, whatever it might be, had been fulfilled. It was also the easier to keep them on board, since most of them had been selected because, for one reason or another, they were wanted by the police.

Having despatched his subordinate on his curious mission. Captain Brant made a tour of his ship, inspecting every portion of her with as close an attention to detail as if she had been a man-of-war. The luxurious and beautifully-upholstered saloon on the upper deck received a large share of his critical scrutiny; while, in strange contrast, his next visit was to a cabin on the lower deck, down in the bowels of the vessel, which was hardly furnished at all, and was certainly not luxurious. A bare bench, with some sacking on it, suggested that it was meant for a bed, and that was about all. Screwed into the bulk-head over the bench was a massive iron ring, and there lay on the floor a longish chain and a complete set of leg-irons fitted with cruel anklets. The only means of light was a small porthole protected by bars. The place seemed to have been prepared as a lazarettoâ a kind of maritime prison.

Brant smiled grimly at the forbiddmg-looking chamber, then went back to the upper deck to await Cheeseman's return. Punctually at the stipulated time the bullet-headed mate appeared at the gangway.

"Well, where are the things? Where is the stewardness? " the captain scowled at him, perceiving that he was empty-handed and unaccompanied.

"The clothes will be delivered within half an hour; they had to make some alterations," Cheese-man hastened to assure him. "As to engaging a stewardess it's a dead failure. I saw one or two, but they won't join without fuller particulars of where we're bound for and how long we're to be away. I couldn't tell 'em, could I, seeing as I don't know myself."

The captain fired off half-a-dozen foul-mouthed expletives, and only checked them when a telegraph boy skipped across the gang-plank and handed him an orange-coloured envelope. Tearing it open, he glanced at the contents and bade the youth begone. The form contained the single word " Advance." Brant tore it into little pieces, and threw them overboard.

"Sailing orders," he said laconically. " Make things hum, Cheeseman. We must be off as soon as we get a full head of steam on her."

In ten seconds the vessel was in a state of orderly confusion. The crew appeared as by magic from the forecastle and went to their stations; the engine-room staff mustered round the shining monsters that were their especial care; the lazy fumes of blue vapour hovering over the funnel from the banked fires changed to great coils of black smoke as the stokers got to work on the furnaces. Brant took his place on the bridge, and watched his gang of ruffians with sinister satisfaction. The period of suspense was over, and they would give him no more trouble now that the lust of gold was on them, and they were in a fair way to verify Nugent's promises of a princely wage.

It was not long before the mate ran up the bridge stairs and reported a full head of steam and all ready to cast off. As he did so a cab rattled over the cobblestones of the quay road, and drew up opposite the Cobra.

"And here's the lady passenger's outfit, just in time not to be left behind," he added, catching sight of the cab as a young woman jumped nimbly out of the vehicle, and, after paying the driver, came towards the ship. Her progress was somewhat impeded by the weight of two large cardboard boxes which she was carrying.

Captain Brant cocked his bloodshot eye at the draper's assistant who had been entrusted with the delivery of the urgent order, and an inspiration came to him. The girl was not prepossessing, hav- ing strongly-marked, determined features; but she had a powerful, almost masculine frame, for all its size, not devoid of a certain panther-hke grace. Brant uttered one of his nasty cackles, and turned to Cheeseman.

"We'll kill two birds with one stone. Bully," he said. " There's the fair passenger's blooming trousseau, and there, by gosh, is the blooming stewardess. Take the girl down into the saloon, and keep your jaw-tackle busy with her while I get a move on the ship. Say you must check the goods, or any flam of the sort. She'll do as well as another, soon as she knows there's dollars in it. If you're clever we'll be out to sea before she tumbles to it that she's left her native shores."

The mate grinned comprehension, and running down to the deck met the girl at the gangway. The moment they had disappeared into the saloon Brant gave orders to cast off, and as soon as the ropes that had moored the vessel to the quay had been hauled on board he rang the engine-room bell. The Cobra's mighty screw began to churn the still waters of the harbour, and slowly she sidled out into the fairway on the first stage of a voyage that was to lead herâ whither? Twenty minutes later she had passed the green slopes of the Nothe and was heading at half-speed towards the open sea under the frowning heights of Portland.

At the end of that time Brant, from his perch on the bridge, saw the saloon door open and the young lady from the draper's shop come out on deck, followed by Bully Cheeseman. For an instant the girl stared round in evident bewilderment, then turned upon the man who had beguiled her into false security while the ship was being got under weigh.

"What is the meaning of this? " she demanded in a ringing voice that reached the bridgeâ the voice of a woman too angry to use many words.

"Skipper's orders," replied Cheeseman curtly. He had exhausted his limited stock of spurious politeness in distracting her attention, and now that the end was gained was not inclined to exert himself further.

Before he could guard himself his cheeks were tingling under two resounding smacks, his cap was knocked into the scruppers and his lank hair was in the clutch of lithe fingers. But the man who had earned the nickname of " Bully " was no respecter of sex, and, recovering himself, he seized the girl by the throat and shook her viciously. In his rage he might have gone to any lengths if Captain Brant had not run down the bridge stairs and flung him aside.

"Get to your duty," commanded the little atomy in his quavering treble. " You ought to be ashamed of yourself for handling a lady so. A little more velvet glove, and not quite so much iron hand tiu it's wanted, on this ship, if you please, my son."

Catching the wicked wink at the tail of his chief's eye, the mate sheered off in seeming self-abasement, and left the involuntary " stewardess " face to face with Brant. Somehow the courage which had stood her in good stead with the sturdy " Bully " failed her when confronted by this five-foot skeleton who looked as if he had been buried and dug up again. Her firm mouth quivered a little, and there was a suspicion of moisture in the sullen, wrathful eyes.

"Now that you've had your lark perhaps you'll turn your beastly ship round again and put me ashore," she strove to speak bravely. " I shau be fined as it is, for not being back on time."

Brant wheezed and cackled. " You've done with fines, my dear," he said, running an approving glance over the imposing female figure in the shabby black dress. "I'm going to be a father to you and make your fortune. Fact is there's a lady passenger coming aboard presently who'll want different company from us rough sailor-men, and I was bound to find it for her. The moment you stepped out of that cab I spotted you for the job, and there's not a bit of use in making a fuss. It'll be a gold mine for you before you've done with it. You'll never need to stand behind a counter again and be cheeked by rude old women â no, not in your natural."

The tall draper's assistant measured the captain with a calculating eye, and saw that in him that was not to be reckoned in inches. She was already mastering her indignation at the outrage. " You don't mean to put me ashore? " she said firmly.

"I'm d d if I do," was Brant's energetic rejoinder.

She appeared to reflect. " If there's really money in it I don't so much mind," she said at length. " But if you want a quiet time you'll have to meet me on one thing.

You must run into Plymouth on your way down Channel and give me a chance to let my young man know where I am. He's in the Navyâ a petty officer on the destroyer Snipe."

Captain Brant rubbed his chin as if weighing the feasibihty of the proposition. " Well," he said, " it won't be at ah convenient, but I'll stretch a point to oblige you. You don't want to see the gentleman?"

"No, so long as I can send word to him, or get a letter posted, it will be all right."

"Then I'll do that much for the sake of a quiet life."

"You'll have to, or there'll be trouble," replied the matter-of-fact young amazon, little guessing that the villainous skipper had not the slightest intention of fulfilling his promise. A naval port, bristling with warships, was the very last place the Cobra would be hkely to visit after her contemplated doings at Ottermouth that night.

However, having for the time pacified his stewardess, he became civil enough and allotted her a comfortable cabin near the saloon and next to a large, luxuriously furnished state-room which he pointed out as destined for the lady passenger whom they were to call for on their way down the coast.

"By the way," he wheezed with one of his monkey-Hke grins as he prepared to return to the bridge, "I haven't had the honour of an introduction. It might save awkwardness if you'd kindly put a name to yourself, miss."

"Jimpson," was the reply, "Miss Nettle Jimp-son, and you'll find I'm a stinging-nettle, if you don't treat me fair."

Brant bowed with a mock solemnity, the hojlow- ness of which he scarcely troubled to conceal. " Simon Brant has tamed vixens worse than you, my lass," he muttered behind his yellow teeth as he swung himself back to his perch.

And all that lovely summer afternoon the Cobra's powerful turbine engines drove the graceful vessel through the calm waters of the sunht sea nearer to its prey. At sundo Ti speed was reduced in order to conform with the instructions not to arrive off Otter-mouth till after dark. But when the last rose tint had faded from the western sky Brant gave orders to steam slowly round the point at the river's mouth and heave to about three miles from the shore.

"Now the fun begins," he said to Cheeseman, who was with him on the bridge. " Keep your eyes skinned for a blue light followed by a green due north of us. When we see it you'll take the electric launch and drive her to the point where the light is shown. There you'll find a passenger waiting for you. Make the launch travel like hell, for you'll have another trip later. Rat Mullins and Snobby Wilson will go with you. They're about the toughest of the crowd, but I don't figure on trouble for you. The chap that's bossing things ashore will have seen to that."

So " the sleeping snake " lay on the gently heaving swell amid the gloom of the moonless night, and waited.

LESLIE CHERMSIDE stood at the window of the Ubrary at The Hut eating his heart out in black despair. Travers Nugent had finally convinced him that the police held a warrant for his arrest and that his only road to safetyâ not, perhaps, though that was doubtful, from conviction of the murder of Levison, but from exposure of his connivance at Violet Maynard's abductionâ lay in flight. He had consented to go on board the Cohra after dark, and escape to South America or anywhere else. Personally he did not care where he went. Wherever it was it would be out of the life of her who had grown to be to him the very sun of his existence.

Furthermore, Nugent had prevailed on him to come over to The Hut that morning and lie low there till it should be time to start. He had been hoping against hope that he would be able to have one last interview with Violet, but Nugent had been so strongly against it that he had yielded.

"What's the use, my dear fellow? " his plausible mentor had said. " You couldn't take a proper farewell of her if you saw her. If you are to succeed in sparing her the horror of learning of your original offence, neither Miss Maynard nor any one else must know that you are on the wing. That Uttle devil, Louise Aubin, would be sure to get wind of it and inform the police. As it is, I am on tenterhooks lest she should discover what is up. Write Miss Maynard a letter if you like, or, better still, I will explain to her verbally to-morrowâ after you have got clear off."

"What should you tell her? " Leslie asked dully.

"1 should do my best to whitewash your memory by throwing ridicule on the allegation that causes your flight," was the prompt answer. " In fact, I should go somewhere near the truth, and assert that it is not the murder charge that you are running away from, but from the revelation of some escapade which it would incidentally bring out. If you like, I will tell her that you will write when you have reached your destination."

Leslie had jumped at the proposition, as it seemed to make his desertion less abrupt and heartless. Also it deferred for a little while the final severance, though he had no hope but that Violet would despise him utterly, hate the very sound of his name, for what she would deem his cowardice, even if she did not believe him guilty of the graver crime of murder.

"Thank you, I shall be obliged if you will take that course," he had said, though he hated to be placed under an obligation to the man whose cunning greed had brought him to this pass.

"Not at all," Nugent had answered glibly, as if divining his thoughts. " I regard it as a kind of atonement to smooth matters as best I can, for I have come to see the heinoiisness of our joint offence, Chermside. I have been filled with remorse for some time that I did not repent of it as soon as you did, and I can sympathize the more readily with you, who have, I think, a keener pang than that of remorse to bear."

The little touch of right feeling from such an unexpected quarter had broken down Leslie's last guard, and he had placed himself unreservedly in Nugent's hands. Quite early in the day he had left his lodgings, and had sought temporary refuge at The Hut, entering the grounds with due precautions by the secluded garden door from the moor, there to remain till nightfall, when his host would see to it that he was smuggled on board the Cobra. Nugent had stayed in and about the house till late in the afternoon, when he had started out in his motor car, informing Chermside, however, that he would not be long away, and enjoining upon him the advisability of not on any account leaving the library.

In the meanwhile Sinnett, the noiseless butler, who alone of the indoor servants was aware of his presence in the house, was to be depended on to preserve the secret; while outside watch and ward would be kept by a trustworthy man who had come down from London to help in the emergencyâ an old hanger-on, as Nugent described him, by the name of Bill Tuke. Several times during the day Leslie had noticed from the window this individual prowling about the grounds and coming in and out of the door on to the moor. It w as not for him to know that Tuke, with whose raffish appearance he was not favourably impressed, had been dubbed by Enid " The Bootlace Man."

And now, at something after seven o'clock, he saw this unprepossessing ally approach the window at which he stood brooding. The coarse features wore a look of cunning satisfaction as he came and drummed on the pane, requesting admission. Mastering his repulsion, Leslie undid the catch and opened to him, reflecting that as he was supposed to be benefiting by the man's services, it would be unfair to show antipathy,

"Is the boss, Mr. Nugent, back? " Tuke asked, as he stepped over the threshold of the French window into the comfortable apartment.

Leslie was beginning to reply in the negative, when the whirr of a car was heard on the other side of the house, where the approach from the road led to the front door,

"I expect that will be him," he said, as the sound ceased; and a minute later Nugent entered the room, brushing the dust from his coat. He was fresh from his interview with Violet Maynard in the rose-garden at the Manor House. He started at sight of his unsavoury henchman.

"Anything wrong? " he demanded of him.

"I ain't seen any cops, if that's what you mean," replied Tuke with a slight wink that called a quick scowl to his employer's face. " But I've got a prisoner in the stone grotto in the shrubbery, the moor her into the garden through the door from Watched, and nabbed her clean as a whistle as she was hiding from me"

Nugent stopped the flow of self-complacence with a repressive gesture, and strode to the open window.

"Ah, that spying ferret, Louise Aubin," he said hastily. " Well, come with me and let her out, Tuke. You acted for the best, no doubt, but we cannot shut young women up in stone grottos against their will in the twentieth century. We must chance her having seen Mr. Chermside, and try and induce her to keep quiet about it if she has. You'll have to apologize, and I shall have to square herâ if I can."

Tuke, pretending to be abashed, followed into the nearer shrubbery, where, as soon as they were hidden from the window, Nugent stopped short. " You idiot! " he hissed, with suppressed fury. " Why did you blurt that out before Chermside? You ought to have said that you wanted to speak to me in private. It wasn't the Frenchwoman, I know, because she was at the Manor House twenty minutes ago. Who is it that you caught lurking aboutâ that Mallory girl?"

"It's her right enough."

"Hasn't she screamed or made any attempt to attract attention?"

"Not a blessed sound have I heard, and she's been there the best part of twenty minutes now."

"That's curious," said Nugent, puckering his brows in a thoughtful frown. " She's just the sort to yell for release till her voice gave out. She must have been frightened by your ugly mug, I suppose, and doesn't want to fetch you back again. Well, anyhow, she must stay there now till we've done with the Cobra, and then we must make what excuses we can. Of course you know as well as I do that there's no danger of interference from the police, for the simple reason that Aubin hasn't laid her information. I have been merely holding them over our friend in the library as a bogey to induce him to go quietly on board the steamer."

"I tumbled to that much," rephed Tuke, with a cunning smile.

"Well, don't relax your vigilance on that account," was Nugent's injunction. " There may be other prowlersâ this girl's father, for instance, or the onion-seller, Pierre Legros. Either of them might upset our arrangements. And, above all, be within call when I want you."

Tuke growled assent, and Nugent returned to the library. " I am sorry to have left you alone so long to-day, but there has been much to do," he said pleasantly, adding, as he noted the restless irritation in Leslie's face, "Your suspense will soon be over. It is growing dark already, and by the time we have had some dinner it will be time for you to start for the chine. There are no signs of anything to prevent your safe departure."

"That girl, Louise Aubinâ you let her out of the grotto, I hope? " said Leslie. " I should be sorry if she was ill-treated on my behalf."

"Chivalrous as ever! " Nugent could not resist the sneer. " Oh, yes; she's half-way to the Manor House by now, reduced to a proper sense of her misdemeanour. A little palm-grease works wonders with a Frenchwoman."

Presently the silent Sinnett served dinner, and during the meal Nugent unobtrusively continued to work the repentant vein he had developed earlier in the day. He waxed eloquent on his own difficult position as a man of birth and expensive tastes, thrown by force of adverse circumstances into a social groove that was really beyond his means.

"I had not, perhaps, your excuse of abject misery, Chermside," he remarked pathetically, " but the Maharajah's bribe was an enormous temptation, and I yielded to his importunities the more readily as I had incurred obligations to him. I shall look back upon our association with shame to the end of my days."

The proper feeling shown by his former accom-phce called forth Leslie's sympathy. " I hope that Bhagwan Singh has no hold on you? " he said. " He is a vengeful beast, and from my knowledge of him he is not likely to overlook your aiding my escape in his yacht after throwing him over. He has the long arm of boundless wealth."

"I am aware of that," Nugent replied gravely. " If he strikes at me, I must pay the penalty. I must regard it as a just retribution."

At ten o'clock Nugent went to the window, opened it, and called softly into the darkness of the summer night for Tuke.

"Have you got the flares? " he asked, when the mottled countenance of his retainer appeared in the stream of lamplight. " That is well. Show the blue first, remember, and then green. Now, Chermsideâ least said, soonest mended. I am not going with you myself, but tliis man will see you through. The captain of the Cohra has orders as to your destination. Good-bye, and may your next venture end in happier fashion."

He held out his hand, and, conquered by his seeming mood, Leslie returned the grasp. A moment later he was following his guide across the lawn, and so out of the door on to the moor. The night air was heavy with the scent of the dew-laden heather, across which they had to grope their way, and the croak of a fern owl alone broke the stillness as they skirted the golf links and came to the head of the chine at the foot of which they were to flash the signals that would summon the Cobra's launch.

They were about to descend the steps cut in the cliff, when from the house they had just left, a quarter of a mile away, the " teuf-teuf " of a motor car was heard. Leslie found himself idly wondering what could have taken Nugent from home again so late. Possibly he was going down to the club for an hour or two, to drown the memory of his villainy in the congenial company of gentlemen who would have spurned him from their midst could they have known the manner of man he was.

"Now, sir; mind where you're going," came Tuke's hoarse whisper. " There's only a handrail in places, and a nasty drop if you fall."

The warning recalled Leslie to himself, and he gave his attention to the steep descent. In a little while they stood on the pebbly beach below, where the incoming tide was making gentle music on the smooth stones. No glimmer came across the dark sea to tell them whether the Cohra lay out yonder in the inky pall, but that meant nothing. Nugent, they knew, had given the captain orders to veil all lights before he arrived opposite the town.

Tuke produced two cardboard cylinders from under his coat, and, striking a match, applied it to the conical head of one of them. There was a spluttering fizzle, and the flare burst out into a brilhant blue flame that shone steadily seaward, but was hidden from the coastguard station and the parade by a jutting angle of the cliff wall. For two minutes it glowed, and when it flickered out he repeated the illumination with the green flare, carefully picking up the empty cases when his pyrotechnic display was over.

"There! " he whispered huskily. " Now all there is to do is to squat down and wait. The boss said the launch is a quick 'un to travel. If the steamer's no more than three miles out she ought to do it in twenty minutesâ with the tide in her favour."

The forecast proved accurate. In a very little over the time mentioned the click-clack of an electric motor was heard approaching the shore from the gloom, and Leslie, catching up the small handbag which was all the luggage he had dared remove from his lodgings, went down to the edge of the waves.

MISS SARAH DYMMOCK threw down the piece of old-fashioned embroidery on which she had been engaged since dinner, yawning aggressively.

"I'm a sleepy old woman, and I shall go to bed," she remarked with a snap. " Young people nowadays are bad company, though I suppose I ought to make allowances for you, Vi, as a what-d'you-call-it."

"That's a vague term, auntie," said Violet Maynard with a wan smile. In the absence of Montague Maynard in London the two ladies had been spending the evening alone, and the girl's nerves were all on edge at the prospect of the coming interview with her lover. The spacious drawing-room at the Manor House had seemed like a prison, and dear Aunt Sarah's fluent talk like the chatter of a persistent parrot. Violet was annoyed with herself for her irritation, but she was nearly beside herself with an intense craving to stand face to face with Leslie and appeal to his manhood not to fly from the charge against him. The dragging hours had seemed interminable, since Travers

Nugent's disclosure of Leslie's intended escape by sea.

"By a what-d'you-call-it I mean a prospective victim on the altar of Hymen," explained the old lady, rising and gathering up her work. " If I had ever been in love, which God in his mercy has spared me, I should have been pirouetting all over the place instead of sitting mum-chance and twiddling my thumbs. By the way, why hasn't your young man been out here to-day. Is he cooling off already?"

"I can hardly expect him to dance attendance on me always, can I, auntie? " replied Violet, making a brave effort to appear playful. She was wondering how she should explain on the morrow that her lover had been skulking somewhere all day preparatory to decamping altogether, if she failed to prevent him from adopting that disgraceful course.

Aunt Sarah sniffed as she took her bedroom candle. " I wasn't thinking of his dancing attendance on you, but on me," she rejoined, working herself into an entirely spurious passion. " I wanted him to sign the documents for the transfer of the securities I am making over to him, but I suppose that he has had other fish to fry. You'll have to teach him manners, child, when you're marriedâ or at any rate attention to his own interests."

The little wizened old woman pecked at the pale cheek which her great-niece offered her, and stumped out of the room. Violet breathed a sigh of relief, for it had been becoming a problem whether her aunt would retire in time to allow her to get away unquestioned. It was quite on the cards that the energetic old spinster might have offered to accompany her if she had said that she was going for a stroll in the gardens before going to bed.

As it was, she was free to make her preparations without interference, and going out into the hall she provided herself with a motoring cap and a heavy golf cloak. Returning to the drawing-room, she was about to leave by one of the French windows when it occurred to her that as her " stroll in the garden " was to-night an excuse for a more extended expedition, it might be as well to take precautions against her being locked out. She rang the bell and ordered the butler not to lock the window, but to merely leave it on latch. She explained that she was going to enjoy the beauty of the night in the open air, and might not have returned when he went his rounds to see that all was secure.

"And don't trouble to sit up for me, Watson," she added. " I have a headache, and may be out some little while."

"Shall I leave the lamps lighted, miss? " asked the butler.

"In the drawing-room and in the hall," was the reply. " I will make myself responsible for putting them out when I come in."

The man bowed and retired, concealing with the tact of the well-trained servant the surprise with which the cap and cloak inspired him. He was aware that his young mistress was in the habit of walking in the grounds at a late hour, but he had never previously received such an order about not sitting up, nor had he known her to take precautions by putting on additional wraps.

"I've got m3 plate chest to think about," the faithful servitor muttered as he made his way back to his pantry. " Miss Violet is always considerate, but I'm blessed if I'm going to turn in while that window's only on latch. It appears to me she isn't in a hurry to come in to-night."

Having got rid of Watson, Violet lost no time in starting to carry out the project on which she was so feverishly bent. Along the noble avenue, lit now by only a few pale stars in an opaque sky, she flitted like a nymph of the night, only checking her footsteps as she passed the lodge, lest she should awake the sleeping inmates. Out on the high road she commenced running, and so neared the clump of trees where she was to find the car. Nugent's carefully modulated voice hailed her from the darkness.

"That you. Miss Maynard? Right! Pray do not distress yourself by undue haste. We have ample time before us. There, let me help you in and make you comfortable. Dixon, take the hoods off the lamps and get in behind. Miss Maynard will sit with me."

Nugent, who was at the wheel, extended his hand, and when Violet had settled herself at his side and the chauffeur had unveiled the great acetylene lamps, he sent the car spinning for Ottermouth at half-speed. But he avoided the road that would take him through the main street of the little town, and struck into a series of country lanes that brought them by a detour to The Hut, without having to pass more than a solitary farmhouse.

"We are in luck so far," he said when they had swept up the drive and he had assisted Violet to ahght. " We didn't meet a soul all the way. Dixon, have the car ready here. I shall want to take Miss Maynard back to the Manor House presently. Now," he added, beckoning Violet to follow him, " we will go round this way, please."

The girl, all her mind set on her purpose, obeyed like one in a dream. She wanted to meet Leslie and bring him to reason. It mattered nothing to her how she reached her goal so long as her task was swiftly accomphshed, and she knew that the shortest way to the sea was through the grounds of The Hut. So without demur she followed Nugent round the house to the lawns and gardens at the back.

"It would be best to be perfectly silent," her guide whispered as they struck across the greensward. " My servants may not all have gone to bed yet, or some one else might be about."

"Iâ I thought I heard something there," rephed Violet, laying a hand on his arm and glancing apprehensively at the spectral outline of the grotto, the walls of which gleamed white amid the gloom of the shrubbery.

"Only the breeze in the foliage," Nugent murmured hastily, and, taking the girl's hand almost roughly, he hurried her to the door on to the moor, opened it, and as quickly closed it when they had passed through.

"There! " he said in a tone of unaffected relief " we shall find no more obstacles in our way but a short walk through the heather and a scramble down the steps to the beach. Chermside will be waiting for us at the foot of Colebrook Chine."

But that prophecy was not to be verified. When at length they stood on the pebbles of the shore the figure which emerged from a nook in the cliff was not Leslie Chermside, but Bill Tuke, " the Bootlace Man."

"Well, where is Mr. Chermside? " Nugent demanded of him angrily.

"It's not my fault that he ain't here, sir," the fellow replied in seemingly surly protest. " Nothing I could say would make him stop. As soon as the launch came he insisted on going off to the steamer."

Violet uttered a cry of anguish. Her self-set task had failed. Not only had her lover fled, but he had fled like a craven without keeping the tryst which he had himself sought.

"Did he leave no message? " Nugent inquired, in a tone of perplexity that sounded perfectly natural.

"He did that," replied Luke. " I was to say that he was frightened to wait about here on the shore lest the coppers should pinch him, but that he would ask the captain, directly he got on board, to keep the yacht out there for a bit, and to send the launch back for the lady. Then she could come out to the steamer and bid him good-bye, and the launch could put her ashore again afterwards."

Nugent turned impetuously to Violet. It was too dark for her to see the expression on his face, but the quiver in his voice was eloquent of hardly-restrained indignation. " Chermside must have lost his head or his nerve," he said. " Though that is no excuse for such a want of consideration. The request is outrageous. I will not worry you with my sympathy, Miss Maynard, for I cannot trust myself to speak. Come! Let me take you home without delay, for of course you will not accede to this preposterous request."

"On the contrary, that is exactly what I mean to doâ if the launch comes for me," replied Violet, straining her wet eyes seaward through the gloom. " You must remember that it was not to say farewell but to prevent him from going that I came here, Mr, Nugent. I am very sensible of your kindness in bringing me, and I regret Mr. Chermside's conduct as an insult to you, even greater than to me. I will not ask you to remain till I return from the steamer. Ifâ if I am alone I shall prefer to make my way home by myself."

"My duty to your father, who is my friend"

Nugent was beginning.

"I have my duty to myself, and to my affianced husband to consider," Violet cut him short. " Pray spare me an argument in my distress, Mr. Nugent. My mind is quite made up to go out to the yacht."

And, as if to fortify her resolve, there sounded from the dark sea the pulsing clack of the electric launch as it sped towards the shore, A few moments later it had been skilfully beached, and a gruff voice inquired in a guarded undertoneâ

"Is the lady there?"

"Yes, I am here and ready," responded Violet eagerly; and she went down across the pebbles to where the bows of the tiny craft nuzzled the shore. A horny hand was stretched out to her, and she was drawn on board. When Nugent had tossed a letter into her, the launch backed off, and, circling round, started for the second time that night on its trip back to the steamer.

"Pray do not wait, Mr. Nugent; I shall be really vexed if you do," Violet's vibrant tones rang from the fast-receding launch.

The reply was uttered so low that it reached no ears but those of Tuke, who, like some foul bird of the night, had hovered round, taking no part in the scene after the delivery of his alleged message.

"I have no intention of causing you any such vexation, dear lady. The wait would, indeed, be a long one," was what Travers Nugent said, as he turned to climb the steps to the top of the cliff.

And the subtle humour of the remark, which was apparently intelligible to " the Bootlace Man," caused that worthy to break into a snigger of servile laughterâ the kind of merriment which the junior bar concedes to a jest from the bench.

"That's a good 'un, sir," he wheezed. " She won't trouble you much more, I'm thinking. But what about the little gel in the grotto? She'll make it nasty for us if she ain't let out soon, I reckon."

"Not for us, Luke," was Nugent's sardonic rejoinder. " But she will probably make it very nasty for you, or rather her father will. I intend you to bear the brunt of Mr. Mallory's displeasure, my friend, on the usual terms. In other words, you will be well paid for any unpleasantness you may incur on my behalf. I am going to release Miss Enid Mallory now, and as the tale I intend to regale her with does not entail your presence, you had better go back to your lodging. And by the first train in the morning you must clear right out for your kennel in London. I will communicate with you by letter as to future requirements."

So at the summit of the cliff they separated, Tuke taking the path to the lower end of the town, where for some days he had been domiciled in a fisherman's cottage, and Nugent striking out across the moor for the back way into his own grounds.

Before he closed the door in the hedge, he turned and looked seaward. Some three miles out a brilliant streak of light was visible. It was moving rapidly westward, like a golden snake gliding on the face of the dark waters. The phenomenon was evidently caused by the port-hole lights of an electrically-lit steamer.

The watcher drew a deep breath of satisfaction. " Brant has lost no time in getting under weigh," he muttered, as he softly shut the door.

LESLIE CHERMSIDE, having taken his seat in the launch, felt more at ease in his mind than he had done for many a day. Ever since he had been told of the suspicion that threatened him in respect of Levison's death, he had been reconcihng himself to the loss of Violet. That dream of midsummer madness had from the first, he realized, from the nature of the circumstances, been doomed to a rude awakening, in spite of Aunt Sarah's generosity. The shattering of his ill-starred love idyll might be borne manfully, as an adequate punishment for his iniquity, and when time had healed his wound he might even rejoice in his expiation.

But with very different feelings had he viewed the possible revelation of his misdeed. That simply would not bear thinking about. That Violet should ever know that he had sought her out in order that her proud young beauty should be offered as an unwilling sacrifice to a licentious Eastern prince was an ever-present nightmare that set him trembling like a frightened child.

And now the strain was over. By his flight he liad escaped the terrible disclosures which would have followed arrest, no matter what the verdict might have been. That Violet would resent his conduct and despise him for it he could not help. Even if Nugent kept his promise of trying to soften it down, the girl's displeasure was inevitable, but it would be as heaven to hell compared with the ignominy he would have incurred by full disclosure. And, to do him justice, he had not been wholly selfish in shrinking from that ignominy. He knew his sweetheart's pure faith in him, and he had been honestly anxious to spare her virginal soul the shock of discovering the loathsome thing from which her short-lived romance had sprung. It might even have been her death-woundâ to hnd that she, the coldly-critical social queen, had surrendered, after so brief a wooing, to a miscreant who had set out to seu her into bondage.

Now, if his luck held, that hideous spectre of disgrace was laid for ever. He would go forth a lonely and a penniless man, to commence life afresh with what courage he could muster in some refuge for human derelicts beyond the seas. If he could not retrieve the past, he might at least lock it up in his own seared heart, as in a chamber of horrors to which he alone had accessâ to be a torment to himself alone.

So, as the launch cleft the calm sea, his troubled spirit caught something of the influence of the summer night, and he began to take an interest in his immediate prospects. Before he left London to come down to Ottermouth on his misguided mission, he had accompanied Nugent occasionally to the docks where the Cohra was fitting out, and he had made the acquaintance of Captain Brant.

In those reckless days he had conceived a great antipathy to the crafty and cruel sailor, and he had reason to believe that the dislike was reciprocated. He wondered how much Nugent had told Brant. of their original scheme, and whether he had informed him that he was the cause of its failure. If so, he was likely to be treated with scant courtesy during the voyage.

He was not long left in doubt as to the captain's attitude towards him when the launch had run alongside the steamer, and he had climbed the ladder to the deck. Brant met him as he stepped aboard, but ignored his presence, and called down to Bully Cheeseman and the two men who had remained in the launchâ

"Now turn her right round and go back again to the same spot. You know what to do. You'll find Mr. Nugent waiting for you, I guess."

"Aye, aye, sir," came out of the darkness, and Leslie heard the tick-tack of the motor as the little craft sped for the shore. He could hardly believe his ears. Why should a second trip be necessary, and why should Nugent, who had declined to accompany him to the beach, be waiting there now, when his car had left The Hut shortly after his own departure?

"Good evening, captain," he said, forcing himself to speak civilly. " Is it not rather risky to hang about off shore now that I am aboard?"

Brant's baleful eyes blazed like coals of fire in the blackness of the darkened ship. " And who the hâ 11 are you, sir, to dictate to me what's a risk and what isn't? " the commander of the

Cobra piped in his shrill falsetto. " I understand that it's your damned foolishness that's made all this jiggery-pokery necessary. A nice one to talk about risks, when we're taking them on your account. You just have patience, and amuse yourself till I have time to attend to you."

He swung on his heel and mounted the stairs to the bridge, where he entered into a low-voiced colloquy with one of his subordinates. Only a few words of it reached Leslie, but they were enough to show that a keen look-out was being kept for the approach of fishing or other small boats to the steamer. That was all in order.

Being engaged in the punishable offence of assisting a fugitive from justice to escape arrest it was intelligible that the captain should be anxious to cover the traces of his misdemeanour. But why the delay? Why the return trip of the launch to the shore, where, so far as he was aware, she had fulfilled her mission in bringing him safely off?

He could find no satisfactory answers to the questions, and, giving up the attempt, he tried to accept the situation philosophically. Not knowing what accommodation had been allotted to him, he could not seek his cabin; so he put his handbag down on the deck and set to pacing to and fro. It was so dark that it was almost impossible to distinguish objects close at hand, and though the crew were evidently alert and at their stations, he could make nothing of them individually. The discipline was perfect.

He passed and repassed ghostlike figures on his promenade, sometimes singly and sometimes in groups, but they never spoke in so much as a whisper. The silence of the dead reigned over the ship.

He tired of walking at last, and, leaning over the stern-rail, let his eyes range towards the twinkling lights of distant Ottermouth. At this late hour they were momentarily growing fewer, only the larger residences on the hill behind the town showing up in bold relief, and the row of lodging-houses on the parade flanked by the more brilliant glow from the billiard-room of the club. The sight of the quiet haven which had yielded him a short and fickle respite renewed his remorse and filled him with regret. Such joys as the placid little pleasure-haunt had to offer were not for him. His proper place was on the scrap-heap of human failures.

The depression found vent in a sigh that was more than half a groan, and he was immediately surprised to hear it echoed near by. Turning sharply, he discerned the dim outline of a woman also leaning over the stern-rail within a few feet of him.

"Don't mind me," she said, noticing his start. " I expect I shouldn't have made any sound if you hadn't let on that you had the blues too. Sighing is pretty near as catching as yawning, I've been told, and now I know it's true."

Leslie could not see her featuresâ only that she was tall and finely-built. He wondered who the woman could be, for he had not been informed by Nugent of the engagement of any female attendants.

"Perhaps your case is the same as my ownâ that you are not looking forward to the voyage with pleasure? " he said kindly.

Miss Nettle Jimpson uttered a short laugh.

"At any rate, you are starting of your own free will," she said. " At least I suppose so, for I was watching you when you came aboard just now, and you didn't make any bones about it. It's different with me. That monkey-faced little devil on the bridge never gave me the option, but just shipped me like a bale of goods to suit his own convenience."

"But surely " Leslie was beginning.

"Oh, don't make any mistake! I was a consenting party as soon as I heard the terms," Miss Jimpson cut him short, drawing a little nearer. " I'm an avaricious sort of beast, and the prospect of a quick haul tempted me to take Captain Brant's practical joke lying down. You see, I've got a young man in the navy, and it seemed a shorter cut to setting up housekeeping than serving behind the counter in a draper's shop. I acted on the spur of the moment, as I always do, and lucky for the captain I did, or he'd have got his ugly face scratched."

"May I ask what position you hold on board â for what duties you were engaged? " asked Leslie. The voluble young person puzzled him.

"Oh, I'm a kind of mix between a stewardess and a maid to the lady passenger, I believe, though that old rascal baited the hook by calling me a companion."

"The lady passenger? " Leshe repeated blankly.

"Yes, and that leads up to what I wanted to ask you? Why didn't she come out to the steamer with you? You see, if it's an elopement, it will smooth it down for me a lot. I'm that romantic I shall be really interested, instead of grizzling all the time till we get back. Some hitch in your young lady's getting off, I suppose, as the launch had to go back to fetch her? Brant has been like a cat on hot bricks ever since we sighted that little town yonder, lest something should go wrong. I hope it hasn't, for your sake. I should be sorry for anything in the shape of an angry parent to break the spell of love's young dream, having been there myself."

Leslie thought he understood. His dimly-seen companion at the stern-rail had been " shipped," as she called it, while the ship was lying in the London docks weeks before, when the original plot for the abduction of Violet Maynard held good. She had been informed of half the vile plot in which he had then been an accompliceâ that the yacht belonged to him, and that it was being used for an elopement. She was still in that belief, the darker side of the story having been kept from her, and she was under the delusion that she would have a lady to wait on during the voyage.

But why, Leslie asked himself, had the delusion been fostered so long after Nugent, and through him, of course. Brant, had been aware of the breakdown of the conspiracy? Why, for the matter of that, was the woman on board at all, since there would be no unhappy captive for whom her services would be required? The obvious thing to have done would have been to put her ashore at Weymouth directly the wicked project was abandoned.

"There must be some mistake," he said. " I am sorry to spoil your romantic anticipations, but I am certainly not eloping with anybody. So far as I know, I am to be the only passenger."

"Then what's that old Har's game? " blurted Miss Jimpson. " Only this morning, when he had the cheek to keep me aboard, he said"

"Only this morning," Leslie interrupted in dull amazement. " Do you mean that only to-day for the first time you made the acquaintance of Brant?"

"That is precisely what I do mean. I never saw him or his ship till this morning at eleven o'clock in the harbour at Weymouth. The yarn he pitched me then was that he was going to pick up a lady down along the coast, and that he wanted one of her own sex to keep her company. 'Tis true he did not say anything about an elopement. It was me who figured that out after you came aboard alone and the launch went back for the lady."

"Went back for the lady!" gasped Leshe, a lurid light beginning to dawn upon his dazed senses.

"Well, I expect it's one of my own sex; I don't suppose all the pretty frilly things Brant ordered and paid for, and which I brought on board, were for you or any other gentleman," was Miss Nettle Jimpson's pert rejoinder. " That's what gave me the elopement notion, don't you seeâ a girl running away on the quiet, and in too much of a pucker to bring her own trunks. And I'm right, after all! Here's the launch back again, and just listen to that!"

Leslie had been conscious of the clack of the electric motor for the last thirty seconds, but now, as it sounded close under the side of the steamer, slowing down at the foot of the accommodation ladder, it was supplemented by the clear tones of a woman's voice â the well-loved tones which he had never thought to hear again, and wliich rather than hear in that place he would gladly have died a hundred deaths.

For it was the voice of Violet Maynard, self-possessed and confident, assuring the crew of the launch that she was quite accustomed to climbing up the side of a yacht in the dark, and that she would need no help but that of her own hands to scale the dangling rope-ladder.

The truth in all its naked horror burst upon Leslie at last. The original object of the plot had been gained in spite of his own defection. Travers Nugent had been playing a deep and subtle part, and by some trick had prevailed on the girl to place herself in the power of her enemies. In another minute she would be hopelessly in the toils, and the Cobra, having gorged her prey, would be steaming at the full speed of her powerful engines on her long voyage to distant Sindkhote.

His memory flew back to the tinselled splendour of the Maharajah's palace, then to the satanic countenance of its owner, and to all the terrors that these implied for the girl in whose foul betrayal he was at any rate a link in the chain. He turned in despair to the odd young woman whose narrative was now quite intelligible.

"I don't know your name, but you sound honest and true, and I'm going to appeal to you," he whispered hoarsely. " They have lured that lady to the ship in ignorance that she is to be kidnapped abroad. I am going to try to prevent it, but I shall probably fail and be killed in the next few minutes. If so, I beseech you to be this poor girl's friend to the best of your power. The vessel is manned by reckless outlaws."

Without waiting for a reply, he sprang forward to the head of the accommodation ladder and shinned down it into the launch. There was not much sense in the forlorn hopeâ only a wild longing to do something, and to stake all, life itself, on the chance that he might prevail by surprise. If he could disable the crew of the launch before they reahzed that they were being attacked he might sheer off and get away in the darkness.

Violet was reaching for the rope rungs of the ladder as he half fell into the little craft, nearly knocking her down in his staggering onrush. Then, steadying himself, he sent his fists crashing right and left into the faces of two men who clutched at him, ducked to avoid a third, and in doing so tripped and fell headlong to the bottom of the boat.

Before he could recover himself a heavy knee was grinding into his chest, and the muzzle of a revolver made a cold circle on his forehead.

"What in thunder is all that racket about? " came down Captain Brant's squeaky hail from the bridge.

"It's the cove we brought off last trip making a bid for freedom, but I've fair downed him," went up Bully Cheeseman's reply. " Shall I shoot?"

"No," said Brant. " I want him for something better than that. I'U send a hand down with some rope. Then you can truss him up, and we'll hoist him aboard."

WHEN the door of the stone grotto in the shrubbery at The Hut was slammed in Enid Mallory's face by " the Bootlace Man " her first sensation was one of relief that the repulsive creature had gone away without maltreating her. This was quickly followed by burning indignation at being locked in, so that her sphere of usefulness was limited to the narrow confines of the mouldy moss-grown chamber. And her anger was in turn succeeded by a humorous appreciation of her plight.

"This is what comes of aiding and abetting father's detective propensities," she laughed, immediately checking her merriment lest it should cause the return of her unsavoury captor.

Now that the door was shut the gloom of the mausoleum-like interior was increased twenty-fold, the meagre light that filtered through the ivy-choked window scarcely showing the walls of her prison. But by degrees her bright young eyes grew more accustomed to the obscurity, and she began to search for means of escape. Having embarked on the venture more or less in a spirit of bravado, and being totally ignorant of the tremendous issues hanging in the balance, she was more concerned to get out of her pother without incurring ridicule than with anything else.

She attached but little importance to the triumphant insolence of Tuke when locking her in. The words he had used suggested that he was acting on his own initiative, and not on specific orders from Mr. Nugent, whose approval he hoped to gain. It was possible that he might meet with reproof instead of praise. But she was aware that there was no love lost between her father and the gentleman on whose property she was an undoubted trespasser, and she was annoyed with herself for having done a silly thing which might make an apology necessary.

"If father has to eat humble pie to Mr. Nugent on my account it will be simply rotten," she murmured, "I wish I could get out of this before that wretched man brings him. If I only could there would be nothing to prove that his story is true, or at worst I could stick it out that it was not me he caught."

But to wish herself out of the grotto was one thing, and to find a means of exit another. The door was of oak, strongly clamped with iron and quite impervious to any battery she could administer. She had her golf clubs with her, and essayed to prise open the lock with her driving iron, but the heavy bolt resisted all her efforts. The window was high out of her reach, and if it had not been it was too small for her to creep through. With tears of vexation in her eyes she had to admit that escape was impracticable. There was nothing for it but to await an ignominious release by way of the door when Nugent should have been apprised of her capture. It was possible, she thought ruefully, that he might pretend he had not been told, and keep her there all night as a punishment for her intrusion.

Having resigned herself to the inevitable, Enid characteristically cast about for means to extract what comfort she could out of her cheerless surroundings. The materials at hand were not very promising, the contents of the grotto consisting of a broken lawn-mower, some empty kegs that had held patent manure, and a few obsolete garden tools. But she now noted, what she had missed before, a bench at the far end, running the whole breadth of the grotto. Upon it lay a lot of matting, such as is used for protecting cucumber frames in frosty weather.

"I'm in luck's way at last," she muttered. " That'll make a ripping sofa on which to take it easy till I'm let out of durance vile."

Suiting the action to the word, she moved one or two of the upper mats more to her liking, and then stretched her lithe young frame luxuriously on the improvised couch. In a moment she was on her feet again, staring in dismay at her hastily vacated nest, while every nerve in her body tingled with apprehension.

Something had movedâ " squirmed," she called it afterwardsâ beneath the mats. Something soft and yielding, horribly suggestive of a human body discomfited by her weight.

But there was no further movement. Relieved of its incubus, the thing that had wriggled its dumb protest had reverted to its previous quiescence, and was as uncannily still as it had been all the time she had been in the grotto. Enid felt that she must do one of two thingsâ either scream at the top of her voice, or fathom the mystery of what, or who, it was that lay concealed.

She was no screamer, so screwing up her lips tightly she chose the second course. A few vigorous tugs sent the mats flying hither and thither, and disclosed a man lying prone upon his face on the wooden seat, flattened out like a gigantic lizard. Enid shrank back a httle as the figure rose slowly, uncoiling its cramped limbs and peering and blinking up at her. Intuitively she recoiled further still when she saw the ferocity in the haggard eyes.

But even as she looked the fierceness died out, giving place to an expression of patient sadness. The man, who was clad in a cotton blouse and blue jean trousers, made a half-respectful, half-deprecating gesture.

"Ah, so it is not Louise," he said gently in French. " So much the better for the traitress, and for me, perhaps." Then he added in broken English. " Ma'amselle must not be frighted. I do her no harm. I only poor sailor man from onion ship, come in naice cool place for rest."

On the instant Enid's self-possession returned to her. She remembered what her father had said to Reggie Beauchampâ that the clue to the murder of Levison was probably connected with a French lugger engaged in the onion trade, at present lying at Exmouth. It was on the cards that her adventure was not to turn out so fruitless as she had feared. But the man would require careful handling, for she did not lose sight of the fact that she might be in the presence of a murderer. And she was handicapped by not knowing what were the relations between Travers Nugent and this foreigner.

In coming to a conclusion on the latter point, her inherited powers of deduction came to her aid. She shrewdly reasoned that if the man were well disposed towards the owner of The Hut, he would hardly be lurking in the grounds, hidden under a pile of matting.

"I was not frightenedâ only startled," she replied pleasantly. " You see I am an intruder here, just as much as I expect you are yourself, I am afraid it will be as awkward for you as for meâ my getting myself locked in by that horrid creature."

Pierre Legros laughed grimly. " It no matter to me, so long as the right person come to unlock the door," he said.

The words were suggestive of some sinister purposeâ if not of some secret relating to the past. Enid reflected quickly that she must draw this man out if he was to be useful to her in either respect. And it also occurred to her that he might be made useful in more ways than as a source of information.

"You thought I was some one else when I sat down upon you? " she said, ignoring his last remark, and trying to read his features in the gloom. It was light enough to enable her to note that her question recalled the ferocity to his deep-sunk eyes, though not for her. His hardening gaze was rather for some one he saw in his mental vision.

"Yes, I t'ink you was anozer person, ma'amselle, and for that I demand of you the kind pardon, for she very weecked person," he said. " Ma'amselle not cruel and weeckedâ I Pierre Legros, tell by her voice. But that ozair, she fille du diable, and trample on the heart of man, and make him more bad than herself. She and her false Ingleesh lover."

The onion-seller had no more terrors for Enid, and she drew a little closer, subtly conveying the idea of confidence in order to win his confidence. She rejoiced that she had been locked up in the grotto now. She guessed that the core of the mystery lay under the cotton blouse of this rugged foreign sailor, and she meant to have it out of him by hook or by crook. Rapidly casting about for the most effective weapon in her equipment, she hit upon friendly sympathy as the bestâ for the opening of the campaign, at any rate. A httle later, perhaps, she would play for all it was worth the sentiment that they were companions in the same dilemma.

"I am sorry that you are in trouble," she said kindly, and wondering what language Reggie would use if he knew how he was to be exploited for her purpose. " I wish I could help you, for I, too, know what it is to have an affair of the heart. I am betrothed to a sailor, and he has gone away and left me miserable. Got half a dozen wives in half a dozen ports, I expect."

Enid Mallory was her father's daughter, and had inherited a strain of the veteran diplomatist's knowledge of human nature. A thrill of victory ran through her veins as she noted the effect of her Parthian shot. For Pierre Legros lifted his brown hands to his swarthy face and wept such a flood of tears as a British seaman could not have secreted.

let alone shed, in a lifetime. She waited patiently till the paroxysm had passed, and then reaped her reward in a flow of excited verbiage which amounted to tliisâ

He was one of the hands on a lugger which had brought a cargo of onions from France, and in the course of vending his wares about the country he had discovered his old sweetheart, Louise Aubin, in service at the Manor House. But her head had been turned by a succession of English admirers, and she would have nothing to do with him. Legros waxed somewhat incoherent about the personality of these swains, slurring over his first efforts to defeat his rivals in a jumble of phrases, from which, however sharp-witted Enid was able to form a distinct suspicion. Her father had hinted that the murder of Levison might be connected with the onion ship; she believed that she was shut up with the actual perpetrator of the crime.

Bringing his narrative down to date, in explanation of his concealment in the grounds of The Hut, Legros became more intelligible. Enid could hardly beheve her ears when it transpired that Mr. Travers Nugent himself was the object of this half-demented creature's jealousy. She was convinced that he was the victim of some ridiculous error, since to associate the fastidious, middle-aged bachelor with a vulgar intrigue with a lady's maid was the height of absurdity. But there was no doubt that, however the misunderstanding had arisen, Legros was firmly convinced of its truth.

He had of late found that Louise was paying frequent clandestine visits to Nugent, and as a conse- qiience he had spent much time in hanging about and spying on them. That very morning he had crept from the moor into the garden for the purpose, and he had been making his way through the shrubbery when he heard Nugent's voice coming towards him. He had taken refuge in the grotto, and had barely had time to conceal himself under the mats when Nugent had entered, accompanied by the man who had just now made them both prisoners by locking the door.

"They made plenty talk, ma'amselle, till my poor head ache," Legros continued with that note of self-pity which seemed his leading attribute. " And their talk was of ' the girl'â always the girl, and how she was to be deportedâ is that your word?â in a steamer that would come off the shore to-night. There was also talk of anozaire â a man, one Jermicideâ who was to be deported and made what you call decoy for tempting her on to the steamer. The girl, cela va sans dire, is Louise Aubin, and Nugent, he run off with her. I not rightly know where Jermicide what you call come in, for I nevair heard of him. He must be one more of the lovers of Louise. She raise 'em like the mushrooms, here in your damp country."

Enid's active brain worked rapidly. The onion-seller had evidently got a bee in his bonnet which it was useless to try to disentangle. The salient fact stood out that Nugent had a project afoot for that night, in which all the principal actors in the Levison mystery, as enumerated by her father, were concerned, and of which her father would wish to be informed without delay. And here was she, his only possible informant, a prisoner without any prospect of release except at the hands of a cunning schemer who would have reason for preventing her from imparting the knowledge she had acquired. The action of " the Bootlace Man " in locking her in took a more sinister meaning by the light of what she had heard, and at the same time made her more than ever anxious to escape.

The suggestion that Violet Maynard's maid was the object of Nugent's machinations she dismissed with scorn, but that Leslie Chermside was to be " deported" in a steamer, either voluntarily or otherwise, was an item which ought to be under her father's consideration before it became an accomplished fact.

"I think that if I was out of this horrid place I could help you," she said. " Miss Maynard, the mistress of Louise, is a friend of mine. I would go to her and persuade her not to allow Louise any liberty to-night. Sailors are so clever, especially French sailors. I am sure that you will be able to hit upon some way of getting out."

The sun- was low in the heavens, and inside the shrub-girt grotto it was scarcely possible to see the walls. Legros peered up at the little window, the top of which was just on a level with the eaves, where the slope of the roof began. Enid followed the direction of his glance, and pointed out that the aperture was not big enough for either of them to pass through. For answer Legros went and collected some of the patent fertilizer kegs, set them one upon the other under the window, and clambered up on to the topmost. By so doing he could easily reach with his hand the upper pane. It was already cracked, and, cautiously removing the broken glass, he thrust his arm through.

"From here I can make a hole in the roof big enough," he called down in a hoarse whisper. " It will take very long time to pick off the slates, they so firm fixed. But it the only way."

"Then, my dear good man, please begin at once," Enid urged him. " And don't make more noise than you can help in dislodging the slates, or we shall have thatldrute, or Mr. Nugent himself, round to stop us."

So she leaned against the mouldy wall and watched the laborious task with growing impatience, and in momentary dread lest the door should be flung open by the " bootlace man" or his employer. For though she was nearly certain that her companion of the grotto was a shedder of human blood her instinct told her that to her personally the forces controlled by Travers Nugent were far more dangerous.

The work of removing the roofing seemed interminable. The interior of the old stone building grew pitch-black before three of the slates had been displaced and gently tossed into the herbage. A distant clock in the town struck eight, nine, and ten and stiu Legros remained on his perch, toiling, with twisted body and arm crooked through the broken pane, in frantic endeavour to enlarge the opening.

At last the clock struck eleven, and before the half-hour the Frenchman slid nimbly to the floor.

"There, ma'amselle! " he panted after his exertions. " I t'ink' there room now for you to pass through. For myself I shall have to make 'im one bit bigger. If you ready I give you what you call a 'and up."

Enid prepared to mount the kegs, grateful that she was wearing a short golfing skirt, but in no wise daunted at the prospect of crawling through the yawning gap in the roof or of the drop to the ground on the other side. But in the act of commencing her scramble on to the improvised stage she paused and clutched Pierre's arm.

"Hush! " she whispered. " I heard some one speaking. There are people close byâ crossing the garden."

In a silence that could be felt they waited, and it was only when the voice which had disturbed her had passed beyond hearing that Enid wished that she had pursued quite other tactics and called outâ called with the full vigour of her lungs.

For all too late she realized that the voice which had arrested her attempted escape was the voice of her friend, Violet Maynard. She tried to rectify her error by calling out now, but there was no response. Her shrill cry shot skjrwards through the aperture towards the blinking stars, but the thick stone walls stood between her and the ears the cry was meant for. Violet and Travers Nugent had passed through the door on to the moor on their way to the beach.

THE commotion caused by Leslie Chermside's descent into the launch, and by his unsuccessful struggle with the crew alarmed and agitated Violet. But she was spared the full extent of the shock, not having recognized her lover in the man who had swarmed down the steamer's side to be ultimately stunned and overpowered. In haste to complete the task which had brought her there, she mounted to the deck of the Cobra without waiting to see the sequel of the disturbance.

As she stepped on board she noticed that the ship, which had been wrapped in complete darkness, suddenly blazed from stem to stern in the full glow of the electric light. She was surprised at this premature disclosure of the vessel's position, as long as it remained stationary off the coast Leslie not being safe from arrest. But she reflected that it did not really matter, since she hoped to prevail on him to go back with her and face his accusers.

The sudden illumination showed her the hairless features of Captain Brant, who had come down from the bridge to meet her at the gangway. The monkeyish limbs and curious leper-hke face of the

Cobra's commander filled her with a repulsion which was increased by the mocking smile and bow of his greeting.

"Miss Maynard, I believe? " he said in his thin, piping treble. " Allow me to introduce myself as the captain of this ship, Simon Brant by n ame, and very much at your service. If you will do me the honour to follow I will conduct you to the saloon, where I think that you will find that everything for your comfort has been"

"My comfort doesn't count, as I shall only be on the steamer a few minutes," Violet cut him short in the rather imperious tone she sometimes used to people she disliked. " If you will take me to Mr, Chermside I shall hope not to delay you very long, for I am anxious to be put on shore again at the earliest possibl emoment."

"Oh, I'll see that you're put on shore again, miss, don't you make any mistake about that. I'm on the job for no other purpose," replied Brant with a chuckle that he made no attempt to conceal.

His insolent manner caused Violet to eye him with growing indignation, and a hot reproof trembled on her tongue. But Bully Cheeseman created a diversion by approaching the captain and handing him a letter.

"The sealed orders, I reckon; the gent gave them to me for you," said the mate, with a cold stare at his late passenger, whose statuesque beauty it had been too dark to appreciate on the way to the steamer in the launch.

Brant tore open the envelope, glanced through the contents, and emitted a low whistle. " Sindkhote, by God! " Violet heard him mutter under his breath, and it struck the first note of vague, uncompre-hended danger. " A long cruise that, but it's all in the day's work."

Aloud he added: " Have you got that swab trussed up?"

"Haven't left him room to wriggle," was Cheese-man's reply, accompanied by an evil grin. " They're hoisting him aboard now. Where would you wish him to be stowed?"

"Is he unconscious?"

"Dazed, but coming round, I reckon."

"Then tell them to take him to his state-room â you know what I mean, the one with the appliances for taming naughty boys," said the captain, winking at his subordinate. " I'll come and read the riot act to him as soon as I've got time. When you've fixed him up safely, sling the launch inboard and take charge of the bridge. You know what to do, but I'U join you as soon as I've seen to this lady. Now, madam, follow me, please."

Violet's eagerness to see her lover was so intense that in spite of the misgivings with which Brant's manner had begun to inspire her she obeyed his curt command. She tried to attribute his rudeness to irritation at having had his start delayed on her account, and she told herself that she ought to be ashamed of her vague alarm. After all the Cohra and her saturnine commander were only incidents in a bad dream which would be past in a few minutes â as soon as she should have persuaded Leslie to return with her to Ottermouth.

But, pursuant on this train of thought, the ques- tion occurred to her: What had the captain meant by ordering his offensive mate to " have the launch slung inboard? " Many happy days on her father's yacht had made her familiar with sea terms, and she knew that the order was incompatible with Nugent's promise that the launch should take her back to the foot of Colebrook Chine, either with or without her lover. If it was required for that purpose there was no reason for hoisting it aboard.

And then, just as she was hesitating how to put her question into words, there came the terrible enlightenment. She had reached the door of the saloon in the deck-house, and Brant, with another of his sardonic bows, was standing aside for her to enter, when the rattle of the launch being raised to the davits fell upon her ears, succeeded without a moment's interval by the sharp beat of the Cobra's engine-room gong. The steamer immediately began to move through the water, gathering speed with every pulse of her powerful turbines.

"Whatâ what is this? " Violet cried, voicing her fears at last. " They have made a mistakeâ have forgotten that I am not going."

The apelike skipper emphasized his amusement with a cackling laugh. " That's where you make a mistake," he said. " Because, my dear young lady, we have been fooling about for weeks for no other purpose than to take you a nice long sea voyage. Come, be a sensible girl and don't quarrel with your luck. I'll explain it au in a brace of shakes."

Throwing off all semblance of deference, he pushed his prisoner into the luxurious and brilliantly lit saloon, and shutting the door, stood with his back to it. Violet, perceiving that she was powerless to resent an outrage so utterly incomprehensible, confronted him in silence, only the cold lightnings from her eyes telling of her anger.

"I like a good plucked 'un, and I can see you're that." Brant resumed in his squeaky tones. " It'll make my job easier, and I'll lay level chalks that by the time we part four weeks hence you'll be giving me a testimonial for gentlemanly conduct and good seamanship. That's what the passengers do on the big liners, and this ship will be quite as comfortable as a mail-boat for you, miss, unless you make trouble for yourself. You'll be telling me so when I land you at Sindkhote."

"At Sindkhote? " Violet repeated faintly. The name seemed famihar, but in her dismay at her present situation she could not remember why.

"Sindkhote, in the Runn of Cutch in the East Indies," said Brant, his base nature leading him to discern acquiescence in the calm that was only due to bewilderment. " This yacht is the property of the Maharajah of Sindkhote, and I, for the time being, have the honour to be his Highness's humble servant at a thundering good wage. Mr. Nugent, who engaged me and the whole bag of tricks, gave me to understand that you and the Maharajah were a bit thick up in London a while back, and that as you drew the line at matrimony, the prince was driven to extreme measures. You ought to take it as a compliment."

No further words were needed to inform Bhag-wan Singh's intended victim of the main issue of the plot against her. She saw clearly that the enormous resources of the Maharajah, aided by Travers Nugent's subtle scheming, had been called into play to avenge her refusal of his preposterous offer of marriage in the conservatory of Brabazon House at the beginning of the London season. The broad hues of the conspiracy stood out in their grim significance, and the minor details of it did not seem to matter. The one thing that concerned her was the part played in it by the man who had so quickly come into her life, and to whom she had given her love.

"Where is Mr. Chermside? " she forced herself to ask.

"Nursing his broken head," was the brutal reply. " You mustn't set any store on having him for a travelling companion. He's going to make the voyage on the silent system, in a cabin of his own. I can't have an impetuous young lunatic like him loose on such a quiet ship as the Cobra."

"It was Mr. Chermside who attacl: ed the crew of the launch just now?"

"No other, but mark you, he never had the ghost of a chance. Bully Cheeseman is equal to taking on half a dozen such shavers as that, and with his pretty temper it's a wonder he didn't shoot. It would have served the dirty turncoat right, but he'll get it hotter by waitingâ hot as hell on this ship, and hotter still when Bhagwan Singh gets his claws into him, from what I hear of his Highness."

It was a trait in Simon Brant's warped temperament to rejoice in the infliction of pain, mental and physical. His brutal answer was designed to create a distress that he could gloat over. But it missed its mark. Violet received it, outwardly at least, with cold disdain.

"Thank you," she said, betraying no emotion save by a little catch in her breath. " I think that I am now fully informed on all necessary points; and I shall be obliged if you will leave me. One moment, please. Is this the apartment I am to occupy? Where is the sleeping accommodation?"

Brant, who had hoped for the luxury of seeing a woman in tears, had begun to open the door, but at her bidding he turned, and the chagrin in his horrible face changed to a grudging admiration which made it infinitely more horrible. The pose of the superb figure, the disgusted scorn in the coolly appraising eyes, the level tones of the musical voice, all reduced him to a temporary servility that would have been unbearingly nauseous to a weaker character, capable of a personal interest in the vile instrument of her persecution. But Violet Maynard, having grasped the main facts, was able to regard Captain Simon Brant from an entirely detached point of view.

"I wiu send the stewardess to you, miss," he said quite humbly. " She has been selected on purpose to be of service to you during the voyage, and if you have any cause of complaint do not fail to let me know."

He was gone at last, and if the devil ever gets his tail between his legs his disciple followed his master's example in the going. But Brant's subdued mood only lasted till he had shut the saloon door. He went storming up on to the bridge, and vented some of his spleen on Cheeseman for being half a point off his course.

"We must keep out of the regular steamer tracks," he growled in conclusion. " There's nothing at sea fast enough to catch us, but the less we're sighted the better for us afterwards."

"That wench that we shipped at Weymouth has been worrying to know when we shall be off Plymouth," said the mate.

"Oh, has she? " sneered Brant. " Go and tell her to attend the lady in the saloon, and if she asks again you can box her ears."

In the meanwhile Violet had sunk down on to one of the couches in the saloon. Though she had thoroughly taken in the meaning of all that Brant had said to her, it was too soon to feel the full force of the blow that had fallen. So stunning had been the shock that she would have to recover from the shock before she would be able to contemplate the prospect ahead in a proper sense of proportion. For the present her thoughts were chiefly busy with her lover, and with the news of him that had enabled her to confound Brant with such stoical calm.

For the fact stood out above all others that Leslie was as much a dupe as she was herself in the train of circumstances that had ended in their being feuow-captives on the steamer. His desperate effort to obtain control of the launch proved that. He had risked his hfe to prevent her coming on board, instead of, as she had been falsely led to believe, leaving the unmanly message which had lured her into the trap. Brant had referred to him as a turncoat, but her heart kept telling her that if he had ever been associated in the conspiracy he had been hoodwinked into itâ just as, later, Nugent had hoodwinked him into acting as the unconscious decoy for her final undoing.

Suddenly her reverie was interrupted by the opening and shutting of the saloon door. Looking up, she saw a tall girl in rusty black advancing towards her, her plain and somewhat bold face showing traces of recent storm.

"You are my female gaoler? " said Violet, rising. On such a ship engaged on such an errand she had not expected a congenial attendant, but the dogged firmness in this young woman's square jaw seemed to foreshadow that present harsh treatment would be added to the terrors of the future. Violet knew enough of human nature to be aware that the same attitude which would quell the loose tongue of a man like Brant would only goad a bully of her own sex to grosser indignities.

The reply which she received came, therefore, as a welcome surprise.

"No, madam, I am not your gaoler, but I will be your friend if you will let me be," said Miss Jimp-son, her clenched hps relaxing into a reassuring smile that changed her into a kindly woman with all the magic of a transformation scene. " I was trapped on to this villainous ship only this morning â same as you were to-night. I'm just as keen to get off it as you can be."

THE daughter of the millionaire and the draper's assistant stood eyeing each other for twenty seconds in growing mutual approval, and then the hearty ring of Miss Nettle Jimpson's rather powerful voice prevailed. Their hands met in a grasp that at once testified to true comradeship and to sympathy for the other's plight. Violet would have drawn the other down on to the couch beside her, but Miss Jimpson, with a glance at the door, resisted the friendly invitation.

"Better not," she said in her matter-of-fact way. " One of those beasts might take it into his head to come in at any minute, and it won't do for them to think that we're going to be thick together. Tve just given one of them a smack in the face that will last him quite a while, but it wasn't exactl ' judicious. They know Fm not fond of them, but my cue isn't open rebellion till I'm driven to it."

So Miss Jimpson remained standing while at Violet's request she recounted the story of her enforced enlistment, and of all that had happened on the Cobra since. She waxed humorous at her own expense over the inducement held out by Brant to pacify herâ that she was to act as companion to a lady passenger; and she described her subsequent surmise that she was to assist at an elopement. Again she went on to relate how Leshe Chermside had shattered that latest theory, first in words and secondly by wild dismay on hearing Violet's voice in the launch alongside.

"I knew then that he might be your sweetheart, but that he certainly wasn't on board the Cobra to run away with you," said Nettle simply. " He was hke a crazy creature in his wish to stop you from coming aboard. He expected to be killed in the attempt, and he begged me to stand by you if he failed to get the better of the men in the launch."

Violet's eyes were moist with unshed tears. " You have been frank with me, and I will be frank with you," she said. " Mr. Chermside is my lover, and the people who are employing Brant in this cruel business induced him by a series of lying tricks to fly on the steamer from a charge of murder. They hoped, as has happened, that I should follow to dissuade him."

"The charge is trumped up, of course? " said Nettle, and it was rather an assertion than a question.

"He might have some difficulty in disproving it, the train was laid with such fiendish ingenuity," answered Violet gravely.

"That is rough luck. Then if he escaped from the ship to land he would be arrested and have to stand his trial? " And there was that in Miss Jimp- son's voice that suggested that she was weighing chances with some definite idea at the back of her active brain.

"I am afraid so, but his arrest would be infinitely preferable to the fate destined for him if he does not escape," rephed Violet. There was a little eager note of inquiry in her voice, for she had been quick to grasp the hesitation in her new friend's tone.

But, ignoring the challenge, Miss Jimpson refused to be drawn at present. " Tell me," she saidâ " that is if you care toâ why Brant has been bribed to do this dirty work, and where the ship is bound for."

Wisely abstaining from forcing her ally's hand, Violet disclosed in such halting sentences as her pride would permit the object of the cunning intrigue that had centred round her. Nettle Jimp-son's fearless eyes grew rounder and rounder as she listened to the crop of mischief sown by the Maharajah of Sindkhote 5,000 miles away to ripen in a quiet English village. And not being the direct object of the villainous outrage, she appreciated more fully than Violet was yet able to the ghastly tragedy looming ahead at the end of the Cobra's voyage.

"There's one chance," she said when the story of the Eastern Prince's passion, aided by a western rascal's guile, came to an end. " Only a little one, but still a chance. On condition that I didn't play the giddy goat over being kidnapped Brant promised to put into Plymouth on the way down channel, so that I could send a letter ashore for my young man. He's a petty officer on the destroyer Snipe."

"The Snipe! " repeated Violet. The name struck her at once as famihar, and a moment later she remembered why. It had been ever on the impertinent hps of Enid Mallory as that of the diminutive warship commanded by her own particular naval hero, Reggie Beauchamp.

"Yes," said Nettle, " the Snipe is attached to the torpedo flotilla there. If I could communicate your position to Ned he'd tell his commander, and something would surely be done to stop this steamer before she reaches her destination. It's a far cry to India, and the authorities would set the cables to work. It would go hard with us if the Cohra wasn't snapped up by a man-of-war somewhere betwixt this and there."

Violet shook her head. " That promise was made to be broken," she smiled sadly. " I fear Brant would never incur such a risk as that."

"If he doesn't this is going to be a hot ship," rejoined Nettle with spirit. " But you are very likely right," she added after a pause. " When I asked the mate Cheeseman when we should be off Plymouth he tried to box my earsâ by the captain's orders, he said. That was why I smacked his face."

Suddenly Violet rose and began pacing the saloon. " Oh, but I have been selfishly thinking of myself! " she cried. " I heard that brute say that Lesheâ Mr. Chermsideâ was only stunned and that he was coming to, but for all that he may be badly injured and in pain. Can you find out for me, you dear kind girl? Not if it will entail insult or ill-treatment for you, though."

"I'll chance that," replied Nettle firmly. " They carried him down on to the lower deck somewhere, and I'll go and see. But I am forgetting my duties. I was to show you your sleeping cabin. It's next door to this,"

Violet waved her away. "As if I could sleep," she protested with a petulance which she instantly regretted.

Nettle, with a large-hearted tolerance for her companion's over-wrought condition, nodded and went out on to the upper deck. The steamer was gliding through the calm water at half-speed, having reached the fishing grounds of the Brixham trawlers off Berry Head. The sturdy little craft were clustered thick as ants on either beam. It was necessary to thread a cautious track through them if an untimely collision was not to furnish a clue to Violet's disappearance as soon as it was discovered in the morning. Nugent's " sealed orders" had been exphcit on this head, and Simon Brant was not the man to risk punishment and the loss of his huge reward for lack of attention to detail.

"The inference at Ottermouth when Miss May-nard is missed will be that she has voluntarily accompanied Chermside on his flight," these instructions run. " On the whole it will serve our purpose as well as another, but it is imperative that the direction of this flight be unknown. I have Mr. Maynard's confidence, and I shall do my best to foster the idea that Chermside, whom he will of course regard as a free agent, will be likely to make for America, blinding pursuit by taking an eastern course up channel, and then a northerly one round the Scottish coast into the Atlantic. In reality you will run down channel to the westward, and in doing so you must therefore avoid undue speed or anything that may draw attention to your vessel as the one in which the ' elopement' has been carried out."

Nettle Jimpson, knowing nothing about the reason, was nevertheless annoyed at the slow speed, because it would delay the " one chance " at Plymouth to which she had pinned her faith. But realizing that the delay was beyond her control, she devoted herself to the matter in hand.

Casting an upward glance at the bridge, where the quartermaster at the wheel and several other figures were dimly visible against the starlit sky, she skulked along in the shadows of the deck superstructure till she came to the companion stairs leading down to the main deck. It was but a short distance from the door of the saloon and she met no one, though both from the stern and the forecastle gruff whisperings told her that it was a wakeful ship. Stealing down the stairs, she reached the main deck unmolested, and looked about her. Evidently it was here that the officers and the engineers were berthed. Open cabin doors yielded glimpses of oilskin coats and tarpaulin hats, while a well-scrubbed table in the centre of the open space was spread with the remains of a meal that had been partaken of by half a dozen people.

But of the prisoner, or of any closed door behind which he could be confined, there was no sign.

She continued to explore, and at the forward end of the deck found an open hatchway with a flight of almost perpendicular wooden steps running down into the pitch darkness of the lower deck. Undaunted by the steepness of the ladder and the absence of light, she descended into the abyss, where the smell of paint and cordage told her that she was near the ship's storeroom. Realizing at once that down here her eyes were useless for the quest, she raised her voice and called

"Where are you, Mr. Chermside?"

Nothing but silence followed, and emboldened by the fact that none of the Cobra's ruffian crew seemed to be on the lower deck, she called louder still, and this time she got an answerâ an inarticulate utterance, half-sigh and half-groan, from out of the inky blackness. Picking her way towards it, her groping hands encountered the blank space of an open door.

"Mr, Chermside, are you in there? " she asked, excitement rather than fear of being overheard causing her to drop her voice to a whisper.

Again that curious sound but no informing reply, and Nettle crept into the cabin. She had penetrated but a few feet when she stumbled over something, and, stooping down, she felt a soft substance which her sense of touch informed her was the body of a man. The next instant she gave vent to a cry of horror when her searching hands came into contact with a steel chain which her busy fingers quickly traced to a metal circlet grasping a man's leg.

"Mr. Chermside! " she scarcely breathed.

"Give me water," came the faint response from the unseen.

Nettle Jimpson's presence of mind, which had never really left her, reasserted itself in full force. " Shan't be a moment," she said, and whisking out of the cabin, retraced her steps as best she could to the ladder, climbed to the main-deck, and seized a jug of water from the table where the ship's officers had supped. She looked around for a portable lamp or candle, but this deck, like the rest of the vessel, was electrically lit, and she had abandoned the hope of providing herself with a light, when she espied a box of wax matches among a heap of tobacco ashes on a plate.

A minute later she was down on the lower deck again, holding the jug to Leslie's parched hps, and by the tiny flare of one of the matches examining the dungeon which

Brant's malevolent spite had devised for his prisoner. Leslie was lying on a plank bench, securely chained from the ankles to an iron ring firmly set in the stanchion over his head. His face was covered with blood, and he was white with the loss of it, though he revived fast when he had drained the water. By the time Nettle had lit her third match she had assured herself that his injuries were not dangerous, though she was equally convinced that to release him from his cruel durance was beyond her powers.

"Miss Maynardâ they have not harmed her? " gasped Leslie, as soon as he could speak.

His ministering angel hastened to reassure him, exaggerating sturdily in a good cause. " She's treated like a queen, with every deference and respect," said the girl, as she eased his cramped position. " Of course, she's worried about you. But see here, Mr. Chermside, we've no time for talking. I must get back to the saloon without being caught if I'm to be of any use. There are only us two women to stand between you and these fiends, and there's only God Almighty to stand between us andâ the end of the voyage. There's a bare chance that we may be able to send word into Plymouth, if I can fool or browbeat the captain, and I must be on hand to run that chance for all it's worth. You understand that I can't stay here with you?"

"Yes, go at once," murmured the injured man. " Never mind me, but for heaven's sake do what you can for her. Above all, let me beg of you not to harrow her with a description of all this."

The clank of the chain was eloquent of what he meant, and, promising to observe his wishes. Nettle withdrew. She regained the saloon after her adventure without meeting any one, and to Violet's eager questions she gave the evasively truthful answer that Leslie was recovering from his injuries, but that he was kept a close prisoner on the lower deck, and that she had had to converse with him without seeing him, leaving it to be inferred that she had not entered his cabin. By this means she avoided imparting the gruesome details of the Cobra's " black hole."

Violet steadily refused to retire to the sleeping cabin prepared for her, and the two girls spent what remained of the hours of darkness in the saloon together. In the grey of dawn Nettle went out on to the upper deck, self-possessed as usual, but despondent of success in the task before her. Brant was on the bridge, stumping to and fro to keep himself warm, for there was a chiuy nip in the breeze that had sprung up during the night. The httle atomy of a skipper seemed in an ominously genial mood, for at sight of Miss Jimpson's fluttering garments he leaned over the bridge-rail and hailed her.

"Hullo, my Weymouth linen-tearer! " he called down. " Shaking into your job nicely, eh? How's her Royal Highness the Maharanee of Sindkhote this morning? I've no doubt that she's confided in you about her brilliant destiny. The day will come when she wiu look on Simon Brant as a sort of fairy godfather."

Nettle looked round warily. Land was visible on the starboard beam, but so far off that its contour could not be distinguished in the blue haze that preceded sunrise. The distance between the coastline and the steamer, which was now running at full speed, was hardly compatible with an intention to make for an English port. Miss Nettle's Sunday walks and talks with a sailor sweetheart had given her a smattering of sea-lore, and she did not like the look of it. But she was there to assert herself, and did not mean to haul down her colours without striking a blow.

"Drat you for a fairy godfatherâ you and your Maharanees! " she exclaimed, with a well-feigned indifference to the larger issue, "It's me and my young man I'm thinking about. When do you run into Pl5miouth, so that I can send my letter?"

"Is it written? " Brant grinned down at her.

"That won't take five minutes. It wiu be ready long before you can put me within reach of a post office."

Brant grinned again as he followed the direction of her gesture towards the distant land.

"Then don't trouble to write it," he'croaked. " I admire your cheek so that Ld break orders for you if I could. But there's five thousand pounds to it, my dear, and the Cobra isn't going to call at Plymouth or any other port till we dump our cargo. If you want a young man, I've no doubt you can be accommodated on board, or if there's none here to your fancy, perhaps the lady will fix you up with a blacky husband in India."

Miss Jimpson's eyes glinted. " Is that your last word? " she said.

"As to calling at Plymouth? Yes, it's my very last word; and now you can start abusing me. I rather like it," came down the captain's shrill treble. And he added maliciously, "We passed the opening of Plymouth Sound an hour ago if it's any use to you to know it."

The girl turned on her heel without further waste of breath. She had never in her heart relied on the miscreant's promise, but she had clung to it as the last chance. And now their last chance had failed.

MR. and Mrs. Vernon Mallory were too accus-tomed to their daughter's erratic habits to be perturbed by her non-appearance at the dinner-table. It came natural to them to account for her absence by an invitation, given and accepted on the spur of the moment, to spend an informal evening at the house of some friend, and they would be quite satisfied if she turned up any time before midnight.

It was Mr. Mallory's practice on three evenings of the week to go down to the club after dinner to enjoy a little bridge or whist with some of his cronies, and this being one of the appointed nights he sallied forth about nine o'clock without giving Enid a second thought. If he had known that she was shut up in Travers Nugent's grotto, his opponents at the card-table would have had reason to rejoice; for, always a sound player, he was more than usually deadly that evening.

On going downstairs at the conclusion of the play, he came upon the lantern-jawed Mr. Lazarus Lowch, the foreman of the adjourned inquest. Mr. Lowch was seldom to be found at the club so late, and he was mooning about the ante-room with an abstracted air which promptly changed to purposeful alertness at sight of Mr. Mallory. A less shrewd observer than the old servant of the Foreign Office would have seen that he was the object of this unwonted visitation.

"I should be glad if you could spare me a few minutes, Mallory," said Lowch, in his funereal tones. " It is rather important and in a way personal to yourself. We are on the eve of some striking developments in this murder case, I think."

In common with most of his fellow-members, Mr. Mallory had no great liking for the dismal Lazarus, but, like the old war-horse he was, he pricked up his ears at the reason for the desired interview.

Glancing into the reading-room, he saw that it was unoccupied. " Come in here," he said shortly. " There is no one to overhear us."

"Your mention of overhearing brings me at once to what I want to say," Mr. Lowch proceeded ponderously. " The other day, in this very club, I overheard the most astonishing confirmation"

"I know. I saw you listening on the stairs when Nugent and Chermside were together in the card-room," Mr. Mallory could not resist the interruption. " Incidentally, you led me into a bit of eavesdropping too, for when I was at pains to inform myself who it was who was so engrossed in that conversation, I couldn't help hearing a few words of what was interesting you."

The sarcasm fell quite flat on Mr. Lazarus Lowch. His hide was as that of a rhinoceros to any such delicate irony. He was one of those who think that the end justifies the means, provided that the end in question entails the discomfort or disparagement of some unfortunate fellow-creature.

"Then if you heard it too, it will simplify my task," he went on serenely. " Mr. Mallory, it will be my duty at the adjourned inquiry to let daylight into the coroner about that fellow Chermside. He is the murderer, as sure as we stand here, and Nugent is shielding him because he wishes to avoid incurring the odium of having introduced a scoundrel into this peaceful spot."

Mr. Mallory could not entirely control the disgust which crept into his face at this open avowal of petty spite. But he was old diplomatist enough to control his voice. " That is not my view of the case," he said, with frigid pohteness. And then, as if stung by a scorpion, he for an instant lost the grip in which he was holding himself, and added quickly, "But why am I the recipient of yourâ what shall I call itâ confession? What have your spy-ings and deductions to do with me more than another?"

Mr. Lowch essayed to impart to his saturnine features an expression of sympathetic concern, and made a failure of the job. Indeed, the facial antics in which he indulged rather suggested the anticipation of malevolent triumph. " You surely, my dear sir, have not forgotten the first sitting of the inquest, and the evidence given thereat by Lieutenant Beauchamp? " he said, trying to adopt an ingratiating tone, but only succeeding in croaking hke a raven.

Mr. Mallory guessed what he was making for, but declined to provide the opening. " Well? " was all he said.

"Mr. Beauchamp admitted that on the night of the murder he was on the marshy close to where the body of Levison was foundâ at least, I elicited as much from him," said Lowch, warming to his work.

"Yes? " snapped Mr. Mallory, stiu refusing to be helpful.

"And that he heard a strange cry?"

"So I understood."

"Leaving an impression on the mind of the jury that he knew more of the occurrence than he chose to tell?"

"Not having been on the jury, it is impossible for me to answer that," Mr. Mallory rejoined drily.

Lazarus Lowch bowed slightly as though willing to make the concession, but conscious of his magnanimity in doing so. " Now Mr. Mauory," he went on, clearing his throat as a prelude to the real issue, "I do not mean any offence, but I am more or less in an official position in this inquiry. Mr. Beauchamp had a companion on that evening, and though the name did not transpire in court, it is common knowledge who that companion was. Gossip may be pernicious, but in a place like this it does not err. It will not be denied, I think, that it was your daughter. Miss Enid Mallory, who accompanied Lieutenant Beauchamp on that evening walk?"

Mr. Mallory contrived to keep the curb on himself. He was very angry, but lie wanted to know what was coming. Evidently this fatuous busybody had not yet sprung the full force of the tremendous battery with which he believed himself armed.

"There is no need for any mystery," Mr. Mallory replied suavely. " Enid and Reggie Beauchamp are engaged to be married. I am aware that they were together that evening, and with my entire sanctionâ if that is what you are driving at."

Mr. Lazarus shook his head, as one who is misjudged. " Really, no," came his protesting croak. " I should be the last to impute that kind of secrecy to Miss Mallory. On the contrary, I am sure that she would be quite open about anything of that sort. Nor would it be my business if she wasn't."

"Well, look here, Lowch, What the devil is it that she hasn't been open about that is your business? " exclaimed Enid's father, losing patience at last. " You have got something up your sleeve, I can see. Would it not be better to pull it down and have done with it? But I warn you first that you must be careful how you handle my daughter's good name."

The chronic scowl that made little children run when the local kill-joy approached lifted at the prospect of striking a blow beneath the belt. Lowch even smiled in sickly fashion as he struck it.

"I was on the golf hnks this afternoon," he began his indictment, " and I happened to see Miss Enid leave at the end of her round, as I thought, for home. Instead of accompanying her friends, however, she parted from them outside the pavilion, and went away alone in the opposite direction. In fact, entirely in the interests of justice, I watched her"

"Where from? " came the knife-hke interruption.

"From behind a gorse-bush," was the unblushing rejoinder. " She went into Mr. Travers Nugent's garden door, which, as you know, abuts on the moor. In a little while she was followed by a disreputable-looking man, who also disappeared into Nugent's garden. He, too, had been taking advantage of a convenient gorse-bush. The deduction is obvious. Nugent and his friend Chermside are deeply imphcated in the murder which I am officially investigating, andâ erâ it looks very much as if Miss Enid, innocently perhaps, is mixed up in it too."

Mr. Mauory's clean-shaven, ascetic face had gone as white as snow. The absence from dinner took on a new complexion by the light of this misbegotten information that she had ventured into the danger zone, and had been shadowed into it by one of its dangerous master's creatures. But the old man's sudden pallor was due as much to the contemptuous rage that overmastered him as to fear for his only child.

"You amazing idiot! " he cried. " Why couldn't you have told me the bare fact of my daughter having been to The Hut at first, without your string of silly insinuations? The delay may meanâ but there, words are wasted on such as you"

He turned to hurry from the room, and there in the doorway, where she had stood for the last half-minute, in defiance of the most stringent rule of the club, was the pretty subject of his anxiety, her sun-browned cheeks all seamed with bramble scratches, her corona of golden hair tumbling over her shoulders, her golf skirt in tatters.

"Don't look so scared, father," she said. " I'm all right. But that person has hit the correct nail about my being very mixed up in it, and you must come away at once, please. I have a lot to tell you."

Ignoring the incoherences of the inquisitive Lazarus, whom they left babbhng his willingness to overlook the infraction of the rule against the admission of ladies if they would only have their say out there, father and daughter passed out of the club into the quiet and deserted street. Alive to the value of every second, Enid condensed the narrative of her experience in the grotto into a few words, but she missed no vital point, from her imprisonment by " the bootlace man " to her escape twenty minutes ago by the aid of her fellow-prisoner, the French onion-seller. Nor did she omit to repeat the fantastic notions held by Pierre Legros, and the final mystery of Violet Maynard's voice being heard in the garden so late at night.

In his absorption in the momentous tale, Mr. Mauory came to a halt under a street lamp, for they had intuitively turned their steps up the hill homewards. Enid saw the dawn of a great fear in the well-chiselled features she knew so well. But she would not have abstained from slang on the Judgment Day.

"What is it, dad," she said, laying a grimy paw on the sleeve of her father's dinner jacket. " Have I enabled you to spot the winner?"

"Tliis is what I make of it on a rough calculation' Mr. Mallory replied. " The Frenchman's suspicions as to Nugent taking Louise Aubin away on a steamer are, of course, all moonshine. It is Violet Maynard who is being decoyed on to the steamer, with Cherm-side and the murder of that miserable Jew as items in a nice little plot of Nugent's. I have had inquiries made in London lately, and I find that he was thick with that Indian prince whose-name was coupled with Violet's in the society rags. I know Bhagwan Singh for an arrogant and pitiless libertine, Enid. That steamer is bound for India."

The old man and the girl stared at each other, comprehending the tragedy in all its naked horror.

"How long ago was it that you heard Miss Maynard passing through the grounds of The Hut on her way to the beach? " Mr. Mallory asked, breaking the strained silence.

"It must have been more than half an hour. I got o ut through the roof of the grotto almost immediately afterwards; then I went home, and, finding you out, ran down to the club as hard as I could," Enid rephed. Then, glancing up at her father's stern, set face, she said abruptlyâ

"What time does the telephone exchange close?"

"Hours agoâ at eight o'clock, and it's now nearly midnight," replied Mr. Mallory, looking at her as if she had gone daft.

"But if we made it all right with the exchange people we could get the wire, I suppose?"

"If you could persuade or bribe themâ certainly," said Mr. Mallory, with a touch of impatience. " But what good would it do? You cannot tele- phone to any one who can prevent Miss Maynard from going on board a steamer which, by your own showing, must have been reached by her long ago."

Enid Hnked her arm in her father's and began dragging him to the shop where the exchange was worked. " Come along and see," she exclaimed excitedly. " The worst of you clever people is that you never give any one else credit for a gleam of intelligence."

A couple of minutes later they had rung the bell at the private door of the shop, and were parleying with a sleepy individual at an upper window, who was at last induced to come down and open to them.

LIEUTENANT REGINALD BEAUCHAMP had been dining at the officers' mess of the Royal Naval Barracks at Devonport, and was making his way back to the dockyard, where he expected to find his boat's crew ready to put him aboard what Enid irreverently called his floating sardine-box. The Snipe was anchored in the Hamoaze, not far from the docks for the convenience of victualling.

Reggie, being a youth of convivial but temperate habits had dined wisely, to the extent of feehng at peace with all the world. The fine digestive powers of eight-and-twenty had served to assimilate the excellent fare provided by his hosts; he had enjoyed the society of many old comrades, whose pockets he had afterwards lightened at snooker pool; and the few glasses of wine he had drunk had done him no greater harm than to render him, out here under the stars, mildly sentimental about his little girl at Ottermouth,

"A rattling good sort, Enid, and no flies on her for a young 'un," he summed up his mental recapitulation of his sweetheart's virtues, "But if she tries to boss me afloat as well as ashore the little witch will have to look out for squalls, that's all."

As he passed through the dock gates his musings were suddenly but respectfully broken into by the police-constable who admitted him. Reggie was the kind of officer who is known by sight, and was remembered even by those who had but little to do with him.

"You're wanted on the telephone, sir," said the man, leading the way into the gate-house. " Sounds like a lady. Been holding the wire and ringing up every two minutes for the last half-hour."

Needless to say that there is an all-night telephonic service into his Majesty's dockyards, and for the commander of a " destroyer " to be rung up at any hour was nothing out of the common. All sorts of official instructions fly about irrespective of the sun's position in the heavens. Port admirals never go to bed, or if they do they leave some wakeful person to harass their subordinates with ill-timed change of orders. But a lady on the telephone at 12.30 at night was a novel experience, considering that the common or garden species has not access to telephonic communication in the small hours. It must be the port admiral's wife, Reggie told himself, doing her lord and master's dirty work for want of an available secretary.

"Who is it? "he asked, when he had been shown to the instrument, and had made his presence known to the other end.

The reply, which was also in the form of a question, fairly staggered him, "Is that you, Reggie? It's me, Enid. Yes, you old sillyâ Enid Mallory at Otter-mouth. The most awful thing has happened, and I want your help. You are the only person in the whole world who can help. Are you listening? Are you ready to attend to every word I say?"

"Go ahead! " was Reggie's laconic reply, the flippant gibe that rose to the tip of his tongue checked by the reflection that the Ottermouth exchange was not ordinarily open at that time of night."Allowing for Enid's fondness for exaggerated phrasing, there must be some foundation for the " something awful," or she would not have been able to get through to him on the telephone.

And when at last he took up his own parable and spoke his answer into the transmitter he knew that there had been no exaggeration at all, and that had she been so minded his saucy sweetheart might have used more lurid language without going astray. So impressed was he by what he had heard that he condensed his reply into the crisp sentencesâ

"What infernal scoundrels! All right, girlie; I'll do it if they break me. Off at once. Good night!"

Hanging up the receiver, and thanking the janitor of the gate, he threaded his way along the deserted quays to the stairs, where his boat was waiting for him.

"By George, but it's a tall order I " he repeated several times as his bluejackets bent to their oars. " Just as I'd settled it, too, that she should never interfere in professional duties. But, damme, it's a good cause to go down in, and perhaps old Maynard will buy me a penny steamboat if I get the sack over the job."

It was, indeed, a " tall order," coming from a minx in her teens to a naval officer enjoying liis hrst independent command, being no less than to employ one of his Majesty's ships on a private enterprise. An enterprise, too, which an ingenious counsel, before a judge of less than average intelligence, might very easily contort and twist into an act of piracy. None knew better than Reggie Beauchamp that for one ship to stop another on the high seas, and do things to her by armed force unbacked by supreme authority was a serious matter indeed.

And yet that was the task which the sunny-haired maiden, with eager red lips to the telephone at the other end of the county, had set him. So graphically had Enid done her bit of descriptive 'phoning that he was under no illusions as to what he had to do. Violet Maynard had been " carried off " in a large steam yacht which had just started from Ottermouth for India. In a few hours' time at most the yacht would be off Plymouth. Enid was aware that the Snipe was leaving port very early every morning for gun practice, and she implored him and threatened him in the same breath to intercept the yacht and rescue Miss Maynard. The few words which Enid had added as to the fate in store for the victim of the outrage had decided Reggie to make the attempt, even at the hazard of his career.

But he was by no means assured that he would succeed. The whole vile scheme must have been planned with deadly deliberation, and with the resources of vast wealth behind it. The vessel chosen for such a lawless errand would certainly be of high speed, and would avoid the regular steamer tracks. The little S iipe, for all her thirty-knot engines, might well be outpaced by the craft bought or chartered by Bhagwan Singh's agent; but before he could put that vital question to the test he would have to find herâ no easy matter in the crowded waters of the Channel, when he had no description of her to guide him, and he was entirely in the dark as to the course she would steer.

But in all things pertaining to his profession the young commander was astute beyond his years, and, having once decided to treat the Maharajah's yacht as a hostile ship, he made his calculations as thoroughly as if his promotion depended on stopping her. As soon as he stepped aboard his destroyer he routed out of their bunks the two men on whose co-operation he would have to rely, one being the only other commissioned officer, Second-Lieutenant Ellison, and the other the petty officer who was acting as gunner, a smart young fellow by name Parsons.

Having tersely explained to them the situation, and at greater length demonstrated that his would be the sole responsibility for what he proposed to do, he succeeded in rousing their enthusiasm, and from that moment he was loyally served by both. The three promptly constituted themselves a council of war in the poky little mess-room, and Ned Parsons was ready with some valuable advice.

"You'll pardon me, sir," he said with a friendly grin, " but if it was my girl instead of yours who was on that yacht I shouldn't fumble for my tacticsâ not for a single minute."

"It isn't my girlâ only a friend of my girl," Reggie corrected him. " But no matter as to that. What would the tactics be, Parsons? You were always a helpful chap."

"Well, you see, sir, I'm thinking, as every man on the ship will be, how to get you out of this without blame," replied the acting gunner. " I don't know the lady that these blackguards are making off with, but if it was my Nettle there'd be only one way to it. I'd lay the Snipe as close as may be to the yacht and trust the girl to do the rest. She'd holler for help, or clout the helmsman over the head, or do something that would justify us in interfering, and in asking questions afterwards. But there! she's a fair cough-drop, though only a draper's assistant at Weymouth."

Reggie had to smile in the midst of his dilemma. The idea of the stately Violet Maynard " clouting the helmsman," or even " hollering for help," was not to be imagined. Still, the notion of getting as close as possible to the yacht and trusting to some stroke of good fortune making it unnecessary to fire on her was a good one. Enid had mentioned on the telephone that by some inexplicable means Leshe Chermside was also on the steamer, and Reggie was as good a judge of men as he was a sailor. That there was some mystery about the reserved young soldier he was shrewdly convinced, but he did not think that his presence on the fugitive yacht was due to collusion with the enemies of the girl he was popularly believed to be in love with. Chermside, he argued, might be trusted, given the chance, to fill the part which would have fallen to Ned Parsons' " cough drop," if she had been on board.

"Very well," he said. " We will start as passive resisters anyway, and trust to luck afterwards. Now as to the course this steamer is likely to steer. She will want to keep clear of vessels bound for Plymouth which might report a craft making clown Channel at high speed. For that reason she would leave the Eddystone well to the northward, and she won't travel more than ordinarily fast at first. That being so, if we up anchor at once and choose the sea beyond the Eddystone for our firing practice this morning we ought to sight her before she has slipped away to the westward."

The necessary orders were given, and, the rumour spreading through the ship that some unorthodox adventure was afoot, the crew achieved a record in getting under weigh. In less than twenty minutes from the time of Reggie coming aboard the Snipe was steaming down past Drake's Island on to the broad bosom of Plymouth Sound, and so to the open sea. There were still three hours to dayhght, and Reggie's intention was to utilize them in reaching the spot where his judgment told him he would stand the best chance of intercepting the runaway.

The break of dawn found the destroyer patrolling the sea some ten miles south-west of the great lighthouse, in the comparatively lonely stretch of water that lies between the track of vessels making for Plymouth and the route of those whose destination is further to the eastward. In the immediate vicinity were only a few trawlers finishing the harvest of the night, but away to the north and south faint smears of vapour on the skyline showed the main lines of the Channel traffic.

And then, suddenly, from his place in the miniature conning-tower Reggie saw a great blur of black smoke crossing the southern edge of the vacuum he had selected for his hunting-ground. His binocu- lars flew to his eyes, and intuitively he knew that, though he had been right in his main conjecture, he had made a shght miscalculation of distance. The cause of the smoke-blur, magnified by his powerful lenses into a graceful steamer running southward at a high rate of speed, was neither a man-of-war or a liner, but a huge yachtâ just such a one as would have been selected for a long ocean voyage. And a cry of chagrin escaped him as he perceived that he had not taken the Snipe far enough out to stop her. She had in fact already passed him, and was now between him and the mouth of the Channel, thus being nearer to the open door of the trap he would have closed than he was.

"What's her speed? " he asked, passing the glasses to his second-heutenant. " I put it at about twenty-five."

The other, after a careful scrutiny of the receding vessel, gave it as his opinion that twenty knots was nearer the mark. Anyway, bar fog, the Snipe, with her thirty-knot engines, ought to be able to catch her in something under five hours.

"Yes, if she is doing her best now," said Reggie doubtfully. " She may be keeping a bit up her sleeve for an emergency. But we'll shove this old hooker along at her top notch anyhow."

So, with disrespect, do the boys to whom the nation entrusts its mosquito fleet speak of the Uttle spitfires they loveâ a disrespect which they would swiftly and haughtily resent if it was evinced by any but themselves.

A word to the man at the wheel caused the Snipe's ugly snout to swing round for her quarry, and then the engine-room gong clanged its sharp command, "Full speed ahead." Reggie, with his eyes glued to his glasses, watched like a cat for any increase of speed or suggestive manoeuvre on the part of the chase, but she held on her way as if supremely indifferent to, or unconscious of, the fact that she was being pursued by the destroyer.

"She's slowing down a trifle, isn't she, sir? " Parsons called up to his chief after the pursuit had lasted twenty minutes or so. " That doesn't look as if she had a guilty conscience."

Reggie was of the same opinion on both points. The yacht certainly was not travelling so fast as when first sighted, and her slackened speed suggested that her commander had no reason for showing his heels to a navy shipâ was, perhaps, moved by curiosity to learn why the spiteful little man-of-war was tearing after him. Whatever the cause might be the result was that in less than an hour the Snipe s lean black hull was within a mile of the yacht, and that objects on the deck of the latter were plainly distinguishable by the aid of Reggie's binoculars.

"By Jove! " he exclaimed, " there's a woman" on board right enoughâ about Miss Maynard's height, too. And, good God! she's waving to us Uke blue murder. But no, her face gets clearer every secondâ no, it isn't the lady we're after."

"We shall soon know what's wrong," said the second-heutenant. " The yacht has pretty nearly stopped. She's only keeping enough way on her for steerage."

The acting-gunner, Ned Parsons, who had also been examining the mysterious vessel through his own pair of cheap inferior glasses, here uttered an exclamation of combined incredulity and dismay.

"If you'd be so good, sir, as to let me have a squint through those binos of yours," he said, "I might be able to tell you something."

Reggie handed over his own splendid pair, the last word in telescopic art and a present from his mother. They had hardly bridged Parson's sun-browned nose when they were lowered again, and the gunner turned a face full of whimsical concern upon his commander.

"Asking your pardon, sir, but it's a funny thing," he said, " but that gal behaving like a semaphore yonder is my young ladyâ the one I was telling you of, seeing as there have been othersâ Miss Nettle Jimpson, of Grigg and Winter's drapery warehouse, Weymouth. How the Holy Moses you've gone and got her mixed up with the lady the Rajah has his eye on licks me, but what licks me most is how Nettle came to be aboard that steam yacht. She ought to be in her beauty sleep on Grigg and Winter's top floor, preparing for a busy day behind the underhnen counter."

"You're sure? " said Reggie, receiving the binoculars back.

"Sure as eggs," responded Parsons. " I could see that she was holding language towards the little monkey on the bridge, him being the captain, I reckon. That's Nettle Jimpson all over."

"Well," said Reggie, after a moment's reflection, " if your girl hails from Weymouth it's fair proof that that is the steamer we want, for Weymouth was her last port of call."

"Didn't I tell you, sir, that she was a cough-drop," rejoined Parsons excitedly. " You can stake your shirt she's bested that dirty little captain somehow. That's why he's stopping for us."

"But he isn't stopping for us," chimed in the second-lieutenant, and his dictum was emphasized by his slight hsp. " See, he's started at full-speed, and that means that he has scored the trick, for his rascally packet is fitted with turbine engines. He's been fooling us, sir."

Reggie Beauchamp was generally a clean-mouthed man, but the tea-party old ladies of Ottermouth would have banned him for evermore could they have heard the sultry oath that flew from his lips as he realized the truth of the assertion. Simon Brant, near enough now for his loathsome personality to be appreciated, was making insulting gestures at them with the hand which he had just withdrawn from the engine-room telegraph. And like a hound slipped from the leash the Cobra leapt forward and went racing to the south-west at forty knotsâ a speed which would quickly reduce her to a speck upon the horizon.

And after thatâ chaos!

AFTER letting himself in through the door from the moor into the grounds of The Hut, Travers Nugent paused irresolute. Should he punish that impudent hussy Enid Mallory by keeping her in the grotto all night and have her accidentally " found " in the morning, or should he go and release her now?

In either case he meant to throw the blame on Tuke, whom he could describe as an irresponsible lunaticâ or anything else that came into his head at the time. He need not be too nice about his excuses, for, after au, the girl, as a trespasser on his private property, was the real offender. It would be interesting to know what account she would give of herself.

On the whole he decided that it would be wiser to go and let her out at once, and so have done with an incident which he regretted as a blunder on the part of his too zealous follower. Mr. Vernon Mauory was a dangerous man to annoy, and, conscious as he was of his veiled antagonism, Nugent did not want to give him cause for open quarrel. Till the Cobra had reached her destination, and all traces of her had been obhterated, Bhagwan Singh's agent knew that he would have to walk warily indeed.

So he struck into the shrubbery, and on coming to the grotto unlocked the door with the key which Tuke had left in the keyhole. With a curious qualm that was not exactly alarm he saw that his kind offices would not be needed, and that the lies he had framed might remain unspoken. For the electric torch which he flashed on the gloomy interior showed it to be untenanted, while the gaping hole in the roof told of the way of escape.

Nugent stared at the improvised ladder of fertilizer kegs, and at the aperture over-head, with a thoughtful frown.

"That is hardly girl's work, yet she cannot have had help," he muttered. " If she had contrived to attract attention, no one would have been at the pains of breaking open the roof for her when the key was on the outside of the door all the time. Certainly she had hours to do it in; and she's more than half a boy."

He turned away, and, crossing the dewy lawn, entered his library by the unfastened French window. The shaded lamp had been lit, shedding a pleasant glow over the cosy bachelor room, and he gave a little sigh of content. He was fain to admit that he was tired with the day's exertions, and glad to be home again. He rang the bell, and the soft-footed Sinnett appeared.

"Mix me some whisky and soda water and give me a cigar," he said. " You have nothing out of the common to report?"

"Nothing that you do not know already, sir," was the reply. " Tuke will have informed you about Miss Mallory and the stone grotto."

"That is why I asked," rejoined Nugent. " The young lady has gone, and part of the roof of the grotto has been removed. You have heard or seen nothing that would account for it?"

"Nothing at all, sir. I have not been in the garden, but no sound reached me in the house. And I have been listeningâ in case she called out."

Nugent nodded, knowing the man's ways. " And that mad French seller of onions, he has not been here to-day? " he continued.

"No, sir; I haven't seen him for a day or two,"

"Thank you, Sinnett. Then that will be all now I think. Don't go to bed just yet. I may want you to go out and post a letter for the early collection."

The butler having retired, Nugent lay back in his luxurious lounge-chair and sipped his drink and watched the blue wreaths from his Havana coiling upwards. He was filled with a delightful sense of achievement. The thing which had seemed so easy at first, and had then threatened dire failure through Chermside's defection, had been carried out in spite of the temporary obstacle. That band of electric light stealing away across the dark sea had been the signal that he had won the game, the stakes of which were the Maharajah's twenty thousand pounds. Not bad pay for six months' work, of which his pawns had taken the most arduous share.

He did not anticipate any trouble from these pawns, except perhaps, from one. Leslie Cherm- side was safe on board the Cobra, and Bhagwan Singh might be trusted to see to it that he was never heard of again. That vain puppet, Louise Aubin, could do him no harm if she would, since she would believe, as all the world would believe, that Violet had voluntarily fled with her lover. And if the flighty French maid was disappointed in her preposterous aims with regard to himselfâ well, a little palm-grease would effectually staunch the bleeding of her fickle heart. Simon Brant, Bully Cheese-man, Tuke, and Sinnett were his accomplices rather than his tools, and they might be trusted to keep silence for their own sakes; if not, he knew enough to hang each or all of them. The crew of the Cohra were to be paid off in India, whence they would doubtless be scattered to the four winds of heaven; and, besides the captain and the mate, not one of them was aware of his connection with the affair.

The remaining exception, which had cost him more uneasiness than all the rest combined, was Pierre Legros. The onion-seller's insane and vindictive jealousy of himself in respect of Louise might grow into a factor to be reckoned with, entaihng unpleasant, if not actually perilous, consequences. Well, it would be surprising if he, Travers Nugent, the finished schemer, were not equal to dealing with a half-demented foreign sailor, whose position was, to put it mildly, somewhat insecure.

"A hint to the fair Louise to revert to her original suspicion would satisfactorily settle Monsieur Pierre Legros, without my having to make an open move myself," he mused aloud, as he summed up the situation.

Sitting there lazily in the lamp-glow, he felt like a general reviewing a victorious battlefieldâ " cleaning up the mess," as he put it to himself, with the advantage that there was no visible mess to clean up. He had scored another of those easy wins in the great game of lifeâ the game he had played so long and so successfully, with men and women as counters and gold as the final stake.

But as he murmured that last self-gratulation there came a sudden sound, very faint, but near at hand, to break his train of thought. He had left the long window open so that he could watch the fire-flies on the dew-frosted grass of the lawn; but he was not sure if the sound came from out there in the garden or from inside the room. It was an ill-defined sound, that might have been the intake of a heavy breath or the stirring of leaves gently moved by the sluggish air. The chair he sat in backed on to a beautifully-carved sandalwood screen which covered the angle at one side of the hearth, and he was smiling, half contemptuously, at an impulse to rise and look behind the screen, when it was checked and driven clean out of his head by quite a different sort of noise.

From the back premises, prolonged and imperative, there reached him the metallic clamour of the electric bellâ the bell at the front door. He glanced at the clock on the mantelpiece. It was half-past twelve. Who could be calhng upon him at that time of night?

A moment later Sinnett knocked and entered, and the man's usually imperturbable face, white and quivering, struck the keynote of danger. With an apologetic gesture, as though to convey that his outer defences had been forced, he stood aside and announcedâ

"Mr. Mallory, sir, and Sergeant Bruce. I told them I didn't think you would see them so late, but they insisted."

Nugent rose, somewhat heavily, to greet his visitors. He was wondering where was the flaw in the web he had woven. There must be a loose thread somewhere, or these men would not be here. That little devil Enid must have been complaining about Tuke's behaviour, and if that was all there was no harm done. So there was no trace of disquiet in the sleepy smile and stifled yawn which he affected.

"Ah, my dear Mallory; I was dozing, I think. And you, Bruce," he murmured, with a pleasant nod for the police-officer. " This looks very formidable. What is wrong? If it is nothing urgent, perhaps you will sit down."

Vernon Mallory ignored the civility. " I have just seen my daughter," he began, with a quiet directness that duly impressed its hearer. " She has been shut up in the grotto in your grounds all the afternoonâ whether with or without your knowledge is immaterial. The point is this: her imprisonment led to her learning that you had planned to entrap some female on to a vessel to-night, using Chermside in some unexplained manner, which, however, I can guess at, as a decoy. Now, a few moments before she escaped from your grotto Enid heard Violet Maynard's voice in your garden, apparently on the way down to the shore. I have telephoned to the Manor House, by favour of the exchange, and I am informed that Miss Maynard cannot be found in or about the house. What have you to say?"

Travers Nugent felt as if an icy finger had touched his spine. The indictment put forward with such inexorable precision comprised the very core of his whole vile plot. This terrible old man had even hinted that the means employed to drive Chermside on to the Cohra were no secret to him. This was a bolt from the blue which only a bold front could avert. Everything depended on the source of Enid Mallory's amazing discovery; till he had ascertained that, it would be childish to abandon his position.

He gave an amused little laugh. " Really it is too bad that I should be dragged into Miss Enid's home-made romance," he protested. " Did she give you chapter and verse, may I ask?"

"My daughter is not a fool," Mr. Mallory rephed quietly. " She happened to have a fellow-prisoner in the grotto, who had earlier in the day heard you discussing your plans for this evening with one of your creaturesâ the same man who shut her into the grotto. To be quite frank with ycu, Mr. Nugent, the sergeant accompanies me because I intend to charge you with serious crime."

â ' And anything you say will be taken down and used against you," the policeman interjected with official gravity. This was the first time the worthy man had had to arrest a gentleman, and he hardly knew whether he liked the job or not.

"Serious crime is a comprehensive phrase,"

sneered Nugent. " Means anything from pitch and toss to manslaughter. Come, sir! What do you charge me with?"

"With a crime one degree more heinous than the worst of those you have namedâ with murder, as an accessory before the fact," the accuser's clear voice cut the silence. " I charge you with indirectly inciting one Pierre Legros to kill Levi Levison under circumstances that would throw suspicion on Mr. Chermside. I charge you with using the state of terror to which you reduced that unhappy man in order to induce him to fly in such a manner that he might be deemed to have eloped with the lady whom you have been suborned to snatch from her home and friends for"

Mr. Mallory checked himself. His ancient training in international politics saved him from the indiscretion of naming the Indian prince who was behind the culprit. And, sub-consciously, he was also checked by a movement behind Nugent's chair. The great carved sandal-wood screen swayed, and was surely going fo fall forward on the man who was fingering his long moustache in a vain effort to frame an answer. But no, the screen righted itself, and Nugent's tongue moistened his dry lips into power of utterance.

"Very pretty, very pretty," he said, striving for calm. " But don't you see, my dear Mallory, that all your midnight madness topples down like a house of cards unless your daughter's informantâ her fellow-prisoner, as you call himâ is a credible witness. I will make you a small wager that he will never come ffjrward and tell the public the wonderful pack of lies with which he gulled that charming little girl of yours. I"

Again that movement in the screen behind Nugent's chair, and this time with results that shifted the centre of interest with starthng suddenness. Round the corner of the screen came Pierre Legros, gaunt and haggard, his fierce eyes in accord with the furious spasms that made a battle-ground of his unshaven face. Nugent, half turning in his chair to look up at the apparition which had drawn the gaze of the other two, broke off in the midst of his sneer with a sobbing catch in his throat.

"You say I not come forward to spik the truth? " the Frenchman began, in a voice that shook with emotion. " I was hide here to do that to you, and now these gentlemens shall hear the truth also. I only now learn it myself, for it is different from what I think till now. I say to myself, messieurs, that this scelerat desire to depart in steamer with

Louise Aubin, but I was wrong. What you say about Ma'amselle Maynard and that poor Jermicide, monsieur, show me all his wickedness as by flash of lightning. It is true, gentlemens, that I kill Levison, and that this Nugent tempt me to it."

The sergeant made a movement, but changed his mind. The man was in the mood to confess, and confession implied that he meant surrender. No need to lay hands on him till he had made a little more evidence. Mr. Mallory stood like a graven image watching Nugent, who, still preserving the half-turn he had made in his lounge chair, was staring up as if fascinated by the man at his shoulder.

"It is that I desire to make clean the name of a man who is innocent," Legros went on. " This Jermicideâ I not know him, I nevair spik with him, but he do me no wrong, and Pierre Legros is not cruel, messieurs. I would not that Jermicide suffer for me, who am guilty. Nugent, he send for me, and pretend he wish to save Louise from the so deceitful Levison, who made to admire her. He say, did Nugent, that Louise, whom as a boy in Brittany I love, will meet Levison on the marsh, and that he will persuade her to fly with him to London, where Levison will leave her in disgrace. Messieurs, I was madâ my brain was hot like fireâ Nugent he gave me the place and time of meeting, and I was there firstâ with my knifeâ that was all."

The tragedy in the concluding words was dramatic; even more so the silence that followed. The sergeant, good man, felt that the next move was with him, but he was single-handed, and had not bargained for having to convey two murderers to the station when he consented to accompany Mr. Mallory to The Hut. He coughed nervously to attract the attention of his two prospective prisoners, who seemed to have no eyes for any one but each other. Nugent, with his head twisted round, was looking up at Legros; Legros, behind the chair, was looking down at Nugent, his nostrils twitching strangely. The Frenchman, with innate politeness, understood, and obeyed the policeman's claim on his attention, turning a mild and friendly gaze on him.

"You know, you'll have to come along with me, both of you, after this," said the sergeant haltingly. " You won't give any trouble, Legros? " It did not occur to his mind that the gentleman would otherwise than " go quietly."

"Oh, yes," Legros answered gently. " We shall both of us give you nothing of the trouble, monsieur. I myself, Pierre Legros, will see that this wolf in the clothes of the sheep will go from this apartment with complacence the most profound."

Nugent essayed to rise, unsteadily, to his feet, but Legros shot out a brown hand on to his shoulder, and firmly pressed him back into a sitting posture.

"Stay there, chicn, till you have the orders to move," he snarled.

The eyes of the master of the house glittered bale-fully. " Really, sergeant, if you persist in coupling us in this absurd charge, I must ask your protection against this man," he protested. " I was going to ring the bell for my servant to arrange matters before leaving; perhaps you will kindly do it for me.

In answer to the summons Sinnett appeared, furtively scanning his employer's face for some sign of his wishes other than what he might hear in words. A quick look of intelligence passed between them, though Nugent's request sounded simple enough.

"There has been a stupid misunderstanding, Sinnett, which will entail my going with Sergeant Bruce tiu it has been explained," he said quietly. " I want you to put a few things in my handbag, pleaseâ just absolute necessaries, such as a change of linen and a tooth brush. You will know what I am most hkely to need. Don't keep us waiting, there's a good fellow."

The silent-footed servitor bowed and retired, and with an air of contemptuous resignation Nugent lay back in his chair. As he fingered his fair moustache his gaze, lazily contemplative, was all for the observant face of Mr. Mallory, whose attention was directed at the supple form of the French sailor. Legros himself had no eyes for any one but the man over whose chair he hovered, expectant and menacing. The sergeant kept shifting from one foot to another, emphasizing the silence with deprecatory coughs. He was probably the most uncomfortable man in the room.

The tableau was not unduly prolonged, for in less than three minutes Sinnett reappeared, carrying a small leather bag, which he brought to his master. Nugent placed it on his lap, and, idly fingering the catch, proceeded to instruct his servant on various household matters. The gardener was to be careful to attend to the heating of the orchid house; Nugent was minutely particular about ordering his dinner for the following night, as he had no doubt that after explaining to the magistrates at Exmouth he should be at home in good time to enjoy it. Dixon, the chauffeur, was to have the car at the police court at noon, so as to be ready to bring him back.

"And now, sergeant, I think I am ready to end this business," he concluded, looking blandly round. " It really galls me to give you so much trouble, but you, like my dear friend Mallory, have brought it on yourself, you see."

As he spoke the fingers which had been toying with the catch of the bag closed, snapping it open and diving swift as lightning into the interior. At the same moment Pierre Legros thrust his hand into the bosom of his blue blouse, and withdrew it just as Nugent hfted a revolver from the bag. There was a gleam of steel, and a great sheath-knife shot downwards like a streak of fire into the back of Nugent's neck ere he could level the weapon. The point of the knife came out above the collar-stud, and the Frenchman dragged it out with a vicious wrench as the corpse fell forward on to a magnificent tiger-skin rug.

"He make to shoot us all," said Legros calmly. " But most he make to shoot you, Monsieur Mallory, and I glad to save the father of the brave ma'amselle. But I have no love for the Ingleeshrope or theIngleesh madhouseâ so hon voyage, messieurs."

And before they could guess his intention the big knife was driven home, through the blue blouse, into his own tumultuous heart.

THE moment when the Snipe was first sighted from the bridge of the Cohra was immediately after Brant's refusal to put into Plymouth to allow Miss Jimpson to communicate with her " young man." The girl had just turned away to rejoin Violet in the saloon, when her quick ears caught the phraseâ

"There's a torpedo craft of sorts away to the nor'-east, and I'm jiggered if I don't think she's chasing us."

The speaker was Bully Cheeseman, who thus passed on his discovery to the captain. The latter took a long survey of the distant destroyer through his telescope, and then, cocking his eye to see if Nettle was within earshot, assented to the mate's statement in a string of imprecations, the pith of which was that the stranger was travelling thirty knots to their twenty.

Which was perfectly true as far as it went, though had he so wished Brant might have added that the Cohra, fast as she was moving through the water, was only going at half her possible speed of forty knots. But he was seized with a malicious desire to raise false hopes on the part of his prisoners, and he wanted Nettle to draw the inference that the war vessel could easily overtake them.

To add to the disappointment of the girl who had flouted him he sent verbal instructions to the engine-room to reduce the speed still further, with the result, as we know, that the Snipe began to rapidly creep up. Nettle, after taking in the situation as she beheved it to exist, ran excitedly into the saloon and imparted the glad tidings to Violet.

"The brute refused to call at Plymouth, but we've beat him for all that," she cried. " There's a Navy ship chevying us and catching up like mad. Your friends must have got news through to the admiral at Plymouth, and he's sent that dear dirty little boat after us. We shall soon be all right now, Miss Maynard."

The girl's cheery optimism was infectious, and Violet roused herself from the apathy of despair. " I hope so, dear," she said, leaping up from the couch where she had spent the miserable night. " Shall we go out on deck and watch Brant's discomfiture?"

But Nettle was wise according to her lights. I think it would be better for you to stay here," she advised. " The captain is such a beast that he might be rude if you showed on deck. He might hide you away somewhere till the danger was past," she added, remembering the ghastly inferno on the lower deck, to which Leslie Chermside had been relegated.

"Then how shall we know what happens?"

"I will keep you posted," Nettle rejoined eagerly. " It doesn't matter about me. Anyhow, I'll stay on deck till I'm stopped, and run in here now and again. What a lark it would be if that was the Snipe, with my Ned aboard. I was reading a tale the other day where they hung a pirate at his own yard-arm, which is a thing I don't believe they've got on this ugly up-and-down steamer. But I'll bet a pair of Grigg and Winter's best one-and-eleven-penny white kids that Mr. Edward Parsons, of his Majesty's destroyer Snipe, will find something to hang Captain Simon Brant on if that's him out yonder."

She skipped out on to the deck without waiting for an answer, and her stout heart pulsed with joy as she saw the lean, venomous hull of the warship much nearer than when she had entered the saloon. Her appearance was the signal for a violent flow of language from Brant, who had confided the secret of his mummery to the mate. Cheeseman, with his tongue in his cheek, played up to the lead of the apelike skipper, simulating the wildest terror of the oncoming destroyer.

Nettle leaned over the rail not far from the saloon door, into which she darted at brief intervals with the latest news. Each time she was able to improve on her last reportâ that she could make out objects on the deck of the pursuer clearer than before. But the highwater mark of ecstasy was reached when Nettle ran in with the announcement that it was indeed the Snipe which was after them, that she had recognized her Ned, and had received an answer to her signals.

"They'll be alongside in a few minutes," she cheered Violet. " Brant and Cheeseman are tearing their hair with rage."

But disaster followed swift on her triumph. Running back to the rail, she saw to her dismay that the distance between the two vessels had increased, and that the reason was not far to seek. The Snipe was steaming as fast as ever; but the Cohra was tearing through the calm sea at the pace of an express train. During Nettle's absence in the saloon Brant had rung down to the engineers to let loose the full power of the mighty turbines, and the fugitive was running away at ten knots an hour faster than the little war-vessel could follow.

From behind the wind-screen on the bridge the evil face of the captain peered down at the girl he had mocked with false hopes. Miss Jimpson was engaged in a dumb-show demonstration of her requirements to her lover, whose stalwart figure as he conversed with his officers in the conning-house of the Snipe seemed to be growing momentarily smaller. Her gestures did not conform to the correct motions as laid down in the gunnery drill-book, but they conveyed a fair impression of what she wanted.

Brant's sinister face was creased in a malignant grin. " Go it, my vixen," he jeered down from his eyrie. " Living statues ain't in it with you for showing off the female figure in the wrong pose. But you can spare your antics, for they'll never dare fire on us without orders, and them I'll lay a whale to a herring they haven't got."

Nettle bit her ripe red lip to keep back the retort that surged up. It was no time for wasting breath in futile insults, when something had to be done, and done cjuickly, if the tragedy implied by the escape of the Cobya was not to be consummated. But, if the Snipe would not use her guns or torpedoes, how was she, with the pluck of the devil but only the experience of a draper's girl, to enable a slower ship to catch a faster one? If only she had a man to help her, with knowledge equal to her determination.

And then, suddenly, it flashed across her brain that there was such a man on board if only she could get to him unobserved. Chermside, chained in the black hole on the lower deck, had risked life once already in Violet Maynard's cause, and would doubtless do so again, were he granted the opportunity. Or if that were not possible he might tell her what to do.

Deciding for the present not to harrow Violet with news of the altered situation, she spent a grudged five minutes in lulling suspicion by sauntering about the upper deck. The crew were too interested in the game their captain was playing with the destroyer to pay any attention to her movements, and, watching Brant out of the tail of her eye, she at last slipped down the companion stairs on to the main deck. In another minute she had clambered down the ladder into the obscurity of the lower deck, and so safely reached the den where Leslie was confined.

Revived by the water she had given him on her last visit, he was suffering now from little more than the discomfort of cramped limbs, and was able to follow intelligently the breathless story which the girl poured out to him. At the conclusion he groaned at his own impotence.

"If I was only free I might find a way of stopping the ship," he said. " Do you think if you could get tools you could draw the staple to which the chain is fastened?"

Nettle stood on tiptoe, and, after a careful scrutiny in the half light, was compelled to admit that the task, even with the aid of tools, would be beyond her powers. The staple, which was really a heavy iron ring, was firmly driven into the oak bulkhead, and without mechanical leverage would remain immovable.

"But what should you have done supposing you were loose? " she asked. " Find a pistol and shoot Brant and the mate? I am afraid I should miss them, or I'd have a try myself."

"You would have to shoot the whole crew," rephed Leshe, with a weary smile for her eagerness. " No, I should endeavour to hit upon some plan for damaging the engines. Those of a turbine steamer like this are a very delicate piece of mechanism, and a comparatively trifling injury, not necessarily entailing great violence, would do the trick. Ever such a little delay for repairs would enable the Snipe to catch up if they have allowed her to come as close as you describe."

"Then the sooner I set to work the better," said Nettle, knitting her brows, as the germ of an inspiration was born. " Good-bye, Mr. Chermside, and keep your pecker up. Miss Maynard doesn't know the hobble we're inâ still thinks we're on the point of being rescued."

"God bless you for that," Leslie flung after his departing visitor.

But she was already half-way to the ladder to the main deck. In her exploration of the steamer during the run from Weymouth on the previous day she had been idly interested in what Chermside had called the delicate piece of mechanism, so far as its throbbing pulses were visible through the dome-shaped skylight of glass on the upper deck over the engine-room. The glass was opaque and thickly corrugated, but a slide in the dome had been opened for ventilating purposes, and through the aperture Nettle had been fascinated by the antics of gyrating fiy-wheels and sucking piston-rods below. As she emerged into the free air of the upper deck she wondered if that convenient slide was open now.

But her first glance was for the pursuing warship, and it told her that the destroyer was a good half-mile further astern since her plunge into the bowels of the Cobra. Her second anxiet was about Brant, and she was comforted to see that he was not on the bridge. As a matter of fact he had gone to his cabin for breakfast, tiring of a joke which had lost its zest with Nettle's disappearance from the deck.

The glass dome over the engine-room was amidships, abaft the funnel. Thither she strolled with seeming carelessness, passing on forward without stopping, but satisfying herself as she did so that the ventilating slide was open. She walked nearly to the bows, and then, on turning to come back, struck a gold mine in the way of good fortune, though it took the humble shape of a zinc bucket full of cinders. It had been placed by the cook outside the door of the caboose, ready to be thrown overboard by one of the sailorsâ a duty which had been neglected in the excitement of the chase by the Snipe.

Miss Jimpson looked slyly round. With the exception of the look-out man in the bows the crew were all aft, watching the outpaced war vessel and exchanging ribald jests at the expense of her commander. But between the cook-house and the superstructure in which were the saloon and the state-rooms was an open stretch of deck in clear view of the bridge. And on the bridge Bully Cheeseman was stalking to and fro, in charge of the ship.

To reach her objective, the skylight over the engine-room, she would have to traverse the open space as far as the deck-house, when the latter would furnish some sort of cover; but the real danger would be after she had passed under the bridge into the after-part of the vessel. The eyes of the mate, who was watching the destroyer, were naturally turned in that direction. The only compensation was that the skylight was close to the bridge, and that she would not be long in the perilous zone of Cheeseman's vision before attempting her self-set task.

Anyhow, the danger had to be faced, and, timing her start so that the mate should be at the opposite end of the bridge from the side of the ship she selected for her rush. Nettle seized the bucket and raced for the shelter of the deck-house. She reached it without, so far as she knew, being observed, and so came to the alley under the bridge, where she waited till the lighter sound of Cheeseman's heavy steps overhead told that he had again receded from the side where she meant to operate.

' Looking' up, slie cauglit lliu Jurious eve ol Cheeseinau glaring at her along the blue barrel of his still levelled pistol."

A Trail or's Wooing

Then, with a queer little sob of expectancy, she darted forward to the glazed cupola and raised the bucket shoulder high over the open slide. As she stood there, her splendid young figure posed like a Greek goddess, a hoarse oath was yelled from the bridge, followed instantly by the simultaneous crack of a revolver and the ping of a bullet on the bucket. The missile glanced off and seared the bloom on the girl's cheek.

Looking up, she caught the furious eye of Cheese-man glaring at her along the blue barrel of his still levelled pistol. She smiled up at him, and before he could fire again she dumped the contents of the bucket into the whirling tangle of machinery below.

THE cinders fell with a clatter among the pistons and the fly-wheels, and Nettle Jimpson, too absorbed in watching results, forgot to notice that the ruffian on the bridge had not fired a second shot at her. For almost immediately there began a jarring and a scrunching in the engines which told that the delicate mechanism was trying to assimilate in its vitals the rough food she had fed it with, and found it indigestible. Cold-blooded murder was quite in Mr. Cheeseman's line as a preventive, equally so as a cure had that been possible. But those ominous sounds were eloquent of mischief done, and he was not the man to run his neck into a noose for the empty pleasure of revenge.

Three feeble revolutions followed, and then the engines stopped altogether, and the Cobra, quickly exhausting the way on her, lay like a log on the oily swell. Brant came running from his cabin, and at the foot of the bridge stairs met Cheeseman, who had descended, and the chief engineer, who had hurried up from below.

"How long will it take to pick the stuff out? " asked Brant, when he had been informed of what had happened.

"It will be from two to three hours before we can get a move on the ship," was the engineer's verdict. " A lot of the muck has got into the governors and cylinders. If I hadn't shut off steam sharp there'd have been such a mix up that the steamer would have had to dock for repairs."

This meant that the Snipe would be up with them in twenty minutes. Brant cocked a wicked eye at the oncoming destroyer, and then began to walk to where Nettle was still standing by the engine-room hatch. So diabolical was the menace on the horrible hairless face that the girl was fascinated as by a snake, and could not fly, though she knew that her fate was trembling in the balance. Brant addressed her very quietly.

"Will you jump overboard yourself, or shall I shoot you first and then throw you over? " he said, drawing a vicious Derringer from his hip.

Unflinchingly Nettle returned his stare. She even laughed a little. " I am certainly not going to commit the crime of suicide to save you from committing the crime of murder. I don't love you well enough for that," she rephed.

And then the swift thought came to her that the wretch meant to slake his thirst for revenge and trust to his cunning to avoid the penalty for it. When the warship's men boarded the Cohra he would have to explain the kidnapping of Violet Maynard and his treatment of Chermside as best he could, and he would doubtless have to suffer for it. But he had been guilty of no capital offence against them, and might contrive to throw much of the blame on other shoulders.

"I'll give you thirty seconds to reconsider that decision," said Brant, cocking and raising the pistol.

"It will be about long enough for you to reconsider yours," Nettle rejoined promptly. " You are relying on the crew of that destroyer not being aware that there are two women on board your ship. You think that if they saw me on deck they will have taken me for Miss Maynard, and that with her rescue assured they will ask no questions about me."

"And they won't," said Brant, though there was a note of interrogation in the assertion. " How are they to know that I shipped a d d wild-cat at Weymouth?"

"That is the hole you have dug for yourself to tumble into," returned Miss Nettle Jimpson sweetly. " You thought you were being funny at my expense in allowing the torpedo-boat to nearly catch you, but you overdid your joke, Captain Brant. That ship is the Snipe, with my young man as acting gunner. You let her come so close that we were blowing kisses to each other half an hour ago. When my Ned steps on to your deck five minutes hence he'll ask for me, if he's still the affectionate youth I've educated him into. And you won't be able to gammon him with any yarn about my having jumped overboard. He knows jolly well I'm not built that way."

Brant looked up at her, mouthing and gibbering; then he spat on the deck, and, turning away without a word, flung his Derringer over the rail into the sea.

And the helpless Cobra, her poison-fangs drawn.

lay on the swell like a wilted weed while the Snipe, vomiting black fury from her three funnels, swooped down.

Mr. Montague Maynard passed the decanter, and beamed upon his guestsâ Mr. Vernon Mallory and Reggie Beauchamp. Through the open window they could catch glimpses of Leslie Chermside, who had taken a lover's privilege to leave the dessert table early and join Violet on the Manor House lawn. Somewhere out there in the twilight there were also Aunt Sarah and Enid Mallory, the elder lady listening for about the twentieth time to the adventure of the 3'ounger in the grotto at The Hutâ an adventure which had been the direct cause of her great-niece's rescue.

"Roughly speaking, then, this is what you make of it," Mr. Maynard was saying. " From first to last Levison's murder was a job put up by Travers Nugent in order to render my future son-in-law the bait for getting Violet on to the Cobra?"

"That is established from the mouth of Pierre Legros, from Brant's brutal frankness to Violet, and by Nugent's evident intention to kill Sergeant Bruce, Legros and myself the other night," replied Mr. Mallory. " He would not have embarked on wholesale murder, which must have been brought home to him, unless he had known that the game was up, and that his only resource was flight."

"Yes, that is all clear enough," the Birmingham magnate assented. " But what I am most concerned with, as I like the chap and he is going to marry my daughter, is Chermside's extraordinary conduct in being frightened into bolting on to that infernal steamer. There seems to be no rhyme or reason to it, he being obviously innocent of the crime. I shouldn't like to think that Violet was going to marry a fool or a coward."

The old civil servant made patterns on his plate with walnut shells before replying. He was thinking of an interview he had had with Leshe Chermside that morning, at which the young ex-Lancer had made full confession to him of his early implication in the plot, and had sought advice as to what as a man of honour he ought to do. Mr. Mallory, after very earnest consideration, had given that advice, and it was in sustentation of it that he now replieda

"My view is thisâ that Chermside was duped by Nugent into becoming an accomplice in this atrocious scheme, without in the least understanding the enormity of the offence he was to aid, that he discovered how and for what a vile purpose he had been duped, and that in the meanwhile, having fallen in love with your daughter, he was terrified lest his comphcity should come out. Nugent then deliberately engineered the murder of Levison so that he might play upon Chermside's fearâ not of the legal consequences of arrest for murder, but of the revelations that would follow, Levison, I have reason to beheve, having played a minor part in the conspiracy. The affair fell out exactly as Nugent anticipated, and Chermside lost his head and ran awayâ with the results we know."

Montague Maynard puckered his brows in a judicial frown quite unsuitable to his jovial features. But the cloud passed.

"Yes," he exclaimed, " the boy has acted straight enough, though he would have been wiser to put us on our guard instead of trusting that Nugent had abandoned the plot. He tells me, however, that he intended to write me about it at the first opportunity, and I have not found him other than truthful. I remember when I tackled him first about Violet, he confessed that the yacht, waiting to take him on that accursed cruise, and credited to him by local gossip, was not his property. No false pretence about that."

"I am sure he tried to act for the best in a very difficult position," Mr. Mallory interposed quietly.

"And his behaviour on the Cohra in tackling, single-handed and unarmed, the crew of the launch, shows he's got grit," Maynard continued warmly. " I reckon we'll leave it at that. He has tried to chuck away his life to save Vi; he has suffered the tortures of the damned for her, and as he's good enough for her, he shall be good enough for me."

Mr. Mallory heaved a sigh of content, which, coming from him, was not of the kind that is noticed. He had achieved his purpose without betraying a confidence.

"You arranged the hushing-up process deuced cleverly," the screw manufacturer went on. " All that transpired at the adjourned inquest on Levison, I understand, and at those on Legros and Nugent, was that Nugent, had been engaged in a plot to kidnap Violet, and that it had failed. Some idiot in Parliament might have raised Cain if Bhagwan Singh's connection with it had been made pubuc."

Mr. Mallory smiled. " I was certainly careful not to let the worthy sergeant into the secret of the Maharajah's iniquity," he said. " But we have chiefly Beauchamp here to thank for the veil we have been able to draw over the inner history of the conspiracy. His prompt action in putting to sea, and his judicious handhng of Brant after boarding the Cobra, crowned my humble efforts with success. The idea of letting Brant and his crew of cut-throats go scot-free, with the advice to finish their voyage and demand payment and explanations from Bhagwan Singh, was a masterpiece which augurs well for our young friend's career. One can imagine the kind of payment that the Maharajah will mete out when he gets that pack of failures into his dominions."

"I had to handle the wicked httle demon judiciously to save my own skin," said Reggie modestly. " I had no orders to rove the seas in search of lost heiresses or eloping couples, and my career might have been nipped in the bud if I'd taken the Cobra into Devonport as a prize. My lords of the Admiralty are not kind to independent action by junior officers, and if I had pleaded that I had been ordered to sea by Enid it would hardly have mended matters. But as we are apportioning rewards and punishments, we mustn't forget the real heroine of the pieceâ Nettle Jimpson, my gunner's best girl. If she hadn't fired that bucketful of cinders into the engines we shouldn't be all sitting here shaking hands with ourselves to-night."

Montague Maynard filled his glass and drained it incontinently. " Grigg and Wynter, drapers, of Weymouth, ceased to exist as a firm to-day," he remarked oracularly.

"As to how? " demanded Reggie, genuinely puzzled.

"I have bought their business as a little reward for Miss Jimpson," the man of money replied. " She will have the transfer as soon as ever my lawyers can put it through."

"Then you've done his gracious Majesty an ill turn in losing him the most promising acting-gunner in the service," said Reggie. " Ned Parsons, as his wife's principal shop-walker, will be a standing disgrace to you, Mr. Maynard, to the end of your days. His only prospect of safety is that his future spouse is not, from what I saw of her, the sort of person to tolerate flirtations with the girls behind the counter. But while you are making everybody happy with that magic touch of yours, sir, what are you doing for Mr. Lazarus Lowch, the champion juryman. I hear that he was foreman at the other two inquests, as well as finishing up Levison."

The millionaire laughed boisterouslyâ so boisterously that it devolved upon Mr. Mallory to explain.

"Mr. Lazarus Lowch is as tame as a sucking dove," he said, with mock solemnity. " He has had his claws clipped and has been taken into custody by that sly little mischief-maker. Mademoiselle Louise Aubin."

"Good Lord! " cried Reggie. " Miss Maynard's maid?"

"Yes; she is a very astute young lady, and the only actor in our drama whose actions have been not quite clear to me, except that she was a bone of contention between Pierre Legros and Levison, and also figured as one of Nugent's puppets. Be that as it may, she contrived to get hold of Lowch, who, as you know, is a widower, as he was hanging about outside the pohce-station ready to get summoned on the two later inquests. She set her cap at him so effectually that he gave the coroner no trouble, and proposed to her the same evening."

"It must have been her figure that fetched him," said Reggie, with the air of a connoisseur. " She's great on corsage."

"And the figures in old Lowch's pass-book fetched her, I expect," roared Montague Maynard, rising. " Come, let's go and cool off on the lawn. It is time some one put a stopper on old Sally Dymmock. She's worrying the love-birds, and demoralizing that girl of yours, Mallory."

Butler Tanner, The Selwood Printing Works, Frome, and London.

The Daily Mail. â " A triumph of cheery, resolute narration. The story goes along like a wave, and the reader with it."

STRONG MAC. 6s.

The Morning Post. â " At the very outset the reader is introduced to the two leading characters of what is truly a drama of real life. So vividly s the story told that it often reads like a narrative of things that have actually happened."

LITTLE ESSON. 6s.

The Scarborough Post. â " One of the most popular of Mr. Crockett's books since ' Lilac Sunbonnet.""

MAX PEMBERTON

PRO PATRIA. 6s.

The Liverpool Mercury. â " A fine and distinguished piece of imaginative writing; one that should shed a new lustre upon the clever author of ' Kronstadt.""

CHRISTINE OF THE HILLS. 6s.

The Daily Mail. â " Assuredly he has never written anything more fresh, more simple, more alluring, or more artistically perfect."

A GENTLEMAN'S GENTLEMAN. 6s.

The Daily Chronicle. â " This is very much the best book Mr. Pember-ton has so far given us."

THE GOLD WOLF. 6s.

Illustrated London News. â " From the beginning Mr. Pemberton weaves his romance with such skil 1 that the tangled skein remains for long unravelled. marked by exceptional power, and holds the attention firmly."

THE LODESTAR. 6s.

The Standard. â " It impresses us as an exceedingly poignant and effective story, true to real life. Written with cleverness and charm."

ROBERT BARR

YOUNG LORD STRANLEIGH. 6s.

The World. â " Mr. Barr gives us a remarkable sample of his power of blending so deftly the bold imaginative with the matter-of-fact as to produce a story which shall be at once impossible and convincing. That a feat of this kind, cleverly accomplished, is attractive to most novel readers goes without saying, and his latest work is certain to please."

THE LONG ARM. 6s.

"The Long Arm " is unlike any of Mr. Oppenheim's other popular stories. The hero, Mannister, a powerfully drawn character, is the victim of a cruel plot of a band of conspirators. Undaunted by the great odds against him, he proceeds to revenge himself. The ingenuity of device and boldness of execution of his astounding adventures keep the reader enthralled to the very end.

THE GOVERNORS. 6s.

The Globe. â "'The Governors' is by Mr. E. P. Oppenheimâ need more be said to assure the reader that it is as full of ruses, politics and sensations as heart could desire."

THE MISSIONER. 6s.

The Huddersfield Examiner. â " We have nothing but the very highest praise for this book. It is a remarkable success for Mr. Oppenheim in every way. Deeply engrossing as a novel, pure in style, and practically faultless as a literary work."

CONSPIRATORS. 6s.

The Daily Telegraph. â " The author must be congratulated on hav ing achieved a story which is full of liveliness."

THE SECRET. 6s.

The Standard. â " We have no hesitation in saying that this is the finest and most absorbing story that Mr. Oppenheim has ever written. It glows with feeling; it is curiously fertile in character and incident, and it works its way onward to a most remarkable climax."

A LOST LEADER. 6s.

The Daily Graphic. â " Mr. Oppenheim almost persuades us into the belief that he has really been able to break down the wall of secrecy which always surrounds the construction of a Cabinet, and has decided to make an exposure on the lines of a well-known American writer. He also touches upon the evils of gambling in Society circles in a manner which should be applauded by Father Vaughan, and, in addition, treats us to a romance which is full of originality and interest from first to last."

MR. WINGRAVE, MILLIONAIRE. 6s.

The British Weekly. â " Like good wine Mr. Oppenheim's novels need no bush. They attract by their own charm, and are unrivalled in popularity. No one will read this present story without relishing the rapid succession of thrilling scenes through which his characters move. There is a freshness and unconventionality about the story that lends it unusual attractiveness."

A MAKER OF HISTORY. 6s.

The Standard. â " Those who read ' A Maker of History ' will revel in the plot, and will enjoy all those numerous deft touches of actuality that have gone to make the story genuinely interesting and exciting."

E. PHILLIPS OPPENHEIM-con nued.

THE MASTER MUMMER. 6s.

The Dundee Advertiser. â " It is a beautiful story that is here set within a story. A remarkable novel such as only E. Phillips Oppenheim can write."

THE BETRAYAL. 6s.

The Dundee Advertiser. â " Mr. Oppenheim's skill has never been displayed to better advantage than here. He has excelled himself, and to assert this is to declare the novel superior to nine out of ten of its contemporaries."

ANNA, THE ADVENTURESS. 6s.

The Daily News. â " Mr. Oppenheim keeps his readers on the alert from cover to cover and the story is a fascinating medley of romance and mystery."

THE YELLOW CRAYON. 6s.

The Daily Express. â " Mr. Oppenheim has a vivid imagination and much sympathy, fine powers of narrative, and can suggest a life history in a sentence. As a painter of the rough life of mining camps, of any strong and striking scenes where animal passions enter, he is as good as Henry Kingsley, with whom, indeed, in many respects, he has strong points of resemblance."

A PRINCE OF SINNERS. 6s.

Vanity Fair. â " A vivid and powerful story. Mr. Oppenheim knows the world and he can tell a tale, and the unusual nature of the setting in which his leading characters live and work out their love story gives this book distinction among the novels of the season."

THE TRAITORS. 6s.

The Athenaeum. â " Its interest begins on the first page and ends on the last. The plot is ingenious and well managed, the movement of the story is admirably swift and smooth, and the characters are exceedingly vivacious. The reader's excitement is kept on the stretch to the very end,"

A MILLIONAIRE OF YESTERDAY. 6s.

The Daily Telegraph. â " We cannot but welcome with enthusiasm a really well-told story like ' A Millionaire of Yesterday.'"

THE SURVIVOR. 6s.

The Nottingham Guardian. â " We must give a conspicuous place on its merits to this excellent story. It is only necessary to read a page or two in order to become deeply interested."

THE GREAT AWAKENING. 6s.

The Yorkshire Post. â " A weird and fascinating story, which, for real beauty and originality, ranks far above the ordinary novel."

AS A MAN LIVES. 6s.

The Sketch. â " The interest of the book, always keen and absorbing, is due to some extent to a puzzle so admirably planned as to defy the penetration of the most experienced novel reader."

E. PHILLIPS OPPENHEIMâ con nued.

A DAUGHTER OF THE MARIONIS. 6s.

The Scotsman. â " Mr. Oppenheim's stories always display much melodramatic power and considerable originality and ingenuity of construction. These and other qualities of the successful writer of romance are manifest in ' A Daughter of the Marionis." Full of passion, action, strongly contrasted scenery, motives, and situations."

MR. BERNARD BROWN. 6s.

The Aberdeen Daily Journal. â "The story is rich in sensationa incident and dramatic situations. It is seldom, indeed, that we meet with a novel of such power and fascination."

THE MAN AND HIS KINGDOM. 6s.

The Freeman's Journal. â "The story is worthy of Merriman at his very best. It is a genuine treat for the ravenous and often disappointed novel reader."

THE WORLD'S GREAT SNARE. 6s.

The World. â " If engrossing interest, changing episode, deep insight into human character and bright diction are the sine qua non of a successful novel, then this book cannot but bound at once into popular favour. It is so full withal of so many dramatic incidents, thoroughly exciting and reahstic. There is not one dull page from beginning to end."

A MONK OF CRUTA. 6s.

The Bookman. â " Intensely dramatic. The book is an achievement at which the author may well be gratified."

MYSTERIOUS MR. SABIN. 6s.

The Literary World. â " As a story of interest, with a deep-laid and exciting plot, this of the ' Mysterious Mr. Sabin ' can hardly be surpassed."

NORMAN INNES

MY LADY'S KISS. 6s.

A Seventeenth Century Romance.

The Sheffield Independent. â "The book is imbued with the spirit of the times. The story goes with a surge and a stir that makes the blood of the reader quicken and his spirit keep pace."

THE LONELY GUARD. 6s.

Dublin Daily Express. â " The author is to bo congratulatod on this book; it is one of the best that has come under oiu: notice for a con-sidrable period. It is not only full of stirring incident, but highly instructive as to frontier life in the Aubtria of Maria Thertsa's day."

THE CRIMSON BLIND. 6s.

The Sheffield Telegraph. â " ' The Crimson Blind ' is one of the most ingeniously conceived ' detective ' stories we have come across for a long time. Each chapter holds some new and separate excitement. It is the sort of story that one feels compelled to read at a sitting."

THE CARDINAL MOTH. 6s.

The British Weekly. â " A brilliant orchid story full of imaginative power. This is a masterpiece of construction, convincing amid its unlikeliness, one of the best novels of the season."

THE CORNER HOUSE. 6s.

The Western Morning News. â " The book is crammed with sensation and mystery, situation piled on situation until one is almost bewildered. It is an excellent romance which will be eagerly read."

THE WEIGHT OF THE CROWN. 6s.

The Dublin Daily Express. â " Mr. F. M. White is one of the princes of fiction. A stirring tale full of the spice of adventure, breathless in interest, skilful in narrative. Who could refrain from reading such a story?"

THE SLAVE OF SILENCE. 6s.

The Sheffield Telegraph. â " Attention is arrested at the outset, and so adroitly is the mystery handled that readers will not skip a single page."

A FATAL DOSE. 6s.

The Standard. â " This novel will rank amongst the brightest that Mr White has given us."

CRAVEN FORTUNE. 6s.

Daily Telegraph. â " A tale of extraordinary complexit ', ingeniously conceived, and worked out to a conventionally happy conclusion, through a series of strange and thrilling situations, which command and hold the reader's attention to the end."

THE LAW OF THE LAND. 6s.

Daily Telegraph. â " Mr. White's new novel may be strongly recommended. It contains enough surprises to whip the interest at every turn."

A CRIME ON CANVAS. 6s.

This is a story of mysterious crime and it is interesting to recall that when published serially prizes were offered to the readers who guessed the solution of the many mysteries divulged in the development of the story. It is a deeply engrossing tale.

JOURNEY'S END. 6s.

The Court Journal. â " Surprisingly fresh, abounding in touches of observation and sentiment, while the characters are drawn with exceptional skill, the ' red-haired young woman ' being a haunting figure."

MONSIGNY. 6s.

The Daily Telegraph. â " The novel is admirable, the idea is very cleverly worked out, and is of an interesting character. The book is worthy of much praise."

THE GARDEN OF LIES. 6s.

The Daily News. â " This novel is far in advance of anything that Mr. Forraan has hitherto accomplished. ' The Garden of Lies ' belongs to that class of story which touches the heart from the first. It contains scenes which are alive with real passion, passages that will stir the blood of the coldest, and whole chapters charged with a magic and a charm. It is a real romance, full of vigour and a clean, healthy life."

TOMMY CARTERET. 6s.

The Daily Chronicle. â " This is a fine book, thoroughly fine from start to finish. We willingly place our full store of compliments on Mr. Forman's splendid and successful book."

BUCHANAN'S WIFE. 6s.

The Daily Telegraph. â " ' Buchanan's Wife ' may be regarded as another success for an already successful author. It contains all the elements to attract, and is WTitten in such a graceful manner that the reader is held delighted and enthralled to the end."

A MODERN ULYSSES. 6s.

People's Saturday Journal. â " Full of exciting incidents handled in a bright, crisp style."

THE QUEST. 6s.

A tense, emotional and romantic drama, surpassing in interest even that notably successful novel and play " The Garden of Lies " by the same author.

HAROLD BINDLOSS

THE LIBERATIONIST. 6s.

Morning Leader. â " This is the author's best novel, and is one which no lover of healthy excitement ought to miss."

HAWTREY'S DEPUTY. 6s.

The action of this novel once again takes place in Canadaâ a country he has made especially his ownâ and in this story is a plot of quite unusual power and interest.

A FATAL LEGACY. 6s.

The Scotsman. â " In all the annals of fiction a more ingenious or startlingly original plot has not been recorded."

RAINBOW ISLAND. 6s.

The Literary World. â " Those who delight in tales of adventure should hail ' Rainbow Island ' with joyous shouts of welcome. Rarely have we met with more satisfying fare of this description than in its pages."

THE ALBERT GATE AFFAIR. 6s.

The Birmingham Post. â " Will worthily rank with ' The Fatal Legacy ' and ' Rainbow Island ' both books full of wholesome excitement and told with great ability. The present volume is an excellent detective tale, brimful of adventure. Told in Mr. Tracy's best style."

THE PILLAR OF LIGHT. 6s.

The Evening Standard. â " So admirable, so living, so breathlessly exciting a book. The magnificent realism of the lighthouse and its perils, the intense conviction of the author, that brings the very scene he pictures before the reader's eyes with hardly a line of detached description, the interest of the terrible dilemma of the cut-off inhabitants of the ' Pillar ' are worthy of praise from the most jaded reader."

HEART'S DELIGHT. 6s.

The Dundee Advertiser. â " The name of Louis Tracy on the cover of a volume is a sufiicient guarantee that the contents are worthy of perusal. His latest novel, ' Heart's Delight," establishes more firmly than ever the reputation which he founded on ' The Final War '; like that notable book it has a strong martial flavour."

THE WHEEL 0' FORTUNE. 6s.

The Publisher's Circular. â " Conan Doyle's successor, Louis Tracy, has all the logical acuteness of the inventor of Sherlock Holmes without his occasional exaggeration."

FENNELLS' TOWER. 6s.

North Devon Journal. â " An absorbing tale of love and crime from the clever pen of Louis Tracy. The secret of the crime which forms the basis of the plot is most skilfully covered, and the solution is a genuine surprise."

THE SILENT BARRIER. 6s.

"The Silent Barrier " is a breezy romance of love and adventure in Switzerland, comparable to an adventure story by the late Guy Boothby.

SIR Wm. MAGNAY. Bart.

THE RED CHANCELLOR. 6s.

Lloyd's News. â " A story full of action, with its characters strongly drawn. Adventure and hairbreadth escapes abound; the style is refreshingly crisp, and the book altogether is one that can be most heartily recommended."

FAUCONBERG. 6s.

The Field. â " The book has a grip, and should be a success. The ultimate fate of Fauconberg is always in doubt from the beginning to the unexpected ending."

THE MASTER SPIRIT. 6s.

The Court Journal. â "A capital story. The intensely interesting situation is developed with much ingenuity and power. A really fascinating novel."

THE MYSTERY OF THE UNICORN. 6s.

The Glasgow Herald. â " This work illustrates the author's dexterity in plot-construction, his skill in setting appropriate dialogue, and the facility with which he is able to develop and embellish an engaging narrative."

THE PITFALL. 6s.

People's Saturday Journal. â "In 'The Pitfall," Sk Wm. Magnay has given to the world his best work, for not only is the story of an engrossing character, but it has the virtue of being completely off the beaten track."

THE RED STAIN. 6s.

The Dundee Courier. â " One cannot but admire the adroit manner in which the author continues the mystery; how he eventually straightens things out is quite clever, and well worth reading."

HEADON HILL

THE HIDDEN VICTIM. 6s.

The Aberdeen Journal. â " To those who revel in sensational fiction, marked by hterary skill as well as audacity and fertility of invention, this story can be confidently commended."

RADFORD SHONE. 6s.

The Dundee Advertiser. â " I recall ' The Hidden Victim ' as one of the best of Mr. Hill's books, and alongside it I shall now put ' Radford Shone.'"

HER SPLENDID SIN. 6s.

Perthshire Courier. â " Headonhill gives us good reading with plenty of thrilling incident. He has never told an intensely absorbing story with more dramatic directness than this one. The story is admirably written, the interest never flagging."

A TRAITOR'S WOOING. 6s.

A splendid story which will be much liked by readers who care for â ' A Woman in White " and similar stories.

THE RACE OF LIFE. 5s.

The English Review.â " Ahead even of Mr. Cutcliffe Hyne and Sir Conan Doyle, Mr. Boothby may be said to have topped popularity's pole."

FOR LOVE OF HER. 5s.

The Court Journal. â " This book shows vivid imagination and dramatic power. Moreover, sketches of Australian life, from one who knows his subject, are always welcome."

THE CRIME OF THE UNDER SEAS. 5s.

The Speaker. â " Is quite the equal in art, observation, and dramatic intensity to any of Mr. Guy Boothby's numerous other romances, and is in every respect most typical of his powers."

A BID FOR FREEDOM. 5s.

The Sheffield Telegraph. â " As fascinating as any of its forerunners, and is as finely handled. A fully written romance, which bristles with thrilling passages, exciting adventures, and hairbreadth escapes."

A TWO-FOLD INHERITANCE. 5s.

Punch. â "Just the verv book that a hard-working man should read for genuine relaxation. This novel is strongly recommended by the justly appreciating ' Baron de Bookworms.'"

CONNIE BURY. 5s.

The Birmingham Gazette. â " One of the best stories we have seen of Mr. Boothby's."

THE KIDNAPPED PRESIDENT. 5s.

Public Opinion. â " Brighter, crisper, and more entertaining than any of its predecessors from the same pen."

MY STRANGEST CASE. 5s.

The Yorkshire Post. â " No work of Mr. Boothby's seems to us to have approached in skill his new story. The reader's attention is from first to last riveted on the narrative."

FAREWELL, NIKOLA. 5s.

The Dundee Advertiser. â " Guy Boothby's famous creation of Dr. Nikola has become familiar to every reader of fiction."

MY INDIAN QUEEN. 5s.

The Sunday Special.â " A vivid story of adventure and daring, bearing all the characteristics of careful workmanship."

LONG LIVE THE KING. 5s.

The Aberdeen Free Press. â " It is marvellous that Mr. Boothby's novels should all be so uniformly good."

GUY BOOTUBYâ continued.

A PRINCE OF SWINDLERS. 5s.

The Scotsman. â " Of absorbing interest. The exploits are described in an enthralling vein."

A MAKER OF NATIONS. 53.

The Spectator. â "'A Maker of Nations' enables us to understand Mr. Boothby's vogue. It has no lack of movement or incident."

THE RED RAT'S DAUGHTER. 5s.

The Daily Telegraph. â " Mr. Guy Boothby's name on the title-page of a novel carries with it the assurance of a good story to follow."

LOVE MADE MANIFEST. 5s.

The Daily Telegraph. â " A powerful and impressive romance. One of those tales of exciting adventure in the confection of which Mr. Boothby is not excelled by any novelist of the day"

PHAROS THE EGYPTIAN. 5s.

The Scotsman. â " This powerful novel is weird, wonderful, and soul-thrilling. There never was in this world so strange and wonderful a love story."

ACROSS THE WORLD FOR A WIFE. 5s.

The British Weekly. â " This sturing tale ranks next to ' Dr. Nikola ' in the list of Mr. Boothby's novels. It is an excellent piece of workmanship, and we can heartily recommend it."

A SAILOR'S BRIDE. 5s.

The Manchester Courier. â " Few authors can depict action as brilliantly and resourcefully as the creator of Dr. Nikola.""

THE LUST OF HATE. 5s.

The Daily Graphic. â "Mr. Boothby gives place to no one in what might be called dramatic interest, so whoever wants dramatic interest let him read ' The Lust of Hate '"

THE FASCINATION OF THE KING. 5s.

The Bristol Mercury. â " Unquestionably the best work we have yet seen from the pen of Mr. Guy Boothby. ' The Fascination of the King ' is one of the books of the season."

DR. NIKOLA. 5s.

The Scotsman. â " One hairbreadth escape succeeds another with rapidity that scarce leaves the reader breathing space. A story ingeniously invented and skilfully told."

THE BEAUTIFUL WHITE DEVIL. 53.

The Yorkshire Post. â " A more exciting romance no man could reasonably ask for."

A BID FOR FORTUNE. 5s.

The Manchester Courier. â " It is impf)ssible to gi 'e any idea of the verve anfi brightness with which the storv is told. The most original novel of the year."

GUY BOOTUBYâ continued.

IN STRANGE COMPANY. 55.

The World. â " A capital novel. It has the quality of life and stir, and will earrv the reader with curiosity unabated to the end."

THE MARRIAGE OF ESTHER. 5s.

The Manchester Guardian. â " A story full of action, life, and dramatic interest. There is a vigour and a power of illusion about it that raises it quite above the level of the ordinary novel of adventure."

BUSHIGRAMS. 5s.

The Manchester Guardian. â " Intensely interesting. Forces from us, by its powerful artistic realism, those choky sensations which it should be the aim of the human writer to elicit, whether in comedy or tragedy."

SHEILAH MclEOD. 5s.

Mr. VV. L. Alden in The New York Times. â " Mr. Boothby can crowd more adventure into a square foot of canvas than any other novelist."

DR. NIKOLA'S EXPERIMENT. 55.

Illustrated by Sidney Cowell.

THE MAN OF THE CRAG. 5s.

ARTHUR W. MARCHMONT

WHEN I WAS CZAR. 6s.

The Freeman's Journal. â " A very brilliant work, every page in it displays the dramatic talent of the author and his capacity for writing smart dialogue."

BY SNARE OF LOVE. 6s.

The Outlook. â " As a writer of political intrigue, Mr. Marchmont has scarcely a rival to-day, and his latest novel worthily upholds his reputation."

THE QUEEN'S ADVOCATE. 6s.

The Liverpool Courier. â " Mr. Marchmont is at his best in this tale. One has sometimes wondered in reading this author's works when his invention will give out. But his resource seems inexhaustible, and his spirits never flag."

A COURIER OF FORTUNE. 6s.

The Dundee Courier. â " A most thrilling and romantic tale of France, which has the advantage of being exciting and fascinating without being too improbable."

BY WIT OF WOMAN. 6s.

The Leicester Post. â " The novel rivets the deep interest of the reader, and holds it spellbound to the end."

IN THE CAUSE OF FREEDOM. 6s.

The Daily Telegraph.â " A well-sustained and thrilling narrative." THE LITTLE ANARCHIST. 6s.

The Scotsman. â " A romance brimful of incident and arousing in the reader a healthy interest that caities him along with never a pauseâ a vigorous story with elements that fascinate."

AN IMPERIAL MARRIAGE. 6s.

A tale of Continental intrigue in its author's best and most original vein.

ROGER TREWINION. 3s. 6d.

T. P."s Weekly. â " It is a foregone conclusion that Mr. Hocking will always have a good story to tell. ' Roger Trewinion ' can stand forth with the best, a strong love interest, plenty of adventure, an atmosphere of superstition, and Cornwall as the scene."

THE COMING OF THE KING. 3s. 6d.

The Glasgow Hekald. â " Mr. Hocking's latest romance exhibits no dimunition of ability, and is marked by insight and dramatic power. His imagination is fertile, and his skill in the arrangement of incident far above the average, and there is an air of reality in all his writing which is peculiarly charming."

EASU. 3s. 6d.

The Outlook. â " Remarkable for the dramatic power with which the scenes are drawn and the intense human interest which Mr. Hocking has woven about his characters. ' Easu ' is sure to be one of the novels of the season."

GREATER LOVE. 3s. 6d.

The Newcastle Chronicle. â " Though of a totally different character from ' Lest We Forget," Mr. Hocking's latest story is entitled to take rank along with that fine romance. The story arrests the attention from the first chapters, and soon becomes highly dramatic."

LEST WE FORGET. 3s. 6d.

Public Opinion. â " His story is quite as good as any we have read of the Stanley Weyman's school, and presents an excellent picture of the exciting times of Gardiner and Bonner."

AND SHALL TRELAWNEY DIE? 3s. 6d.

The Weekly Sun. â " An engaging and fascinating romance. The reader puts the story down with a sigh, and wishes there were more of these breezy Cornish uplands, for Mr. Joseph Hocking's easy style of narrative does not soon tire."

JABEZ EASTERBROOK. 3s. 6d.

The Rock. â " Real strength is shown in the sketches, of which that of Brother Bowman is most prominent. In its way it is delightful."

THE WEAPONS OF MYSTERY. 3s. 6d.

"Weapons of Mystery " is a singularly powerful story of occult influences and of their exertion for evil purposes. A tale which it is not easy to put down when once commenced.

ZILLAH: A ROMANCE. 3s. 6d.

The Spectator. â " The drawing of some of the characters indicates the possession by Mr. Hocking of a considerable gift of luiniour. The contents of his book indicate that he takes a genuine interest in the deeper problems of the day."

JOSEPH noCKlnGâ continued.

THE MONK OF MAR-SABA. 3s. 6d.

The Star. â " Great power and thrilling interest. The scenery of the Holy Land has rarely been so vividly described as in this charming book of Mr. Hocking's."

THE PURPLE ROBE. 3s. 6d.

The Queen. â " Mr. Hocking's most interesting romance. It is exceedingly clever, and excites the reader's interest and brings out the powerful nature of the clever young minister. This most engrossing book challenges comparison with the brilliance of Lothair.

THE SCARLET WOMAN. 3s. 6d.

The Methodist Recorder. â " This is Mr. Hocking's strongest and best book. We advise every one to read it. The plot is simple, compact and strenuous; the vriting powerful. It brings out sharply the real character of the typical Jesuit, his training, motives, limitations, aims."

ALL MEN ARE LIARS. 3s. 6d.

The Christian World. â "Ihis is a notable book. Thoughtful people will be fascinated by its actuality, its fearlessness, and the insight it gives into the influence of modern thought and literature upon the minds and morals of our most promising manhood."

ISHMAEL PENGELLY: AN OUTCAST. 3s. 6d.

The Athen um. â " The book is to be recommended for the dramatic effectiveness of some of the scenes. The wild, half-mad woman is always picturesque wherever she appears, and the rare self-repression of her son is admirably done."

THE STORY OF ANDREW FAIRFAX. 3s. 6d.

The Manchester Examiner. â " Rustic scenes and characters are drawn with free, broad touches, without Mr. Buchanan's artificiality, and, if we may venture to say it, with more realism than Mr. Hardj-'s country pictures."

THE BIRTHRIGHT. 3s. 6d.

The Spectator. â " This volume proves beyond all doubt that Mr. Hocking has mastered the art of the historical romancist. ' The Birthright ' is, in its way, quite as well constructed, as well written, and as full of incident as any story that has come from the pen of Mr. Conan Doyle or Mr. Stanley Weyman."

MISTRESS NANCY MOLESWORTH. 3s. 6d.

The Scotsman. â " ' Mistress Nancy Molesworth ' is as charming a story of the kind as could be wished, and it excels in literary workmanship as well as in imaginative vigour and daring invention."

FIELDS OF FAIR RENOWN, 3s. 6d.

The Dundee Advertiser. â " Mr. Hocking has produced a work which his readers of all classes will appreciate. There are exhibited some of the most beautiful aspects of disposition."

THAT PREPOSTEROUS WILL. 6s.

The Daily Graphic. â " We could wish that every novel were as pleasant, unsophisticated and readable as this one."

HOPE, MY WIFE. 6s.

The Gentlewoman. â " Miss Moberly interests us so much in heroine, and in her hero, that we follow the two with pleasure through adventures of the most improbable order."

DIANA. 6s.

The Scotsman. â " So cleverly handled as to keep its interest always lively and stimulating; and the book cannot fail to be enjoyed."

DANâ AND ANOTHER. 6s.

The Daily News. â " Must be considered one of the best pieces of work that Miss Moberly has yet produced."

A TANGLED WEB. 6s.

The Daily Mail. â " A ' tangled web," indeed, is this story, and the author's ingenuity and intrepidity in developing and working out the mystery calls for recognition at the outset."

ANGELA'S MARRIAGE. 6s.

Irish Independent. â " That Miss Moberly has a delightful and graceful style is not only evident from a perusal of some of her former works, but from the fascinatingly told story now under review."

THE SIN OF ALISON DERING. 6s.

Miss L. G. Moberly is making a big reputation for herself as a writer of strong emotional stories, and this story will add considerably to her popularity.

GUY THORNE

FIRST IT WAS ORDAINED. 6s.

The Pall Mall Gazette says:â " ' First it was Ordained ' is a long way ahead of ' When it was Dark." Mr. Guy Thorne has the gift of the great orator or preacher in holding your attention."

THE ANGEL. 6s.

Dundee Advertiser. â " Another of those daringly original, graphic, and popularly influential stories that Guy Thorne loves to write. Both as a story and as an argument for the reality of the spiritual in men and affairs, it is strong and persuasive."

THE SOCIALIST. 6s.

The subject of his new novel is indicated by its title, and the story is one likely to attract enormous attention, and be everywhere discussed

THE TRIFLER. 6s.

The Daily Express. â " A most cleverly contrived farcical comedy, full of really fresh incidents, and a dialogue that is genuinely amusing; there is not a character who is not always welcome and full of entertainment."

THE "custodian. 6s.

The Morning Post. â " An exceptionally clever and entertaining novel; the reader is compelled to finish the book when he has once taken it up. It is impossible to resist its attractions."

THE GIRL IN WAITING. 6s.

The Daily Mail. â " This is quite a dehghtfui book. The note is struck ingeniously and hilariously on the doorstep. It is a most enjoyable comedy, which must be read to be appreciated. We can cordially recommend it."

THE LEADING LADY. 6s.

Daily Express. â " A good stirring, moving novel, one which retains the attention and compels a sustained interest. It is a good book."

CHARLES G. D. ROBERTS

THE HOUSE IN THE WATER. 6s.

The Press says:â " As a writer about animals, Mr. Roberts occupies an enviable place. He is the most literary, as well as the most imaginative and vivid, of all the nature writers."

"Poet Laureate of the Animal World, Professor Roberts displays the keenest powers of observation closely interwoven with a fine imaginative discretion."

KINGS IN EXILE. 6s.

Another beautifully illustrated volume of nature and animal stories, in the writing of which the author is without a compeer.

MARIE CONNOR LEIGHTON

SEALED LIPS. 6s.

The Daily Express. â " An excellent story, well constructed, and the interest is kept going till the last page."

PUT YOURSELF IN HER PLACE. 6s.

The Sheffield Daily Telegraph. â " Marie Connor Leighton is well known as the authoress of ' Convict 99," and in her latest work she present a novel equal to anything her pen has written. Many dramatic incidents are introduced, and the work may be safely recommended as containing all the elements of a successful novel."

MONEY. 6s.

"For what shall it profit a man if he shall gain the whole world and lose his own soul? " This is the keynote of this stirring novel by the author of " Convict 99."

Lightning Source UK Ltd.
Milton Keynes UK
UKOW03f1911080914

238259UK00001B/296/P